Atlantic Ocean waters
Sea 4, 18, 23, 45, 50, 55, 63, 70, 71, 73, 74, 77, 78, 132, 184, 295, 303, 310, -314, 320
3, 46, 48, 70, 73, 77, 292, 307, 320

295, 304
0, 49, 55, 70, 71, 297, 303
mpany 56
finery 55, 56
ational coastline 291
anding Universal Value
) 27, 310, 312, 313

ership(s) 16, 296, 297, 317
enger port(s) 26, 27, 50, 74, 76, 77, 293, 302
dependency 23, 26, 35, 37, 301, 305
64, 291, 295
ers 52, 54, 55, 58, 65, 79, -297, 316, 317
ing 9, 11, 13, 22–27, 33–35, 2, 43, 50, 52–59, 63, 64, 8, 79, 291–298, 300, 303, 307, 311, 315, 316
ing cultures 54, 58
ing pattern 292
ing process 54, 58, 295,

ing rules 58
ing tasks 58
ymaking 20, 26, 34, 310
ion 21, 35, 64, 65, 296, 312, 316
ation density 65, 74, 77, 32, 184, 237, 306, 319
ccess 294
rea 3, 4, 35, 38, 46, 53, 58, 4, 78, 292, 293, 296, 308
uthority 25, 32, 36, 52, 04, 311, 315
basin 52, 306
ityScape 21, 291
onstruction 53
evelopment 24–27, 54, 92, 301, 315
xpansion 55, 295
acilities 15, 21, 294

Port function 3, 36, 46, 54–56, 58, 77, 291, 292, 303, 306, 313, 314
Port governance 56, 57, 58
Port infrastructure 34, 52, 64, 72, 292, 294, 314
Port location 3, 55, 307
Port operations 55, 311
Port planning 8, 27, 52–54, 56, 59, 64, 78, 292–294, 297, 300
Port refinery 296
Port regions 296
Port service 55
Port specialization 293
Port structure 52
Port terminal 52, 303
Port, mono-functional 53
Port, poly-functional 53
Public health 64, 297
Public participation 58

Q
Qualitative data 20
Quantitative data 22

R
Rail infrastructure 64, 317
Renewable energy 297
Resilience 15, 34, 38, 297
Resources 22, 71, 296
River 3, 4, 13, 18, 21, 27, 38, 54, 55, 64, 78, 92, 94, 114, 168, 182, 186, 190, 194, 200, 204, 206, 208, 210, 212, 216, 224, 226, 228, 292, 302, 308, 312, 313, 314
Road infrastructure 55, 313
Rural development 76
Rural territory 304

S
Scalar/scale 4, 17, 20, 23–26, 33, 34, 38, 39, 42–47, 62–65, 72, 77, 78, 303, 311, 312, 317
Sea 13, 15, 16, 18, 20–24, 26, 27, 30, 32, 33, 37–40, 42, 44–47, 50, 52, 54, 55, 58, 62–65, 70–74, 76–80, 132, 184, 236, 291, 292, 295, 300, 302, 306, 307, 310–314, 317
Sea depth 52, 78, 294
Sea-level rise 20, 30, 32, 65, 297, 311

Seaport 8, 16–18, 20, 26, 27, 32, 40, 44, 53, 62, 6
77, 294, 296, 31
Security 56, 29
Service Port 57
Sheltered bay 5
Ship(s) 3, 21, 34,
52, 56, 63–66, 71, 72, 78, 291, 295, 296, 302, 306, 312, 314–316, 319
Shipping company 25, 55, 64
Social cohesion 197
Social integration 54, 58
Socio-cultural function 78
Socio-economic activity 78
Spatial development 22, 33, 42, 49, 63, 65, 71, 291, 297, 300
Spatial growth 295
Spatial patterns 44, 47, 49, 300
Spatial planning 52, 53, 58, 78, 292, 301, 317
Spatial relation(ship) 45, 48, 292, 303
Stakeholder 13, 20, 22–25, 32–39, 53, 54, 58, 73, 78, 296, 297, 300, 306, 307, 310, 311, 315–317
State 20, 21, 30, 46, 48, 53, 56, 57, 59, 62–64, 71, 72, 292, 294, 305, 315
Statistical data(set) 43, 46, 47, 49, 306, 307
Strategic decision 292
Sustainable development 22, 25, 33, 36–40, 56, 59, 62, 296, 300, 307, 310, 311, 316, 317
Sustainable Development Goals 13, 33, 297, 317

T
Telecommunications network 294
TEN-T Network 38, 50, 294, 306
Terminal 25, 30, 52, 53, 55–57, 64, 78, 303, 316
Terrain 78
Territorial assessment tool 292
Territorial development 20, 32, 56
Throughput 3, 8, 10, 26, 44, 46, 50, 65, 66, 74, 77, 293, 302, 311
Tonnage 3, 46, 77, 80, 132, 184, 237, 301

Tool Port 57
01
14,
56,
94, 301
Transitions 36, 38, 42, 292, 296
Transmission 53, 76
Transport hubs 304
Transport network 3, 4, 18, 45–48, 73, 78, 295, 306

U
Underwater sediments 294
UNESCO 3, 4, 9, 11, 16, 27, 39, 49, 310–317, 319
United Nations 3, 13, 297
Urban area 23, 53, 59, 66, 77, 292, 303
Urban Audit 3, 4, 40, 50, 306, 307
Urbanization 24, 44, 47, 48, 63, 64, 71, 292, 304
Urban centre 50, 303–305
Urban development 23, 25, 33, 37, 58, 311, 316
Urban planning 16, 22, 24, 43, 52, 53, 59, 71, 292, 293, 303
Urban Type 307

V
Vessel 3, 8, 10, 15, 18, 40, 46, 49, 50, 52, 56, 66, 73, 80, 132, 184, 237, 294, 319

W
Warehouses 21, 24, 52, 64, 313, 314
Waste management 296
Water-land intersection 9, 76, 78
Waterfront 15, 21, 22, 24, 35, 55, 293, 316
Waterway 4, 25, 38, 40, 58, 63, 294, 302, 306
Western Waters 4, 70, 77, 78, 295
Wharf 291, 313
World Heritage Properties 3, 9, 11, 27, 49, 310–313, 315–319

100 European Port City Territories

BALTIC SEA

ID	Port Name
HEL	Helsingborg, SE
HLS	Helsingør, DK
CPH	Københavns, DK
TRG	Trelleborg, SE
MMA	Malmø, SE
RNN	Rønne, SE
STO	Stockholm, SE
LLA	Luleå, SE
TKU	Turku, FI
NLI	Naantali, FI
HEL	Helsinki, FI
SKV	Sköldvik, FI
TLL	Tallinn, EE
RIX	Riga, LV
VNT	Ventspils, LV
LPX	Liepaja, LV
KLJ	Klaipeda, LT
BOT	Butinge, LT
GDN	Gdansk, PL
GDY	Gdynia, PL
SZZ	Szczecin, PL
SWI	Swinoujscie, PL
RSK	Rostock, DE
ROF	Rødby, DK
PUT	Puttgarden, DE
SLM	Sillamäe, EE
LBC	Lübeck, DE
KEL	Kiel, DE
FRC	Fredericia, DK
AAR	Århus, DK
SST	Statoil-Havnen, DK
SJO	Sjaellands Odde, DK

NORTH SEA

ID	Port Name
AAL	Aalborg, DK
FDH	Frederikshavn, DK
HIR	Hirtshals, DK
EJB	Esbjerg, DK
BRB	Brunsbüttel, DE
HAM	Hamburg, DE
BRE	Bremen, DE
WVN	Wilhelmshaven, DE
BRV	Bremerhaven, DE
DZL	Delfzijl, NL
EME	Emden, DE
AMS	Amsterdam, NL
RTM	Rotterdam, NL
ANR	Antwerp, BE
GNE	Ghent, BE
ZEE	Zeebrugge, BE
DKK	Dunkirk, FR
DVR	Dover, UK
CQF	Calais, FR
MED	Medway, UK
LON	London, UK
FXT	Felixstowe, UK
HRW	Harwich, UK
IPS	Ipswich, UK
IMM	Immingham, UK
HUL	Hull, UK
MME	Tees & Hartlepool, UK
TYN	Tyne, UK
FOR	Forth (Edinburgh), UK
BGO	Bergen, NO
TON	Tønsberg, NO
OSL	Oslo, NO
GOT	Göteborg, SE

ATLANTIC

ID	Port Name
CYP	Clydeport (Glasgow), UK
CYN	Cairnryan, UK
BEL	Belfast, UK
LAR	Larne, UK
DUB	Dublin, IE
LMK	Limerick, IE
ORK	Cork, IE
HYM	Heysham, UK
LIV	Liverpool, UK
HLY	Holyhead, UK
MLF	Milford Haven, UK
BRS	Bristol, UK
SOU	Southampton, UK
PME	Portsmouth, UK
LEH	Le Havre, FR
NTE	Nantes Saint-Nazaire, FR
LRH	La Rochelle, FR
BOD	Bordeaux, FR
BIO	Bilbao, ES
GIJ	Gijón, ES
LCG	La Coruña, ES
FRO	Ferrol, ES
LEI	Leixões (Porto), PT
LIS	Lisboa, PT
SET	Setúbal, PT
HUV	Huelva, ES
LPA	Las Palmas, ES
SCT	Santa Cruz de Tenerife, ES
CAD	Cádiz, ES

MEDITERRANEAN SEA

ID	Port Name
ALG	Algeciras, ES
CEU	Ceuta, MA
CAR	Cartagena, ES
VLC	Valencia, ES
CAS	Castellón, ES
TAR	Tarragona, ES
BCN	Barcelona, ES
MRS	Marseille, FR
TLN	Toulon, FR
GOA	Genova, IT
SVN	Savona, IT
SPE	La Spezia, IT
LIV	Livorno, IT
CVV	Civitavecchia (Roma), IT
NAP	Napoli, IT
PFX	Porto Foxi, IT
CAG	Cagliari, IT
PMO	Palermo, IT
SIR	Siracusa, IT
MSN	Messina, IT
MLZ	Milazzo, IT
GIT	Gioia Tauro, IT
REG	Reggio di Calabria, IT
TAR	Taranto, IT
RAN	Ravenna, IT
VCE	Venezia, IT
TRS	Trieste, IT
KOP	Koper, SI
MNF	Monfalcone, IT
RJK	Rijeka, HR
SPU	Split, HR
PIR	Peiraias (Athene), GR
PER	Perama, GR
EEU	Elefsina, GR
SKG	Thessaloniki, GR

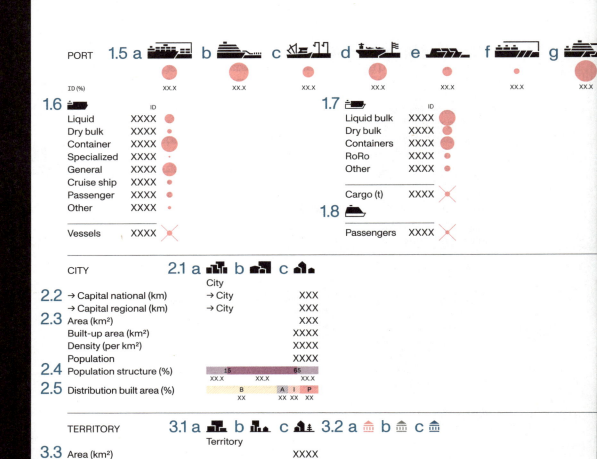
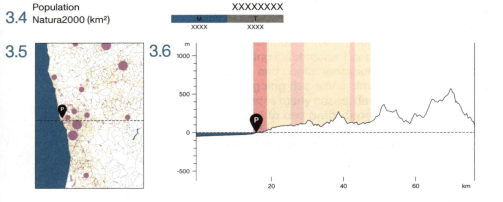

PORT

Port's UNLOCODE
UNLOCODE is the United Nations Code for Trade and Transport Locations.

Official name and nationality of the port according to Eurostat
Eurostat Maritime transport data/ GISCO Transport networks-port 2013.

Main type of transit
a Cargo b Passenger
Eurostat Maritime transport data 2019.

Water-land category based on ESPON and the name of the water
a Embayment, Protected Coast or Marine Inlet
b Engineered Coastline c River d Estuary
ESPO Port Performance Dashboard 2013.

Port functions in % of the total extent of port sites within the administrative entity of the adjacent city
a Cargo b Passenger c Fishing d Naval
e Marina f Shipyard g Local multi-functional
Typologies calculated on the basis of the Copernicus Coastal Zone 2018 dataset. Note: This is not the total surface of the port area in the territory; part of the port may be outside administrative boundaries.

Number of vessel types in thousands and percentage of total number of vessels calling at the port.
Below the line the total number of vessels in thousands and in relation to the other selected ports.
Eurostat Maritime transport data 2019—Vessels in main ports by type and size of vessels.

Tonnage of cargo types in thousands and % of total cargo handled in the port. Below the line, the total tonnage of cargo in thousands and in relation to the other selected ports.
Eurostat Maritime transport data 2019—Gross weight of goods handled in main ports by direction and type of cargo.

Total number of passengers in thousands embarking and disembarking in the port and in relation to other selected ports.
Eurostat Maritime transport data 2019—Passengers embarked and disembarked in all ports by direction, excluding cruise ship passengers and private vessels.

Note to 1.6 & 1.7: The total tonnage of cargo or numbers of vessels does not always correspond to the sum of the typologies. In case of missing data for 2019, available numbers from previous years have been used.

CITY

Official name and local typology of the city according to Eurostat
a Greater City b City c LAU
Eurostat Urban Audit data 2020 (City and Greater City) or Local Administrative Units (LAU).

2.2 Distance of the port to the nearest national or regional capital
Calculated in GIS based on port location in Eurostat in relation to National & Provincial Capitals of Europe.

2.3 Total area of the local administrative entity according to Eurostat and the extent of built-up area
Eurostat Urban Audit data 2020 and Local Administrative Units (LAU) data 2019.

2.4 Population structure of the administrative entity
Eurostat Urban Audit data 2020 and Local Administrative Units (LAU) 2019, or the nearest year for which data is available.

2.5 Built-up area of the administrative entity in typologies and % of the total built-up area
B: Built-up area, A: Airport, I: Industrial, P: Port
Calculated in GIS based on Copernicus Corine Landcover 2018 data and rounded to whole numbers.

TERRITORY

3.1 Official name and urban typology of the territory (NUTS 3) according to Eurostat
a Urban b Intermediate c Rural
Eurostat Territorial typologies data-urban-rural typology of NUTS 3 2018: predominantly urban regions, intermediate regions, or predominantly rural regions.

3.2 Presence of UNESCO World Heritage properties
a Cultural b Natural c Maritime related
UNESCO World Heritage Convention, World Heritage list 2022.

3.3 Total surface area and population number of the NUTS 3
Eurostat NUTS 3 regions in 2019, or the nearest year for which data is available.

3.4 Total area of Natura2000 areas in the NUTS 3 in km², both marine (M) and terrestrial (T)
Calculated in GIS based on EMODnet Natura2000 data in combination with NUTS 3. The marine Natura2000 sites are calculated within a 25-kilometre offset of the coastline of the NUTS 3 region.

3.5 Map indicating position cross-section of the height profile and the configuration of the LAU in combination with urban settlements with at least 5,000 inhabitants
OSM places 2021, combined with population numbers

50,000 250,000

3.6 Height and depth profile of the water- and landside of the port city territory with a projection of the land cover
Calculated in GIS based on EMODnet Bathymetry data in combination with Copernicus Corine Landcover data 2018.

Further note:
No data means that data is not registered with Eurostat, not that there is no throughput.

GENERAL FEATURES

Administrative division of the European maritime waters (EMODnet, Regional Advisory Councils, 2014)

- Atlantic (North Western Waters)
- Baltic Sea
- Mediterranean Sea
- North Sea

Bathymetric contour lines with 50, 100, 200, 500, 1000, 2000, 5000-metre intervals (EMODnet, Bathymetry WMS)

- Depth contours

Land mass and elevation pattern (Copernicus, Land Elevation dataset EU-DEM V1.1, 2017)

- Elevation from 0–5000 metres

Protected areas within the Natura2000 network (EMODnet—Human Activities, 2021)

- Natura2000 Marine
- Natura2000 Terrestrial

European network of rivers and canals (Eurogeographics, EuroGlobalMap (EGM), 2021)

- River or canal

LANDCOVER

Morphology of land cover pattern (Copernicus, Corine Land Cover dataset (CLC), 2018; port area is also based on Coastal Zone dataset, 2018)

- Airport
- Built-up area
- Industrial area
- Port area

TRANSPORTATION

European transport network of motorways (Eurogeographics, EuroGlobalMap (EGM), 2021)

- Primary road
- Secondary road
- Ferry lines

European transport network over rail (Eurogeographics, EuroGlobalMap (EGM), 2021)

- Primary railway, station
- Secondary railway, station

BOUNDARIES

National, urban and municipal administrative boundaries (Eurostat, Local Administrative Units (LAU), 2019; Urban Audit, 2020)

- Country border
- Municipal border
- Administrative border of selected port city

LOCATIONS

Infrastructural functions within the transport network of goods and people (Eurogeographics, EuroGlobalMap (EGM), 2021)

- A — Airport (public)
- P — Port selected for the atlas
- P — Port selected for the atlas, cross-section
- F — Ferry terminal

Cultural, health, education, and local government (OpenStreetMap (OSM) points of interest, 2021)

- U — University
- T — Town hall of selected port city
- N — UNESCO World Heritage property
- H — Hospital (public)

Scale 1: 450,000
1 cm on the map corresponds to 4.5 km on the ground, Pseudo-Mercator projection

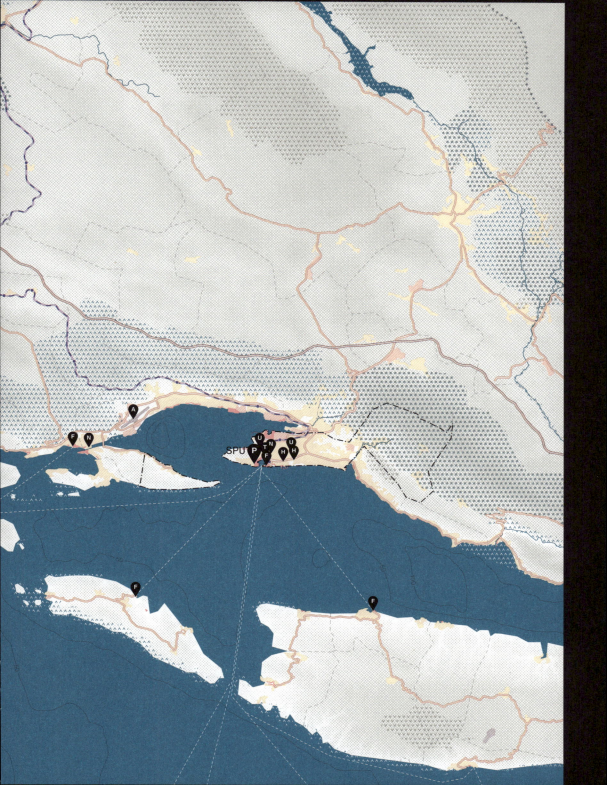

Port City Atlas
Mapping European Port City Territories:
From Understanding to Design
Carola Hein
Yvonne van Mil
Lucija Ažman-Momirski

nai010 publishers
TU Delft
LDE PortCityFutures

		Foreword: Edouard Philippe, President AIVP	13
		Foreword: Isabelle Ryckbost, Secretary General ESPO	14
		Acknowledgements	16
		Global Vessel Density and Port City Territories on Europe's Coasts	18
		Introduction: Mapping European Port City Territories: from Understanding to Design Carola Hein, Yvonne van Mil, Lucija Ažman-Momirski	20
I		**Exploring**	29
		Europe from its Maritime Waters and Coasts	30
	1	European Port City Territories in the Past, Present and Future Carola Hein	32
		Europe through its Ports and Metropolitan Areas	40
	2	How Can Mapping Help to Better Understand Port City Territories? Yvonne van Mil	42
		Europe as a Space of Mobility	50
	3	How Has Port Planning Shaped European Port City Territories? Lucija Ažman-Momirski	52
II		**Mapping**	61
	4	Exploring Europe through the Mapping of Coastal Areas and Seaports: a Comprehensive Approach Carola Hein, Yvonne van Mil, Lucija Ažman-Momirski	62
		Ranking European Ports by Type of Throughput	66
	5	Looking at Europe through the Lens of its Four Maritime Waters: (Re)connecting Nations Carola Hein, Yvonne van Mil, Lucija Ažman-Momirski	70
		Europe through its Four Waters	74

	6	Examining 100 European Port City Territories through Maps and Infographics: (Re)conceptualizing Water-Land Intersections Carola Hein, Yvonne van Mil, Lucija Ažman-Momirski	76
		Baltic Sea Map and Statistics	80
		Map Series and Infographics of 25 Port City Territories in the Baltic Sea	82
		North Sea Map and Statistics	132
		Map Series and Infographics of 25 Port City Territories in the North Sea	134
		Atlantic Map and Statistics	184
		Map Series and Infographics of 25 Port City Territories in the Atlantic	186
		Mediterranean Sea Map and Statistics	236
		Map Series and Infographics of 25 Port City Territories in the Mediterranean Sea	238

III Interpreting 289

	7	Planning Challenges and Opportunities in Port City Territories: an Analysis through Infographics and Maps Lucija Ažman-Momirski	291
		Maps and Infographics for the Planning of Port City Territories	298
	8	What Can We Learn from the Maps and Mapping Process about European Port City Territories? Yvonne van Mil	300
		Interpreting the Morphology of Port City Territories	308
	9	Port City Territories and UNESCO World Heritage Properties: an Opportunity for Implementing the UNESCO Historic Urban Landscape Approach Carola Hein	310
		European Port City Territories and UNESCO World Heritage Properties	318
		Comparative analysis of the Port City Territory	320

Global Vessel Density and Port City
Territories on Europe's Coasts   18

I   Exploring
    Europe from its Maritime Waters and Coasts   30
    Europe through its Ports and Metropolitan Areas   40
    Europe as a Space of Mobility   50

II Mapping
    Ranking European Ports by Type of Throughput   66
    Europe Through its Four Waters   74

Baltic Sea		North Sea	
Map and Statistics	80	Map and Statistics	132
Helsingborg, SE/		Aalborg, DK	134
Helsingør, DK	82	Frederikshavn, DK/	
København, DK	84	Hirtshals, DK	136
Trelleborg, SE/Malmö, SE	86	Esbjerg, DK	138
Rønne, SE	88	Brunsbüttel, DE	140
Stockholm, SE	90	Hamburg, DE	142
Luleå, SE	92	Bremen, DE	144
Turku, FI/Naantali, FI	94	Wilhelmshaven, DE/	
Helsinki, FI	96	Bremerhaven, DE	146
Sköldvik, FI	98	Delfzijl, NL/Emden, DE	148
Sillamäe, EE	100	Amsterdam, NL	150
Tallinn, EE	102	Rotterdam, NL	152
Riga, LV	104	Antwerp, BE	154
Ventspils, LV	106	Ghent, BE	156
Liepaja, LV	108	Zeebrugge, BE	158
Klaipeda, LT/		Dunkirk, FR	160
Butinge, LT	110	Dover, UK/Calais, FR	162
Gdansk, PL/Gdynia, PL	112	Medway, UK	164
Szczecin, PL	114	London, UK	166
Swinoujscie, PL	116	Felixstowe, UK/Harwich, UK/	
Rostock, DE	118	Ipswich, UK	168
Rødby, DK/		Immingham, UK/Hull, UK	170
Puttgarden, DE	120	Tees & Hartlepool, UK/	
Lübeck, DE	122	Tyne, UK	172
Kiel, DE	124	Forth (Edinburgh), UK	174
Fredericia, DK	126	Bergen, NO	176
Århus, DK	128	Tønsberg, NO	178
Statoil-Havnen, DK/		Oslo, NO	180
Sjaellands Odde, DK	130	Göteborg, SE	182

Atlantic		Mediterranean Sea	
Map and Statistics	184	Map and Statistics	236
Clydeport (Glasgow), UK	186	Algeciras, ES/Ceuta, MA	238
Cairnryan, UK	188	Cartagena, ES	240
Belfast, UK/		Valencia, ES/	
Larne, UK	190	Castellón, ES	242
Dublin, IE	192	Tarragona, ES	244
Limerick, IE	194	Barcelona, ES	246
Cork, IE	196	Marseille, FR	248
Heysham, UK	198	Toulon, FR	250
Liverpool, UK	200	Genova, IT/Savona, IT	252
Holyhead, UK	202	La Spezia, IT	254
Milford Haven, UK	204	Livorno, IT	256
Bristol, UK	206	Civitavecchia (Roma), IT	258
Southampton, UK/		Napoli, IT	260
Portsmouth, UK	208	Porto Foxi, IT/Cagliari, IT	262
Le Havre, FR	210	Palermo, IT	264
Nantes Saint-Nazaire, FR	212	Siracusa, IT	266
La Rochelle, FR	214	Messina, IT/Milazzo, IT	268
Bordeaux, FR	216	Gioia Tau, IT/	
Bilbao, ES	218	Reggio di Calabria, IT	270
Gijón, ES	220	Taranto, IT	272
La Coruña, ES/		Ravenna, IT	274
Ferrol, ES	222	Venezia, IT	276
Leixões (Porto), PT	224	Trieste, IT/Koper, SI/	
Lisboa, PT/		Monfalcone, IT	278
Setúbal, PT	226	Rijeka, HR	280
Huelva, ES	228	Split, HR	282
Las Palmas, ES	230	Peiraias(Athene), GR/	
Santa Cruz de Tenerife, ES	232	Perama, GR/Elefsina, GR	284
Cádiz, ES	234	Thessaloniki, GR	286

III **Interpreting**
Maps and Infographics for the Planning of Port City Territories — 298
Interpreting the Morphology of Port City Territories — 308
European Port City Territories and UNESCO World Heritage Properties — 318

Foreword

This atlas is a valuable tool for visualizing and designing the geography of our port cities, which are on the front line of major contemporary issues such as migration, the energy transition, and digitization. The Covid-19 pandemic and the war in Ukraine are a reminder, more than ever, of just how strategically important they are to the trade of essential goods and to human mobility.

The Association Internationale Villes et Ports (AIVP) brings together public and private stakeholders, all motivated by the same commitment to creating safer, more resilient, more innovative port cities. AIVP's 2030 Agenda provides the organization's members, who come from around fifty different countries, with an initial policy framework for achieving the United Nations' sustainable development goals. By regularly sharing our experiences and best practices, we aim to fine-tune a strategy that promotes global cooperation while taking account of local specificities.

The result of rigorous work, initiated by the University of Delft under the direction of Professor Carola Hein, using data freely available from the European Commission, this atlas reveals the complexity and fragility of land-sea ecosystems. It advocates the pioneering 'port city territory' concept, encompassing all of the various spaces affected by maritime traffic, along coastlines or river-sea corridors. It lays the foundations for analysing these territories from a maritime perspective. It identifies water and port cities as central to a systemic understanding of the European space and its integration.

These maps are intended to foster dialogue by highlighting shared opportunities and challenges from one territory to another, from governance to infrastructure planning, and from health to heritage. Cooperation and solidarity have been AIVP's core values ever since its creation, and I have no doubt that this atlas will be the new gold standard for informing citizens, scientists, and decision-makers in port cities. Happy reading!

Édouard Philippe, President of AIVP, Mayor of Le Havre

Foreword

I very much welcome this new *Port City Atlas*, which visualizes a hundred port city territories in a comprehensive way and brings to the forefront the important role of port cities as essential and unique interfaces between sea and land.

Many historical cities and their surrounding fore- and hinterlands in Europe are what they are today because of their proximity to the sea and the port as a gateway to the world. The economic and cultural wealth of these port city territories reflects the importance of their port. Even today there are some examples of young cities that are developing because of the port. A perfect example is the city of Esbjerg, Denmark's energy metropolis, often called Denmark's youngest city.

The relation between port and city is however not an easy one. Historically, both fought for space and land on and near the waterfront. Then the increasing size of vessels, the expansion of port facilities as well as the broader role of ports meant that ports had to move out of the city into the territory. Real estate, tourism and recreational purposes are now competing for space both on the newly attractive old port waterfronts and in the hinterland. Meanwhile, as the saying goes: 'out of sight, out of mind'—port citizens have more difficulty seeing the added value of having a port or understanding what it means.

The energy transition and ongoing energy crisis could bring ports back to the centre of attention. Ports play a strategic role and are proving to be indispensable links and players as Europe aims at becoming independent from Russian energy. In the pandemic and the energy crisis we are going through, it has become clearer than ever what the port can do for the city and its territory. Ports are essential in keeping supply chains going and ensuring that citizens all have the goods and materials they need. At a time when everyone is looking for alternative energy suppliers and aiming to accelerate the energy transition, ports are again showing resilience in helping to ensure the supply of today's energy, and they will be instrumental in supplying the economies of port city territories with renewables.

The expanding and new roles of ports as hubs of energy, blue economies and blue industries will create new partnerships and attract new job profiles to the port. In this respect, these changes will also bring port, city and territory closer together again.

Taking all these developments into account, I believe that the territorial approach taken in this *Port City Atlas* is of paramount importance. The *Port City Atlas* clearly shows that Europe's borders do not stop on land. The maritime dimension is an integral part of Europe's continent, strength and future. It also demonstrates that the positive impact of the port exceeds the mere boundaries of a city; it also covers the port city territories. I invite all readers to dive into this unique view of Europe from the sea, that is this *Port City Atlas*.

Isabelle Ryckbost,
Secretary General of the European Seaports Organisation

Acknowledgements

This book is the outcome of our long effort to raise awareness of maritime flows across sea and land, through ports, cities, and territories. All three editors are members of the Leiden-Delft-Erasmus (LDE) PortCityFutures Centre, directed by Carola Hein, who also leads the recently established UNESCO Chair Water, Ports and Historic Cities hosted by the Leiden-Delft-Erasmus University consortium.

We are grateful to the student assistants and doctoral students, who, under the supervision of Yvonne van Mil, contributed to the making of the maps and infographics: Stephan Hauser, Batuhan Özaltun, Mees van Rhijn, Myrthe Peet, Lukas Höller, Hülya Lasch and Douwe de Jager. We particularly appreciate the technical support of Lukas Höller, who worked closely with Yvonne on the Mapping Handbook, a technical guide to map port city territories.

The book would not have been possible without the financial support of the Chair History of Architecture and Urban Planning at Delft University of Technology, the Department of Architecture TU Delft, the TU Delft Central Library, LDE PortCityFutures Centre, the University of Ljubljana Faculty of Architecture, the Van Eesteren-Fluck & Van Lohuizen Foundation and the Dutch research organisation NWO who supported the publication through a NWO KIEM grant and NWO Open Access.

We are grateful to Association Internationale Villes et Ports (AIVP) for their support, notably Bruno Del Salle, Jose Sanchez and Martial Dubuisson, who introduced us to their members and the association's president, Edouard Philippe, who kindly wrote a preface for this book. We would like to extend our gratitude notably to those port authorities and city officials who took a preliminary look at the maps and provided us with feedback. We are very grateful and would like to thank the Ports of Bordeaux, London, Marseille, Algeciras, Valencia, Helsinki, Bilbao, Dunkirk, Venice, La Rochelle, Taranto, Rotterdam and Antwerp. Whenever possible, we included their responses. We are equally thankful to the European Seaport Organisation (ESPO) for their support, especially Isabelle Ryckbost. We look forward to continuing to refine the methodology that provides shared and comparable insights on port city territories based on the same type of data, the same territorial scale and the same indicators, even though more concise or up-to-date data may be or become available in select locations.

We are also indebted to our colleagues Reinout Rutte, Dirk Schubert, and Stephen Ramos for valuable insights into the scientific argumentation of the book and the mapping approach, and to Laura Helper for her excellent editorial insights.

Yvonne wishes to thank Jelle, Milou, DJ, Ed and Toos. This work would not have been possible without their love and support. She also thanks Reinout for his mentorship and critical view. Lucija wishes to thank Agnes, Jurij, Silva† and Vlado† for their love and unlimited support, which made it possible to do this work. Carola wishes to thank her family, Patrick, Caya, Aliya, Jolan, Joris, Wuppi † and Walter †, for their love and support and without whom this work would not have been possible.

Carola Hein, Yvonne van Mil, Lucija Ažman-Momirski

Global Vessel Density and Port City Territories on Europe's Coasts

Shipping and ports are essential for international trade and commerce: the EU transports 90 per cent of its external trade and more than 40 per cent of its internal trade by sea, and more than 3.5 billion tonnes of cargo and 350 million passengers pass through Europe's seaports every year.[1] The EU controls 40 per cent of the world's fleet and its leadership in this global industry is indisputable. The map shows the density of shipping around Europe per year and (on the inset map) the global maritime routes. The high density of vessels between the Strait of Gibraltar and the Suez Canal in the Mediterranean and around the Strait of Dover between the Atlantic and the North Sea stand out. It also reflects the many connections between Central America and Europe, and the connection between Europe and Russia along the Norwegian coast. Even though the map does not actually identify the leading European port city territories, it is easy to tell that those ports are located where the density pattern is thickest. These global transport networks on the seas and oceans, in combination with other claims on the maritime waters (as shown on page 31), cumulatively exact a high spatial and temporal toll on the world ocean.

1   Directorate-General for Internal Policies: policy department b: Structural and cohesion policies Transport and Tourism, The evolving role of EU seaports in global maritime logistics (2009).
2   Natural Earth.
3   Eurostat, GISCO NUTS 0, 2019.
4   NCEAS, 2008 https://www.nceas.ucsb.edu/globalmarine.
5   HydroSHEDS, B. Lehner and G. Grill, Global River hydrography and network routing: baseline data and new approaches to study the world's large river systems. Hydrological Processes (2013), 27(15), pp 2171–2186. Data is available at www.hydrosheds.org.
6   Eurostat/ Natural Earth.

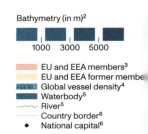

Bathymetry (in m)[2]

1000 3000 5000

EU and EEA members[3]
EU and EEA former member
Global vessel density[4]
Waterbody[5]
River[5]
Country border[6]
National capital[6]

0   500 km

18   Port City Atlas

Introduction:
Mapping European Port City Territories:
from Understanding to Design

Abstract

Europe is a continent surrounded by water on three sides; major seaports and metropolises are located along the coast lines. Public and private responses to contemporary crises—climate change, sea-level rise, migration—all depend on coordinated approaches along Europe's coasts. Yet, the sea borders of Europe are rarely recognized as part of European policymaking and identity creation. The focus internally on nation states, national borders and European unification has distracted policymakers and stakeholders from a maritime perspective on the continent. But looking from sea to land, using an ecosystem approach, we can recognize seaports and their unique role in shaping Europe's future. Moreover, we can see the port and its adjacent port city, marine foreland and terrestrial hinterland as a distinctive type of space: the port city territory. The *Port City Atlas* shines a light on the port city territory as a key player, a key location and a potential steward of water futures. This perspective opens up a critical new opportunity to meet contemporary challenges of climate crises, energy transition, migration and multiple water-related urgencies and to address contemporary challenges at the boundary between sea and land in a coordinated way. Yet this perspective also shows us that stakeholders in these territories are diverse and multiple, governance at the scale of the territory is missing, methodologies to comprehensively understand these territories are lacking and the important impact of ports on territorial development is not fully understood. We need a new type of governance to organize port city territories and to connect the various stakeholders and interests. Naming and conceptualizing the port city territory—its form, governance and culture—as unique, and developing methods to visualize the multiple flows, institutions and practices that occur in these territories is the first step in our new conceptual and methodological approach for understanding and designing coastal areas. This book argues that visualization of quantitative and qualitative data in maps and infographics can provide a foundation for comparative analysis beyond case study

Carola Hein, Yvonne van Mil,
Lucija Ažman-Momirski

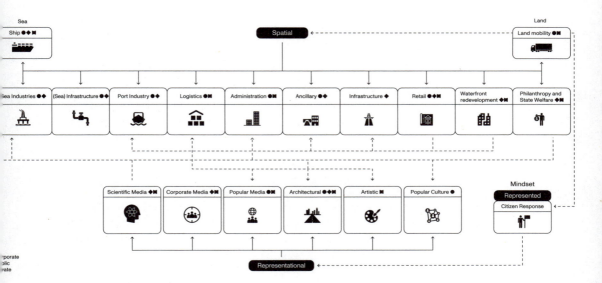

Fig. 1   The PortCityScape (Author: Carola Hein).

approaches that are often locked into national contexts, select languages or disciplinary approaches. It proposes that a comprehensive, mapping-based approach allows for the exploration of a single port city territory as part of a larger system of maritime and transport connections, and for standardized comparison among multiple territories. In doing so, the *Port City Atlas* opens up a new field of study that explores territories from the lens of water bodies, including rivers, and that sets the stage for additional thematic atlases. The chapter posits that such an approach affords local decision-makers novel insights into the complex territories at the boundary between sea and land, and proposes that the *Port City Atlas* provides the foundation for follow-up studies that take a sea-based approach to the understanding and design of Europe.

Introduction

At a time of multiple crises that involve the sea—climate change, environmental pollution, water-related urgencies, migration—the *Port City Atlas* (re)conceptualizes Europe as a continent surrounded by water, with a shared coast, with shared needs and interests beyond national borders, and it visualizes global and local patterns from sea to hinterland. Europe is a maritime continent. None of the other five continental masses has more points of contact with the seas (pages 19 and 31). From the water, we can see that oceans and seas create the highly recognizable form of the European continent: the Arctic Ocean and the Barents Sea are part of its northern border; the Atlantic Ocean, with the North and Baltic Sea, forms its northern and western edges; and the Mediterranean Sea is the southern border. Only in the east the European continent is separated from another land mass by a mountain range rather than water, making the boundary with Asia much less obvious. We rethink the spaces where sea and land intersect as ecosystems where maritime practices engage with urban and rural ones, and as zones of porosity[1] where different types of water meet and mix with land. Coastal areas are among Europe's most vulnerable ecological spaces; they are also shipping-based and industrial economic hubs and population centres. Ports play a unique role in these territories, their infrastructure for transhipment and logistics carrying flows of people and goods. Urban and territorial actors have their own visions for these spaces, imagining them in terms of mobility, housing, and other functions. Each territory mirrors the others while depending on its own local geography, topography, history, politics, economy, and culture. We argue that these marine and terrestrial spaces are unique and require conceptualization, understanding and design, so that they can serve as stewards of a sustainable future. We propose the notion of *port city territory* as a distinctive type of space that includes a maritime foreland and a terrestrial hinterland, a space where ports have major impact on and co-exist with urban settlements and rural areas. We visualize qualitative and quantitative data in maps and infographics, a fresh methodological foundation for comparative analysis of these complex spaces at the boundary between sea and land.

Shipping follows the coastlines; its maritime flows and transhipment historically created port city territories along flat and sandy coasts, against steep mountains or in swamps. Nonetheless, European unification has long connected different nations through land-based infrastructure; no single institution governs the complex economic and ecological dynamics of these areas; and no methodology acknowledges the multiple flows, practices, and interests that act upon spatial development. A 2014 EU directive did establish a framework for maritime spatial planning, taking an ecosystem approach and acknowledging the importance of sea-land interaction, of sustainable development and use of marine and coastal resources, but it does not specifically address the development of port city territories.[2]

The *Port City Atlas*'s concept of port city territories is *first of all a new conceptual and methodological approach* that can help diverse local and global stakeholders gain a comprehensive understanding of the spatial impact of shipping, logistics, commodity flows and other port related activities on nearby maritime, urban and rural areas. The concept of the port city territory builds upon and aims to enrich the large body of research on ports, port cities and waterfronts in multiple fields, including economics, geography and planning (too large to summarize here).[3] It provides a foundation for collaborative approaches that will allow us to plan,

[1] C. Hein (ed.), 'Planning for Porosity: Exploring Port City Development through the Lens of Boundaries and Flows', *Urban Planning*, Vol. 6 (2021). Also online. Available HTTPS: https://doi.org/10.17645/up.v6i3.4663.

[2] 'DIRECTIVE 2014/89/EU OF THE EUROPEAN PARLIAMENT AND OF THE COUNCIL of 23 July 2014 establishing a framework for maritime spatial planning', *Official Journal of the European Union*. Online. Available HTTPS: https:/eur-lex.europa.eu/legal-content/EN/TXT/HTML/?uri=CELEX%3A32014L0089.

[3] For an overview see also: C. Hein, 'Port cities and urban waterfronts: how localized planning ignores water as a connector', *WIREs Water* 3 (2016), 419–438.

govern and design better ecosystems on sea and land. Such new approaches to port city territories that cross land and sea allow for a rethinking of governance structures and the establishment of more comprehensive approaches that connect diverse stakeholders and interests.

The *Port City Atlas* builds from a single important premise to address this diversity in port city territories: a sea-based approach that looks at water as a key connector of ports, cities and nearby territories, for human living as well as for shipping—thus overcoming traditional land-based approaches that depend on national boundaries. The Atlas builds on this premise to pursue three key goals. It first aims to place our understanding of current challenges into their long-term development from the past to the future, building on the discussion of path dependency. It then argues that multi-scalar understanding is needed to explore how maritime flows intersect with urban practices and transport. Finally, it posits that we need new approaches for multi-stakeholder collaboration and frameworks for shared governance among stakeholders of diverse power and territorial control. To address the premise and these goals, the *Port City Atlas* proposes that a combination of quantitative and qualitative approaches—primarily mapping and infographics—allows for a more comprehensive understanding of economic, social and other developments in these specific geographical spaces. The *Port City Atlas* thus newly links a maritime approach to the planning of port city territories.

While multiple disciplinary approaches have contributed to the understanding of economic flows, urban development, planning, heritage and culture, as discussed by Carola Hein and Yvonne van Mil,[4] the *Port City Atlas* integrates quantitative and abstract data-based approaches with qualitative spatial analysis for the first time, and connects global flows to local territories. Making these global flows and local conditions visible in maps and infographics can facilitate communication and collaboration among local stakeholders in one port city territory; it can also provide a foundation for collaboration and shared strategies among diverse stakeholders along the European coast and in its four maritime waters (Baltic Sea, North Sea, North Atlantic Ocean, Mediterranean Sea).

The port city territory as proposed here builds upon long-standing recognition of the importance of maritime flows for development on sea and on land.[5] We acknowledge that the terms *hinterland* and *foreland* have specific historic and conceptual, notably economic connotations, including in the colonial context, and are largely disconnected from specific spatial conditions.[6] But the English terms have recently been more closely aligned with the original German word. In line with Merriam-Webster, we have chosen to use the most straightforward definition of *hinterland*: the area lying inland from a coast, remote from urban areas.[7]

Second, the Port City Atlas *proposes (geospatial) mapping as a methodological approach to the study of port city flows.* All port city territories are the result of investment in port and transport infrastructure, governance systems, policies and regulations aimed at connecting global flows to local territories with their specific topographical, morphological, political, economic, social or cultural requirements. Yet, the port city territory as a whole is not an institutional or statistical entity. On the contrary, it crosses institutional and administrative borders, and is often difficult to recognize due to absence of clear spatial borders and relevant datasets. (To distinguish this concept from administrative language, we opted to not use the term *region*, as in port city region.) Nonetheless, mapping requires delineation. We therefore chose a standardized frame corresponding to 75 by 100 kilometres, centring each frame over a port and its city, or constellations of ports and port cities, as a basis for comparing them. Standardized comparison—across multiple port city territories as part of a larger system of maritime and land-based transport—can help guide European development, helping stakeholders forge shared policies on maritime trade and port development, on health, heritage and ecology, and even forge a shared European identity.

Moreover, mapping can serve as what we call a "gap-finder"—that is, as a tool to identify transitional territories that often cross institutional boundaries without strong, mutually supportive governance frameworks, legal systems, and planning guidelines.[8] Here we build on an important insight from the members of the PortCityFutures research group, who recognized networked spaces in ports affected by commodity flows—infrastructure, warehouses, headquarters, housing, and even leisure or other functions—and termed them a PortCityScape[9] (figure 1). This enabled the research group to investigate the urbanization of the sea,[10] and to reflect on water and its role in connecting diverse spaces—think of industrial ports or rebuilt waterfronts that serve as places of leisure and urbanity.[11] To their concept we have added, among other things, a visualization of each port city territory through the spatial extent of the port itself, the built-up area within and around the port, infrastructure and the hinterland, with detailed information on institutions of health, education and governance. For the mapping of 100 port city territories, with 25 per sea, we have used open-access data and chosen a scale independent of institutional borders that can capture a larger territory. We have opted to map these territories on the same scale and to use both morphological and functional aspects to highlight their shared typology, while examining the unique needs and opportunities of each. The choice of 25 port city territories per sea has allowed us to pay attention to the diversity in terms of location, while also offering a much richer approach to ranking ports or cities.

8   C. Hein and Y. van Mil, 'Mapping as Gap Finder: Geddes, Tyrwhitt and the Comparative Spatial Analysis of Port City Regions', *Urban Planning* 5, 2 (2020), 152–166. Also online. Available HTTPS: https://www.cogitatiopress.com/urbanplanning/article/view/2803/2803.

9   C. Hein, 'The Port Cityscape: Spatial and institutional approaches to port city relationships', *PortusPlus* 8 (2019), 1–8. Online. Available HTTPS: https://portusplus.org/index.php/pp/article/view/190.

10   N. Couling and C. Hein (eds.), *The Urbanisation of the Sea: From Concepts and Analysis to Design* (Rotterdam: nai010/BK Books, 2020). Also online. Available HTTPS: https://doi.org/10.7480/isbn.9789462085930.

11   C. Hein, 'Port cities and urban waterfronts: how localized planning ignores water as a connector', *Wiley Interdisciplinary Reviews: Water* 3, 3 (2016), 419–438. Online. Available HTTPS: https://doi.org/10.1002/wat2.1141.

Third, and finally, the Port City Atlas *establishes a foundation for advanced analysis, informed decision-making and collaboration in these complex areas at a territorial scale for a diverse group of people.* The maps and infographics provide a space-based framework for close reading by all stakeholders. Port authorities can use the maps to gain a better understanding of their impact on nearby cities and territories. Port authorities are often powerful institutions, as ports are economic engines of national relevance with extensive technological and communication capacities. Though they control a limited and very specific area, they also seek to develop spaces beyond that area, and therefore need insight into them. For example, they need to know where road, rail or waterway infrastructure in the territory might be restrained by urban development; where commodities flow; where they can site warehousing (dryports), even located tens or even hundreds of kilometres away from the port itself. They collaborate with stakeholders such as international shipping companies like Maersk, CMA CGM or Sinotrans, and terminal operators—COSCO, DP World or APM Terminals—that have very limited spatial control, but can strongly affect the nearby territory through the growth and decline of their international activities.

City and regional authorities can similarly use these maps and infographics as they search for space to build housing, develop green energy or strive for sustainable development, at times conflicting with port developments. Local citizens, seafarers, port workers and fishermen, who may or may not have a say in port development—even as the port may affect their environment and quality of life—can use the maps to form coalitions. The interests of these locals often compete with the interests of port and city decision-makers, those of a logistic company, a port authority, a local government, a tourist bureau or even an NGO. They also have different degrees of power, longevity and control. This means that compromises have to be made. All struggle with understanding of and planning for the spatial, economic, and social impact of ports, shipping and logistics; all share concerns for environment, health, sustainable development and questions of citizen participation in the limited space they share. Currently, each actor is engaged in their own space, without taking into account the needs and opportunities of the nearby port, city or agricultural space, but such an approach to a limited functional zone is no longer in line with contemporary comprehensive planning.

Overview

The *Port City Atlas* brings together academic reflection and spatial analysis to outline the legitimacy and urgency of the port city territory as a scalar unit for European data collection, mapping, analysis and planning. At the pluri-national, trans-European scale, port city territories are key sites of economic, spatial, cultural, ecological collaboration and integration, which, when identified, can inform planning policy and integration. The book is set up in three parts, each focusing on a specific aspect of the port city territory.

Part I, composed of three chapters, sets out the foundations of the project from three perspectives: conceptualizing port city territories; establishing infographics and geospatial mapping as a method for understanding port city territories; and the role of port development in shaping port city territories. Chapter 1 examines the development of the new concept, the European port city territory. It explores current European port city territories as a result of historical path dependencies and looks at the present and future of their integrated governance. Chapter 2 explores geospatial mapping more deeply, as a novel methodological approach to explore port city territories comprehensively, both across local borders and comparatively across Europe. Chapter 3 shines a light on the role of port development and planning in port city territories. Together these chapters set the stage for conceptual, methodological innovation and for new approaches to policymaking, planning and governance in these territories. European-scale maps (pages 19, 31, 41 and 51) accompany the texts and visualize their sea-based approach to Europe. They show Europe's position in the global trade network, Europe's seaports, related urbanized territories and major sea- and land-based mobilities. They show the importance of these coastal ports, and adjacent urban settlements and territories, and demonstrate their unique geographical, topographical, historical, national and other patterns. The map on page 51 features the 100 largest port city territories in terms of throughput and provides a first glimpse of the unity in diversity of port city territories and the benefits of a shared approach.

Part II is the core of the project, featuring 108 maps in three sections and three short chapters. Each of the sections applies our concept and methodology to the European Union. Each section is composed of a short introductory text and relevant maps that again focuses on each scale of analysis: the European scale, the scale of the four maritime waters and that of the 100 port city territories. The chapters briefly present the geographical and topographical particularities at the scale of Europe, the four maritime waters and the port territory respectively. They address questions of geography, history, and the role of ports in their territories, and they discuss the scale chosen for mapping as a foundation for interpretation and design. Chapter 4 introduces two European maps (pages 67–69) that show how both cargo and passenger ports have an impact on the form and function of the port city territory, respectively. Chapter 5 introduces the level of the four maritime waters, attending to their characteristics, such as depth, size, ecology and location on shipping routes (pages 75, 81, 133, 185 and 236–237).

Chapter 6 introduces the 100 port city territories that form the core of the *Port City Atlas* (pages 81 to 287). Ranking cargo and passenger ports, and taking into account the number of inhabitants of port city territories, we have identified the 25 key ports in each of the four European maritime waters.

Part III provides deeper interpretative analysis, bringing together lessons from the making of the *Port City Atlas* through the lens of port development, and of mapping and conceptualizing European port city territories. Chapter 7 explores the many ways in which port development and port planning have shaped and continue to shape the port city territory. Chapter 8 examines the lessons that can be drawn from the mapping and analysis of individual port city territories. Chapter 9 explores the multiple opportunities and challenges of the location of UNESCO World Heritage properties in port city territories for the protection of Outstanding Universal Values (OUV) for maritime flows and economic growth at a time of climate change and changing water levels.

Together with the dedicated spreads of maps, the articles show both the level of threat that Europe faces in its coastlines and port city territories, and provide a proof of concept for a better understanding of shared challenges and opportunities for these territories.

We sincerely hope that this *Port City Atlas* will serve as a methodological model for international investigation; as a bridge between different disciplines and fields, such as history and design, planning and governance, logistics and urban design, ecology and economy; as a catalyst for new scholarly and professional explorations of the impact of ports on cities and territories—a theme that many ports recognize as being of key importance; and as a foundation for discussion, updates, and innovation within and among port city territories themselves.

Even though not all European countries have access to the sea; they are all dependent on seaport territories through river networks. Landlocked countries such as Switzerland and Austria have major river ports, for example in Basel and Vienna. For the purpose of this *Port City Atlas*, we have focused on seaports; a second volume will study river and channel port territories that are major inland connectors. In a next step this methodology can be used as a foundation to explore how historical development has shaped development patterns today in diverse port city territories; or for citizen engagement, with the goal of developing shared approaches in support of ports that serve nearby territories as well as far-flung fore- and hinterlands.

Introduction

Exploring

Europe from its Maritime Waters and Coasts

The sea is not an empty space, but a territory where multiple political, economic, commercial and military interests coexist and sometimes collide. It is a territory of maritime flows that shape the coasts of Europe independently from national borders and land-bound dynamics. It is also a territory where many challenges play out, including climate change, energy changes, migration, and sea-level rise. The map shows both tangible and intangible features at sea: energy extraction (oil terminals and wind farms) and transport (pipelines and telecom cables), military control (national defense areas), economic and political interests (maritime boundaries and shipping lanes) and nature protection (Natura2000). To manage all these factors, port city territories must forge both far-reaching cooperation and regulation. One example of this work is Maritime Spatial Planning (MSP), by which the relevant Member State's authorities analyse and organize human activities in marine areas to achieve ecological, economic and social objectives.[1]

1 Directive 2014/89/EU of the European Parliament and of the Council of 23 July 2014 establishing a framework for maritime spatial planning, Article 20. Also online. Available HTPPS: http://eur-lex.europa.eu/legal-content/EN/TXT/?uri=celex%3A32014L0089.
2 Natural Earth.
3 EA EuroGeographics EuroDEM, 2022.
4 EMODnet Human Activities, MilitaryAreas 2021.
5 ———, Windfams, 2022.
6 ———, Environment, Natura2000, 2015.
7 ———, pipelines, 2022.
8 ———, Telecommunication and power cables, schematic routes, 2021.
9 ———, Maritime boundaries, 2022.
10 An extension of the territorial sea to a maximum of 24 nautical miles (44.4 km) from the baseline, within which a state can exercise limited control (EMODnet Human Activities, Maritime boundaries, 2022.
11 Based on Eurogeographics, (2020). EuroGlobalMap. Version 2020 Eurogeographics. Retrieved from https://eurogeographics.org/maps-for-europe/open-data.
12 Eurostat/ Natural Earth.
13 EMODnet Human Activities, Oil and Gas, Offshore Installations, 2015.

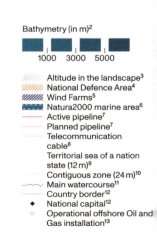

30   Port City Atlas

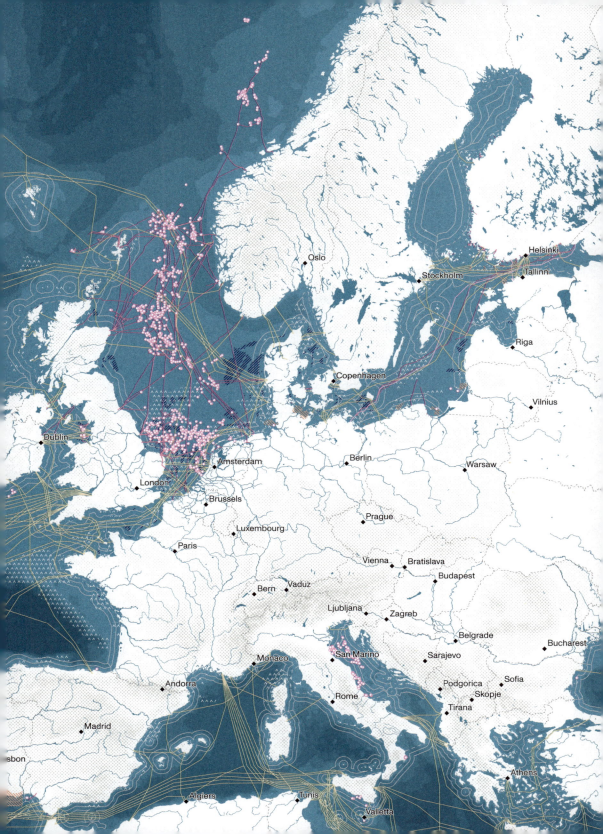

1 European Port City Territories in the Past, Present and Future

Abstract

European port city territories have been at the heart of European development at the edges of the continent for centuries. They are closely interlinked, face similar challenges, and have evolved in relation to each other in continuous global and local exchange. Their shared characteristics start with their relation to the sea and to shipping, and continue in spatial, economic, political, social and cultural patterns. The stakeholders of each port city territory include a port authority—often very powerful and with ties to national authorities—and diverse local actors and groups of citizens, often less powerful. At the same time, each port city territory has developed its own distinctive spatial strategies and constellation of stakeholders over time. Collaboration among these stakeholders depends largely on their willingness to engage with each other, and on the availability of shared spaces and tools. Only a few institutions promote collaboration among these interest groups or across and among these territories. With a stronger awareness of the historic conditions shaping port city territories and their relationships with each other, stakeholders can better work together to overcome spatial, social and cultural challenges today, such as sea-level rise and other climate-related changes in water patterns. This chapter first shows, through the cases of London, Rotterdam and Hamburg, how historic investments and actor constellations influence decision-making today and going forward. It then examines current stakeholders, their collaborations, and tools, and posits that this atlas can facilitate the emergence of shared practices, policies and governance systems for these delicate territories at the boundary between sea and land.

Introduction

Our Atlas starts with a focus on seaports: engines of technological innovation, economic development and prosperity, and agents of urban and European territorial development. Seaports have long served as hubs of transit for global flows of goods; accordingly,

Carola Hein

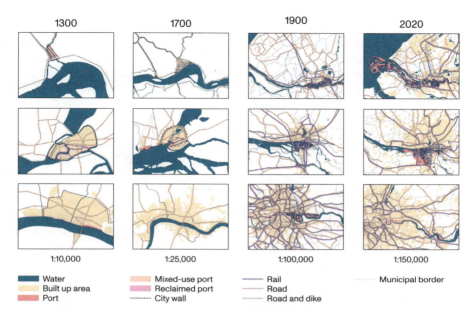

Fig. 2 Comparison of the historical spatial and institutional urban development in three port city territories from 1300 to 2020, with a selected abstraction of land and water, built-up area, infrastructure and administrative boundaries (Authors: Carola Hein, Yvonne van Mil, Blanka Borbely and Batuhan Özaltun).

large numbers of people have settled near them, creating industrial hubs and metropolitan areas where the land meets the sea over millennia. Many developed into global metropolises, leaders in urban transformation and creativity. To serve shipping, and to facilitate local and regional growth, public and private leaders have built harbours, urban spaces and infrastructure in and near the port. They created port city territories that have been key to European development on the borders of the continent. These port city territories have long facilitated the development of new spatial and institutional solutions. They can also be critical in addressing the challenges we face today, such as the energy transition and implementing the UN Sustainable Development Goals (SDG). Given the urgency of the current climate crisis and its impact on water systems, Europe needs comprehensive multi-scalar collaboration with new approaches to governance and spatial development. Recognizing where we stand—in spatial development, in institutional collaboration and in their respective narratives—is a key step in overcoming blockages from long-term petroleum-fuelled unsustainable development.[1]

Port city territories around the world today are the outcome of long-standing stakeholder collaborations (and sometimes their absence) and other historical practices established often over a long period of time. As current stakeholders prepare plans and policies with each other, whether in one or across multiple port city territories, they can collaborate better when they understand these roots at the territorial scale and develop a comprehensive understanding of how flows of goods and people through ports shape port city territories. In Europe, they can contribute to shared values and cohesion policies. This chapter first explores the role of historical processes and stakeholder engagement through a few case studies, identifying historic trajectories, so-called path dependencies and key moments of change, or so-called critical junctures—concepts derived from the political sciences in the context of the theory of Historical Institutionalism.[2] It then addresses stakeholder interaction in a single port city territory and collaboration among stakeholders in multiple port city territories. Understanding these complex situations, in part by mapping and visualizing port- and shipping-related flows, can provide stakeholders with a much-needed foundation for engaging with each other, overcoming disciplinary approaches, and building new coalitions for sustainable planning and policymaking.

The Past Shapes the Present: Historical Processes as the Roots of Contemporary and Future Port City Territories

Historical analysis is important to gain a better understanding of local development and of the goals and often long-standing power interrelations among local actors. While we do not explore the historical development of port city territories, our maps show the outcome of long-term investment and long-standing institutional constellations. As public and private leaders and diverse citizens in Europe built harbours, cities, and infrastructure over the centuries, they developed distinctive social and cultural practices that continue to shape development today and in the future, or path dependencies. These are self-reinforcing practices, in part because their 'embeddedness' in institutional dynamics and physical structures implies that there will be significant costs to changing strategy. Once a development path is established in a port's space—particularly in the capital-intensive port infrastructure[3] of wharves and docks—it can determine port and city functioning and institutional interactions for decades, if not centuries to come. Moreover, in making complicated decisions, stakeholders often rely on familiar, proven strategies. Path dependence theory emphasizes not only this institutionally established continuity, but also the role of critical junctures, decisive interruptions that privilege some pathways over others, in turn reshaping institutions. For port city territories, the arrival of steam ships and containerization have served as such critical junctures. Ongoing decisions almost necessarily follow these privileged paths; in many cases, decisions and built structures cement ('lock in', to use path-dependence terminology) development paths and once again change becomes difficult. The actions of individual actors within and among port city territories

2   Sorensen, 'Taking Path Dependence Seriously'.

3   C. Hein and D. Schubert, 'Resilience and Path Dependence—A comparative study of the port cities of London, Hamburg and Philadelphia', *Journal of Urban History* (2020), 1–31. Also online. Available HTTPS: https://doi.org/10.1177/0096144220925098.

are thus the outcome of historic processes, and in the absence of new critical junctures future decisions will still follow established development paths.

The relationship between ports and city authorities has its own historical path dependencies and critical junctures. Historically, diverse stakeholders collaborated to facilitate the transfer of goods and people across each territory, and they often found ways to balance positive and negative effects of the presence of the port on the territory to make the areas attractive enough for workers and cities. Increased wealth, jobs and education are advantages; environmental pollution, safety risks, and decay of natural ecosystems are detrimental to the health of communities living nearby. Following containerization in the 1960s, the historical balance shifted: people lost their jobs and ports moved from their nearby cities and territories to new deep-water sites for container storage and logistics. In the places they left, waterfront redevelopment for urban activities emerged as a key planning challenge—even as the residual environmental impact of the ports lingered. Air and water pollution, both past and present, clearly illustrate the need for collaborative understanding and governance of port city territories. The exhaust gas of ships, of industries and of logistics travels across the borders of land ownership and the fences of port areas. Citizens in the nearby territories are subject to this pollution and other forms of what are often called negative externalities. Port authorities need these citizens' support for their activities, the 'licence to operate'; they also need new workers to do the work of the ports of the future. Finding novel ways to collaborate with their neighbours will enable port city territories to keep playing their traditional role as places of innovation and will also make them key agents for a collective European future.

Conceptual, Methodological and Planning Innovation

Despite their similarities and shared functions, port city territories differ from each other, often profoundly, as each territory's current form and function is the outcome of centuries of a distinctive history. They can consist of a major port and a large metropolis (e.g., Barcelona); of a large port and a decentralized urban agglomeration (e.g., Rotterdam); of an important port and a tiny settlement (e.g., Bremerhaven); or of multiple ports in a sparsely populated territory (e.g., Las Palmas). These multiple spatial constellations are also shaped by different maritime functions. Transport of containers or bulk cargo (including petroleum) has a different spatial impact than cruise shipping or yachting; another key activity, fishing, is not even included in this analysis. Furthermore, each port city territory also has a multitude of governance structures, institutions and collaborations, each of which has its own data, policies and tools for planning and development.

4   C. Hein and Y. van Mil, 'Towards a Comparative Spatial Analysis for Port City Regions Based on Historical Geo-spatial Mapping', *PORTUSplus* 8 (2019), 1–18. Also online. Available HTTPS: https://portusplus.org/index.php/pp/article/view/189.

Carola Hein and Yvonne van Mil pursued a historical mapping of European port city territories in the first incarnation of this project. However, we found that the analysis of historic maps and archival documents this requires was extremely time consuming and required deep local knowledge. We therefore switched our attention to the contemporary situation, for which open-access data is available. But these barriers would be far lower for local stakeholders, and we encourage readers to consider developing similar historical map sequences for their own port city territories. These will reveal which actors have been the driving force behind change in the past and can potentially be activated to engage with challenges and transitions going forward. To provide an incentive for readers to pursue their own historical geospatial mapping, here are the results of our pilot mapping and comparative analysis of three European port city territories—Rotterdam, London, Hamburg.[4] Reading these analytical maps in conjunction with historical documents reveals continuities beyond moments of extreme change. In all three examples, port, city and territorial activities have close spatial and institutional connections; there are specific relationships that drive future development; and each faced the same challenges of shipping and maritime development. Yet the relationship between different actors, their control of space, and their respect of each other's needs has worked out in very different ways in these port city territories.

In the case of the port city territory around Rotterdam, including its neighbouring cities The Hague and Dordrecht, the historical mapping suggests, and historical investigation confirms, that the port authority has spearheaded local spatial, economic, and social development by introducing novel technologies or developing new spaces; these moments of innovation included the advent of steamships, the growth of petroleum storage, and containerization. Even today, the Port of Rotterdam takes the lead, addressing challenges of energy transition and digitization. Meanwhile, in the case of London, stakeholders privileged the urban function over port activities. London's historic dependence on private shipping and the strength of its financial system ultimately separated port and city functions: port stakeholders and urban decision-makers developed new sites for shipping, moving port functions first beyond the borders of the city and then outside the larger London region. Critical junctures, including strikes, did not reverse these roles, and maritime heritage serves as a backdrop for urban activities today. In the case of Hamburg, port and city activities started off intertwined and have been governed together as a tandem; as the city grew, so did the port, and they have developed very much in relation to each other. Local actors responded to critical junctures from both city and port perspectives. It can be expected that strategies for sustainable development will follow similar patterns, the Port leading in Rotterdam, the City in London, and Hamburg working as a tandem.

Historical geospatial mapping helped us visualize these path dependencies and critical junctures in these select territories at specific moments in time. It showed that the historic responses from each territory were different, even as each location dealt with the same challenges.[5] We haven't yet analysed the interaction between port city territories, but this could be an important next research step. This historic overview suggests that today's futureoriented solutions need to acknowledge historical path dependencies as a foundation for current conditions; in other words, current conditions are an outcome of the physical spaces, institutional structures, and cultures established over centuries, and thus those dynamics and structures will continue to shape the future. This diversity of responses also signals that we need a mixture of global interventions and locality-specific approaches and that different territorial stakeholders must collaborate for sustainable development both within and among port city territories. In finding this balance, port city territories and their governance authorities can effectively contribute to European cohesion and sustainable development.

The Present Shapes the Future: European Port City Territories as Stewards of Sustainable Development at the Boundary between Sea and Land

Path dependencies are embedded in the spaces, institutions, and cultures of port city territories. They are at the heart of hidden designs of spatial strategies, policies and laws with a single port city territory. They also mark shared development among port city territories, as these host the same ships and face the same water-based challenges.[6] With the climate crisis, we are again at a critical juncture. A number of new institutions, collaborations and tools are starting to work to involve different communities of actors in port city territories in the conversation about sustainable development: to offer advice, to collect best practices, and to align the work of port city territories. These include the worldwide network of port cities, AIVP (Association Internationale Villes et Ports), and RETE, the Association for the Collaboration of Ports and Cities. AIVP promotes its own agenda 2030 for sustainable development.[7] RETE aims to bring together diverse actors for port city territory governance.[8] Meanwhile, the UFM (Union for the Mediterranean) is developing tools for collaboration between port city territories on sustainable development, including its Strategic Urban Development Action Plan 2040.[9] The development of infrastructure and sustainable mobility on the sea-land continuum is part of ongoing discussions about the European Commission's European Green Deal.

10 'Directive 2014/89/EU'.

11 EU Commission, 'COMMUNICATION FROM THE COMMISSION Ports: an engine for growth'. Online. Available PDF: https://eur-lex.europa.eu/legal-content/EN/TXT/?uri=CELEX%3A52013DC0295.

12 Trans-European Transport Network (Ten-T). Online. Available HTTPS: https://transport.ec.europa.eu/transport-themes/infrastructure-and-investment/trans-european-transport-network-ten-t_en.

13 S. van der Werf, J. Arts, G. Smit, M. de Bruijn, K. van der Linden, R. Poppeliers and P. Staelens, 'Validated policy recommendation for better integration of urban nodes in the ten-t network.' (2020) Online. Available PDF: https://vitalnodes.eu/wp-content/uploads/2020/01/Vital-Nodes-recommendations_final.pdf.

14 Motorways of the Sea (Mobility and Transport). Online. Available HTTPS: https://transport.ec.europa.eu/transport-modes/maritime/motorways-sea_en.

15 Van der Werf et al., 'Validated policy recommendation'.

16 A. Ghennaï, S. Madani, and C. Hein, 'Evaluating the sustainability of scenarios for port city development with Boussole21 method', Environment Systems and Decisions (2022). Also online. Available HTTPS: https://doi.org/https://doi.org/10.1007/s10669-022-09869-9.

17 J.-F. Vereecke and C. Hein, 'Port city ecosystems and the "canvas" as a tool for analysis, interpretation and planning', PortusPlus 2022-1 https://portusplus.org/index.php/pp/article/view/262/235.

18 ENSURE. Online. Available HTTPS: https://www.espon.eu/ENSURE.

19 Magpie. Online. Available HTTPS: https://www.magpie-ports.eu.

Through the EU directive on Maritime Spatial Planning, the EU promotes planning for a comprehensive ecosystem to connect water and land.[10] The Commission has also recognized the importance of ports with regards to sustainable European development.[11] The proposed revision of the TEN-T Core Network,[12] which contains all modes of transport (roads, railway lines, inland waterways, maritime shipping routes) that are of European importance, addresses questions of sustainability, resilience and future-oriented mobility; sea and river ports are core nodes in this infrastructure.[13] The European Commission's concept of Motorways of the Sea (MoS), a network of short-sea routes, ports and other relevant maritime infrastructure and facilities, aims to achieve a European Maritime Transport Space without barriers.[14] Ports themselves have established institutions to facilitate exchange and best practices for sustainable development, including the European Sea Port Organization (ESPO), the International Association of Ports and Harbors (IAPH), MedPorts, and the World Port Sustainability Program (WPSP). Meanwhile, cities have gathered in organizations such as the C40 Cities Climate Leadership Group, the Resilient City Network, and MedCities to address challenges of the climate crisis. Numerous cities and regions celebrate the annual European Week of Regions and Cities to showcase their capacity of creating jobs and growth, providing good governance and implementing European cohesion policy, as well as addressing the climate crisis.[15]

Other projects aim to promote sustainability at a larger territorial scale. Boussole 21, for example, is a digital tool that helps stakeholders to set priorities and to identify challenges and opportunities to achieve UN 2030 SDGs. Amira Ghennai and colleagues have already applied the tool with stakeholders from Algiers and explored its potential for the port city territory of Skikda.[16] Similarly, the industrial canvas (Toile industrielle®) graphically represents important relationships and exchanges between different industries in the port city of Dunkirk and provides stakeholders with a systemic approach for designing economic strategies based on common goals.[17] It can support projects that aim to help former port areas whose redesign is particularly constrained by costs of decontamination and complex landownership,[18] such as the project European Sustainable Urbanisation through port city Regeneration (ENSURE), a project by ESPON. It can also support innovative ways of accelerating the transition to cleaner energy sources, as proposed by MAGPIE, the European project for smart green ports.[19] Others are introducing alternative modes of transport in port cities across Europe, as in the project CIVITAS PORTIS.[20] Finally, some ports, cities and other entities are already collaborating directly on sustainable development; the cases of Limassol[21] and Barcelona are worth mentioning here.

A focus on port city territories as key agents at the boundary between sea and land, and as a collective agent in European unification and climate change mitigation and adaptation, however, is still largely missing from these sustainable development initiatives. Our atlas provides these projects and actors with a shared framework for potential policy transfers, or more general comparison, providing a visual foundation. It conceptualizes and visualizes port city territories, fostering a governance approach that allows stakeholders on the sea-land continuum to coordinate with each other. It lets people look closely at individual port city territories and across multiple port city territories, providing insights into both shared maritime threats and opportunities, as well as local particularities that require individual solutions. Its comparative detail lets academic and professional stakeholders think about, for instance, how transport infrastructure concretely affects territories, people's lives and heritage sites. Stakeholders can gain a better understanding of the evolving spaces and scales in which they are active.

Conclusion

Port city territories are uniquely suited to guide European development and to serve as stewards of the sea. But the diversity today of European port city territories, of institutions, and of policies and laws, requires a careful analysis both of individual port city territories and of their intersections, while acknowledging the local histories of development and engagement among stakeholders. Understanding both the shared needs and the spatial, social and other differences among port city territories, stakeholders can develop locally adapted strategies and provide a framework for the development of European cohesion policies.

This atlas captures a snapshot of the current situation as a result of past investments and practices. It clarifies the need for the European Union to develop shared perspectives for port city territories and for collaboration among multiple entities. Such a comprehensive approach to port city territories can facilitate discussions on new strategies and tools to (re)shape built-up and agrarian areas, including expropriation and land readjustment or zoning[22] and facilitate solutions for contested projects. European professional organizations such as AIVP, RETE and academic groups such as LDE PortCityFutures and the UNESCO Chair Water, Ports and Historic Cities promote such collaboration through their engagement with professional and academic members, and through new tools and concepts. Their work complements and links to ongoing collaboration among like-minded actors who have formed thematic networks, including port, city and territorial authorities. These and other cross-border collaborations are an important step forward to overcome the limitations of the laws and policies of local, regional, national and international (including European) governance systems, and to address the economic and ecological needs and challenges of spatial systems that flow beyond administrative borders.

Europe through its Ports and Metropolitan Areas

The European territory is dotted with ports, most of them sea ports along the coast; they have been engines of economic development for many centuries. As agents of climate change, they can also be key players in the shift to sustainable development at the border between sea and land. The map shows all the ports—big and small—that report to Eurostat, in relation to high-density metropolitan areas, specifically Cities, Greater Cites and Functional Urban Zones (FUZ, or a city and its commuting zone whose labour market is highly integrated with the city). Inland metropolitan areas are connected to seaports by the main waterways, which cross multiple nations, regions with a variety of governance systems, and a range of geographies. Only a few inland metropolitan areas are not directly or indirectly connected to the sea.

1 Natural Earth.
2 EEA EuroGeographics EuroDEM, 2022.
3 EMODnet Human Activities, Vessel Density Map 2019.
4 Eurostat Urban Audit, 2020.
5 Based on Eurogeographics, (2020). EuroGlobalMap. Version 2020 Eurogeographics. Retrieved from https://eurogeographics.org/maps-for-europe/open-data.
6 Eurostat/Natural Earth.
7 Eurostat, GISCO ports, 2013.

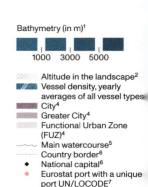

Bathymetry (in m)[1]
1000 3000 5000

∷∷∷ Altitude in the landscape[2]
▰▱▰ Vessel density, yearly averages of all vessel types
▰ City[4]
▰ Greater City[4]
▰ Functional Urban Zone (FUZ)[4]
⌇ Main watercourse[5]
----- Country border[6]
◆ National capital[6]
● Eurostat port with a unique port UN/LOCODE[7]

0   250 km

2 How Can Mapping Help to Better Understand Port City Territories?

Abstract
Understanding the unique spaces of port city territories where global flows meet local geographies, topographies, histories and practices, requires a uniform approach of visualization, specifically mapping a large number of territories in a unified way. Such an approach can also help us understand the relationships between sea and land, and among port, city and territory. It furthermore helps us explore the relationship among multiple port city territories as part of international networks of trade, and it can facilitate the identification of 'gaps' where spatial, institutional or cultural opportunities and challenges exist and where planning can be beneficial. But how do we achieve this mapping method? The challenge is to capture the great diversity of port city territories and to make it possible for readers to explore and compare their spatial particularities. This chapter explores maps and mapping as tools for the analysis of port city territories generally and discusses the availability and interpretation of European datasets for that mapping of European port city territories in particular. It explains the relevance of choices made in the map-making process and points out the challenges of developing a research method that contributes to future spatial development of port city territories.

Introduction
At first glance, port city territories may look similar around the world in terms of location, global connection and infrastructure. However, their scale, form and spatial characteristics, as well as their political, social and cultural structures all vary greatly. We use geo-spatial mapping as a powerful tool to enable a systematic and analytical study of this great complexity within similarity, and to explore how port city territories operate internally, on the seas they border and within Europe. Mapping means discovering all kinds of things and identifying key indicators of port city territory transitions. It can result in a map, of course, but also in other forms, including graphics and narrative analysis. It distils complexity and helps us explore

Yvonne van Mil

the relationship between the spatial characteristics of port cities and their surroundings. Most broadly speaking, we propose a systematic geo-spatial mapping with a uniform approach. This method requires multiple steps of decision-making, including defining the right scales and spatial level for the maps; finding and interpreting sources; and identifying and mapping the most relevant data. These steps are essential and must be carefully assessed and documented; they form the 'black box'[1] of the mapping process.

This chapter describes our mapping method. By separating the various structures that make up port city territories into (thematic) layers in a Geographic Information System (GIS), studying them in a selected and reduced form, and then overlaying them on a map, we make it possible to discern relationships between them. These layers are explained in more detail in this chapter: their relevance for the study of port city territories; how they are identified and represented on the map; and what sources, definitions and decisions they are based on.

Mapping as a Way to Study Port City Territories

How do we devise a mapping method that captures the great diversity among contemporary European port city territories in a uniform way? Maps enable us to form a spatial understanding of things, concepts, conditions, processes and events in the world;[2] they are a means of communication, and they act as an interface between reality and humans. A map is defined by the International Cartographic Association as 'a symbolized representation of a geographical reality, representing selected features and characteristics, resulting from the creative effort of its author's execution of choices'.[3] Mapping is the acquisition and processing of spatial data, which can result in the construction and communication of spatial knowledge though maps.[4] Mapping is a way of doing research; in this case it is a powerful way to see and analyse the spatial structure of port city territories and to see connections or interrelationship between different spatial, social and cultural features and systems that otherwise might remain unnoticed. GIS enables researchers to process, analyse and display complex spatial data. It allows them to combine and compare different spatial and statistical data at multiple scales, and to visualize and analyse these data at a comparable level of abstraction, without losing context or too much detail. Geo-spatial maps and mapping can act as a 'gap-finder', by identifying spatial, institutional or cultural opportunities and challenges, and where planning may be beneficial.[5] The increasing number of spatial datasets available on the internet made it easier for us to collect data. However, these data sources are of limited use if we cannot find meaning in them; perhaps the greatest challenge of mapping is to find a way to use data to create maps that provide new insight into our research questions.

6 J. Bird, *The Major Seaports of the United Kingdom* (London: Hutchinson of London, 1963).

The mapping methodology used in this atlas involved abstraction of spatial features, selection and layering of spatial (related) data, and standardization of the projection, scale, and symbology. We built on the method that geographer James Bird used to arrive at his well-known *Anyport* model (1963).[6] Bird used a series of uniform abstract maps on multiple scales and diagrams of port statistics, to define, compare and examine the collected scientific data; he used mapping to spatially analyse source material to see connections. In his maps as well as his model, Bird aimed to provide an analytical depiction of similarity by abstracting the ports into standard objects and combining them with a particular version of reality. While we also used abstraction, our methodology differs from Bird's, as we include topographical aspects that are key to development. Our temporal, spatial, and disciplinary approach are new. We explicitly focus on the physical reality of port cities, analysing them in relation to their spatial, political, social and cultural context.

For the mapping of 100 port city territories on multiple scale levels, we depended on existing spatial datasets. It is important to note that these datasets record earlier map-makers' definitions and decisions, and they reflect local particularities or political choices that may already shape answers. Without understanding these definitions and adjusting our approach accordingly, we might well make incorrect assumptions or create misunderstandings. Nevertheless, the choices that cartographers make, consciously or unconsciously, mean that a map is far from objective. As geographer Mark Monmonier puts it, 'There's no escape from the cartographic paradox: to present a useful and truthful picture, an accurate map must tell white lies'.[7] In fact, for a comparative analysis of port city territories and to highlight relevant aspects, maps need to give a selective, incomplete view of reality. But we can make this selective view as clear and honest as possible. To this end, we are not only publishing the outcome of the research—the written as well as the mapped results—but also this 'black box'[8] of the study: the underlying reasoning, decisions, definitions and sources.

7 M. Monmomier, *How to lie with maps* (Chicago: University of Chicago Press, 1991), 1.

8 Harley, 'Deconstructing the map'.

Selecting Levels of Scale and Focus Areas

To study European port city territories in light of their global, national and local contexts, we defined three scale levels of spatial interest: Europe, the four maritime waters of the European continent, and the port city territory. As a continent with a long maritime border and historically strong oversea connections, Europe has promoted sea-based transportation for centuries. Shipping, industrialization and urbanization, the growth of ports, cities and neighbouring areas have led to the emergence of port city territories with their shared goal of facilitating the transhipment and throughput of goods and people, which have led to unique spatial patterns. Each of the four maritime waters has distinctive geographical features, with its own long maritime history and position in global transport networks; and each sea creates a unique framework for groups of port city territories and helps explain the configuration of each territory. This sea-based approach allows us to both present the larger spatial context and to zoom in on the level of a single territory. It helps us to explore the ways in which the European coast and the four maritime waters have served as foundation for political, economic and social development; and to link this foundation to the analysis of the port city territories.

The *European* scale means that all port cities are part of the same overarching political entity, with corresponding legislation, regulation, and a common European history. This scale helps us to show how the port city territories are connected through water and over land, and how they are related to each other; to their geographical, topographical and political context; and to the European network of trade. At the same time, the nations are very different from each other, and their borders have changed over time; if we looked only at this European scale, we would end up with a strong emphasis on the North Sea, since the major cargo ports and most of the densely populated regions are located here.

Adding a second scale, and exploring port city territories within and among *the four maritime waters that surround Europe*—the Baltic Sea, the North Sea, the North Atlantic Ocean and the Mediterranean Sea—we can identify special constellations and conditions, such as natural geographical conditions, cultural and political settings and their position in maritime networks, which differ for each sea. This scale allows us to study the interaction between port city territories within the context of a common body of water and a shared hinterland.

The *port city territory* is the third scale, capturing the spatial relationship between the port, the adjacent city and the surrounding landscape, and their geographical location and urban patterns, as well as transport networks and institutional borders. To map each port city territory in a uniform manner, we selected a scale independent of institutional borders and pragmatically chose a format that can be printed in a standardized book format. That is, whereas Europe and the seas can be clearly defined based on statistical and spatial data from the European Commission, the port city territory is not a defined administrative or governance unit. Administrative units are institutional and do not necessarily coincide with the area that the port presence negatively or positively affects. Rather, a port city territory is a functionally connected area, bordering a foreland (sea or ocean) and connected to a hinterland. It cannot be strictly defined on the basis of data, as such areas are changeable over time, can be intertwined with other port city territories and merge into one another in barely perceptible ways. The uniform scale reveals how relatively big or small ports and their urban settlements are—Rotterdam port barely fits into this format, and London actually needs two maps. The maps do not necessarily show the whole territory of a port, as it is difficult to define, and at times ports that have the same throughput cover a larger territory and can have a bigger impact on their environment. Rather, they show (part of) the area under the influence of the port city.

We followed the Eurostat definition of a *port* as 'a place having facilities for merchant ships to moor and to load or unload cargo or to disembark or embark passengers to or from vessels' and classified their data by cargo, and passenger transportation.[9] To test our methodology, we decided to select 25 ports per sea. This number was somewhat random, but multiplied by the four maritime waters it gave us a sample of 100 territories. To enable comparison between the four different waters—to understand how different nations engage with the sea, for example, and how they have historically evolved—we used the same selection criteria or indicators for all four maritime waters. We selected ports based on their throughput of total tonnage of cargo and total number of passengers, with cargo being weighted more heavily. Then, since we focus on *port city territories*, not ports alone, we combined these figures with the population numbers of Eurostat NUTS 3 regions, or regions with at least 150,000 inhabitants and with major settlements.[10] For the following cities, we have also selected some ports that didn't meet these criteria, such as Bordeaux and Oslo. We included them because they are important historical and cultural port cities that have adapted to the transit of freight and passengers for decades or sometimes centuries. Although they have recently lost some of their port function and can no longer compete with modern industrial ports, their urban structure, infrastructure and architecture is still based on that (former) port function, and they face similar future challenges as other port cities, such as the redevelopment of former industrial port areas. Finally, given that all the infrastructure is still there, they have the potential to become important again.

Finding and Interpreting Datasets

To study and compare these European port city territories at three different scales consistently and systematically, we used harmonized datasets that cover all European nation-states with sufficient spatial resolution. National and regional data may be more detailed and accurate, but is often not freely accessible, and each dataset has its own definitions and criteria, which makes combining and comparing difficult. To avoid incompatibility issues across incomparable definitions, we selected spatial and statistical data from open access European datasets: the statistical data for the maps and infographics come from *Eurostat* and are combined with spatial data from *Copernicus*, maritime data from *EMODnet* and data on transport networks from *EuroGeographics*. These agencies are

9 Eurostat, 'Reference Manual on Maritime Transport Statistics version 4.1' (2019), 8. Online. Available PDF: https://ec.europa.eu/eurostat/documents/29567/3217334/Maritime_reference_manual_2019.pdf.

10 Eurostat, 'Regions in the European Union. Nomenclature of territorial units for statistics NUTS 2013/EU-28' (Luxembourg: Publications Office of the European Union, 2015). Online. Available PDF: https://ec.europa.eu/eurostat/documents/3859598/6948381/KS-GQ-14-006-EN-N.pdf/b9ba3339-b121-4775-9991-d88e807628e3?t=1444229719000.

coordinated by the *European Commission* and produce environmental and statistical datasets of the *European Economic Area* (EEA). Understanding by whom, how and for what purpose the data was obtained is important: these dynamics and choices affect how data can be interpreted and used. For example, the spatial datasets are based on satellite imagery and automated photo interpretation, therefore they are not always accurate and detailed. This in turn limits the scale to which the datasets can be applied and the precision of figures shown in the infographics that accompany each map. Matching the detail level of a dataset to the scale of the map is important: more detailed data holds more knowledge, but this knowledge is lost in translation when it is not readable on the map. Less detailed data, on the other hand, can overgeneralize knowledge, which can in turn lead to wrong conclusions.

Port city territories are embedded in their natural and man-made geography. To study the natural geography of port cities, we selected basic geospatial layers: the morphology of land and water, the elevation of the landscape and the depth contours of the sea. To study the relationships between port city territories at the European and sea level, these layers are complemented by maritime statistics, data on the urbanization of administrative units, and global infrastructure networks. At the scale level of the port city territory, we added spatial patterns on the basis of an abstract morphology of the land cover, which is an abstraction of the built and natural details on the surface, mapped and recorded through land cover survey initiatives (EEA CORINE land cover programme by the European Environment Agency;[11] Urban Atlas;[12] Coastal Zones.[13] In order to study shared or conflicting interests between natural location and man-made features, we completed this land cover data with information from Natura2000 areas, a network of protected areas for Europe's most valuable and threatened species and habitats. We overlaid these spatial layers with a layer of European, national and regional transport networks to illuminate the connections between the port and its territory, particularly its hinterland and foreland. Local administrative boundaries are added to show urban and maritime areas in relation to local regulations and interests. The maps are supplemented with infrastructural, political, cultural and social objects of interest to signal the degree of urbanization and centralization in each territory.

Selecting and Mapping Relevant Data
Using European datasets, it is important for the mapmaker to select and identify relevant features per scale level. Selection is a form of generalization, a process of meaningfully removing and abstracting details to support the purpose of the map. Maps are useful not because they represent all of reality in all its complexity, but because they intentionally omit details to make the subject as clear as possible.

Land Cover

Mapping the abstract morphology of land cover—distinguishing between built-up areas, industry, port typology and airports—allows us to analyse urban settlements, the spatial relationships between a port and its adjacent city, patterns of urbanization and the degree of industrialization in the territory. This helps us to identify and better understand the complex urban patterns and densities that characterize port city territories.

Transport Networks

Transport networks over water, land and rail create conditions for urban settlements, economic activities, and mobility of people and things. Mapping this infrastructure gives us another view of how port cities are connected to the hinterland and to the foreland, as well as of their impact on the territory. Each nation-state has its own definitions and classification of infrastructure. To bridge national differences, these networks are distinguished by function and importance rather than by physical characteristic and legal classification. On the maps we show a hierarchy of two classes: the first class represent the main transport routes and corresponds to the comprehensive Trans-European Transport Network (TEN-T) of the *European Commission*; the second class comprises infrastructure of national importance that links larger cities and towns in the territory with national and regional facilities.

Administrative Entities

Mapping administrative boundaries helps us to explore the complex governmental structure of port city territories. Most ports are spread over several local administrative units and have to relate to local as well as regional and state governments. In addition, administrative units are used for analysing data. Harmonized definitions of administrative areas are essential for defining almost all statistics of social, economic, or cultural characteristics. Each nation-state, however, has its own definition and levels of administrative units, which complicates the analysis of port cities within and across multiple nations. In order to avoid incompatibility among administrative definitions, we selected three hierarchical classes corresponding to Eurostat NUTS classification: class one represents a recognized independent state (country), corresponding to NUTS 1; class two is the intermediate or regional level (province, region, county), corresponding to NUTS 3; class three represents local government, including municipalities, communes, and districts, which correspond to the Local Administrative Units (LAU).

Urban Patterns and Objects of Interest

To explore the degree of centralization in the territory, urban functions and the accessibility of nearby towns and villages, we supplemented territorial maps with objects of interest or points of recognition: buildings for the transport of goods and people (railway stations, airports and ferry stations), health care (public hospitals), higher education (universities), culture and heritage (UNESCO World Heritage properties) and politics (city hall of the port city). These objects are no quantitative overview. They should be considered indicators of presence and location in the territory, and the maps show these objects in relation to their surroundings. A port city that for example accommodates all hospitals and universities in the territory has a centre function, but is also a university city; a railway station shows that an area can be reached by train; a city hall indicates the city centre.

Statistical Data

To show more detailed similarities and differences among European port city territories, the territorial maps are displayed in relation to a series of infographics. Each geo-visualization represents the typology and function of the waterbody, port, city and territory, based on statistical data from Eurostat and calculations made in GIS of the land cover, height profile, and distances between the port and nearby capitals. Due to their abstraction and lack of spatial context, these visualizations and graphics make it possible to visualize more and more detailed data not easily represented in maps. Statistics on vessels, for example, show the presence of cruise ships and other vessel types, and statistics on cargo indicate the specialization of ports for oil, containers, or other commodities.

Conclusion

Mapping port city territories and then analysing the resulting maps and infographics helps us to better understand and compare inter-relationships among different components of territories, including their spatial characteristics. The key to our mapping method is the uniform legend and its common definitions. By using standardized datasets from the European Commission and carefully interpreting the data and making informed decisions on how to define and present them on the map, we achieved a mapping method that allows us and others interested in port city territories to better understand their complex spatial patterns. The method also allows readers to further refine the maps, choosing themes, time periods or geographical areas; and combining those choices with the infographics. Thus, it can serve as a guide for scholars and professionals working in urban port territories. Choices made during the mapping process have been accurately documented. Only with their documentation can maps and mapping contribute to answering future questions about the spatial development of port city territories.

Europe as a Space of Mobility

The European territory is connected through maritime flows—the exchange of goods and people and their distribution throughout the continent—along its coasts and water, road, and rail corridors. Supranational or European planning has focused on communication and TEN-T networks and on shipping lanes, so-called motorways of the sea, and has been an important part of European unification strategies since 2000. Ports are key nodes in these flows. The map shows that the nine corridors of the TEN-T network connect important urban centres (ranked by population) to the major European ports, carrying goods and passengers from land to sea networks. The map also shows that ports and port cities have important, albeit diverse, connections to European capital cities. While many European national capitals are themselves port cities (Amsterdam, Tallinn and Lisbon), other leading ports serve non-coastal cities—such as Paris by Le Havre, Brussels by Antwerp, Dunkirk and Zeebrugge (even Rotterdam) and Ljubljana by Koper. A circle around each European capital indicates a distance of 250 kilometres, showing the proximity of ports to capitals.

Bathymetry (in m)[1]

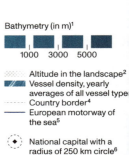

1000 3000 5000

- Altitude in the landscape[2]
- Vessel density, yearly averages of all vessel type[3]
- Country border[4]
- European motorway of the sea[5]
- National capital with a radius of 250 km circle[6]
- 100 largest cargo ports in terms of throughput[7]
- 100 largest passenger ports in terms of throughput[7]

Population numbers Cities and Greater Cities (in M)[8]

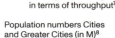

0,1 0,25 0,5 1 5

Reconstruction of the TEN-T corridor network[9]
- Atlantic corridor
- Baltic – Adriatic corridor
- Mediterranean corridor
- North Sea – Baltic corridor
- Orient/East – Mediterranean corridor
- Rhine – Alpine corridor
- Scandinavian – Mediterranean corridor
- North Sea – Mediterranean corridor
- Rhine – Danube corridor

1   Natural Earth.
2   EEA EuroGeographics EuroDEM, 2022.
3   EMODnet Human Activities, Vessel Density Map 2019.
4   Eurostat NUTS 1 data.
5   TEN-T network—European Commission.
6   Natural Earth.
7   Eurostat Maritime transport data, 2019.
8   Eurostat, GISCO Urban Audit, 2020.
9   https://ec.europa.eu/transport/infrastructure/tentec/tentec-portal/map/maps.html?corridor=1&layer=8,9.

0   250 km

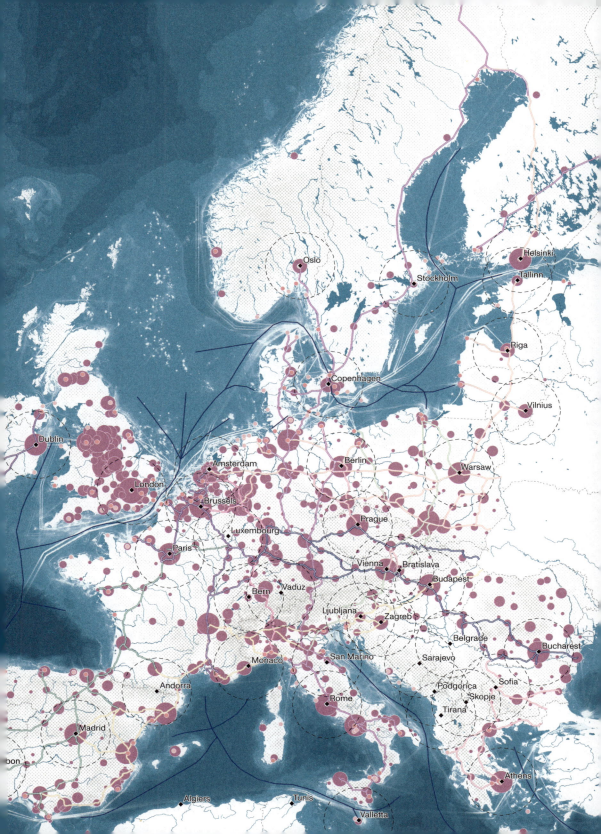

3 How has Port Planning Shaped European Port City Territories?

Abstract

European ports developed in relation to nearby port cities, and port city territories, shaping each other in planned and unplanned ways. Port authorities and other actors have invested in port terminals, docks, warehouses and port infrastructure over time. This construction and planning of ports has a long history as an engineering discipline. Today port planning is part of urban and spatial planning, and engineering plans are part of executive phases. Unlike urban planning, though, port planning is not bound to administrative boundaries; port city territories elude planning boundaries and established planning procedures. Port planners and port authorities have to find planning compromises at local, regional and national levels as they create and plan ports handling a wide range of cargo or ports handling special cargo, terminals with dedicated functions and, more recently, inland port terminals. Thus, port authorities contribute to the shaping of the port city territory.

Introduction

Port authorities' decisions about port structure, development, and requirements can shape an entire port city territory. Since the mid-twentieth century, port authorities have commissioned port planners to design port layout and infrastructure, including port terminals (their functions, dimensions, capacity, components), port basin dimensions, berths, road systems and railway systems. Port planners take into account local geographic conditions on sea and land, the evolution of vessel types and the room they need to manoeuvre—including sufficient sea depth—and the logistics of transit or transhipment to transfer cargo or containers from one ship to another on their way to final destinations. They develop master plans that provide a blueprint for future development and establish the framework within which each port authority must operate, defining and detailing port-related functions by current and planned land use per location and activity. The data underlying this information is available at the EU level through the Lucas survey

Lucija Ažman-Momirski

carried out by Eurostat.[1] This data shows that ports can be poly-functional, handling a wide range of special and general cargoes, or mono-functional, primarily handling one special cargo; it also shows that terminals within port areas are mono-functional.

Yet, the planning powers of port authorities are generally limited to the immediate water and land port areas and do not capture the impact of flows throughout the port city territory on its space. Our maps exhibit the result of *all* past port, port city and port city territory European development and planning. Throughout much of European history, planning for ports was part of the developing, determining, designing and drawing up of plans for urban areas. Ports were embedded in urban plans, like the development of the seaport of Piraeus, the port city of ancient Athens. Port construction evolved as an engineering discipline starting in antiquity, and during the nineteenth century developed into a large and specialized profession. The hydro-engineer and builder of the port of Marseille, Hilarion Pascal (1815–1896), for example, drew up construction plans for Trieste, Rijeka, Varna, Istanbul, Izmir and other ports.[2] Port engineers also included railroad specialists, who planned railways into the port itself and across the port city territory.

In the late nineteenth century, urban planning was established as a discipline and later port planning evolved as part of it. But although there are procedural similarities, port planning in practice differed and continues to differ from urban planning. The port plan is usually defined by property borders, while municipal urban plans are generally defined by administrative boundaries of the municipality or settlement. Port planning at the local level also focuses on the relationship between the port and the city—their separation or merging, and the relationship between the port and the landscape; at the regional level it focuses on wider strategies for parts of the port city territory.

During the twentieth century in today's EU member states, port planning became part of spatial planning, which even more broadly 'sets the frame for the development of a specific area'.[3] The approaches to the making of these plans and the role of key stakeholders vary. In Slovenia, for example, port planning is an integral part of national spatial planning and port master plans are national spatial plans—such as Slovene roads, railways, gas pipelines, transmission lines and power plants.[4] The official initiator of port planning, which is the Ministry of Infrastructure of the Republic of Slovenia, and the investor, the port authorities of the port of Koper, follow the spatial planning procedures in cooperation and coordination with the national and local spatial planning authorities and the public. The government approves the port master plan; then Slovenian local authorities must respect such a plan and adopt its provisions when preparing municipal urban plans. The complexity of the process makes it difficult to amend. Another example is the case of Dublin, where the master plan for the port is not required by law, but has been prepared by the Dublin Port Company as part of EU policy, national, regional and local development plans. The Dublin Port Company Board adopted the master plan 2012–2040 in 2012 and revised it in 2018. During the planning process, stakeholders, customers, employees, interest groups, the local community, the general public and others significantly and extensively participated: the Dublin Port Company received over 300 submissions in response to the Issues Paper published as part of the master planning process and following the publication of the draft master plan.[5]

5 Dublin Port Company, 'Dublin Port Masterplan 2040, Reviewed 2018' (2018). Online. Available PDF: https://www.dublinport.ie/wp-content/uploads/2018/07/DPC_Masterplan_2040_Reviewed_2018.pdf.

The port city territories we mapped provide insight into the outcomes of historical port planning and port development, and help us better understand the impact of port planning at the port, port city, and port city territory level. The following sections outline four themes that illustrate the interrelationship between ports, cities and territories: (1) The influence of the territorial conditions of the four maritime waters surrounding the European continent on the development and planning of its ports and port city territories; (2) the impact of port functions on the planning of ports and their role in European port city territories; (3) the governance of European port authorities that organize, structure, manage and decide on the development of the European ports; and (4) planning culture as a necessary step toward the social integration of European ports into the broader community. While the first is clearly visible on the maps and the second is explained in the infographics, the third and fourth are given as additional explanations to aid reading and understanding our maps.

Ports Located on Water, Land and Territory

Ports are fixed landing places for loading and unloading sea cargo and sit at the heart of their port city territories. Multiple factors influence the selection of a location for a port: territorial conditions come first, before economic growth, social welfare, environmental sustainability or political acceptability. The starting point of any port planning is the choice of a suitable site, where ports take advantage of the local geographical features and port planning strengthens and compensates for unfavourable site characteristics. Cartographic exploration of European port city territories shows that they are mostly located where topographic features sheltered the water. Ports are located on rivers (e.g., Riga, Bremen, Hamburg, London), in estuaries (e.g., Liverpool, Immingham, Hull, Humber), in bays (e.g., Thessaloniki, Koper, Trieste, Monfalcone), and next to maritime waters as engineered coastlines (e.g., Santa Cruz de Tenerife, Rønne, Barcelona, Dover, Calais). In each case, port planners created appropriate conditions for the transfer of goods and people from sea to land and vice versa.

More than half of the ports on the Baltic Sea have developed from their original location towards the shore, which in most cases is not exposed to the open sea but is part of a sheltered bay. The availability of non-freezing ports was particularly important in this region, providing port services to port city territories in Russia, Kazakhstan, Belarus and other countries in all seasons. Port developers found other conditions on the west side of the European continent where it meets the North Atlantic Ocean. There, port founders mainly sought locations on estuaries or rivers, or on sheltered bays and natural harbours. On the south coast of Ireland, the Port of Cork is located in the second largest natural harbour in the world and is at the same time a hugely important catalyst for trade and employment in the port city territory. The Mediterranean topography allowed planners to locate ports right on the coast, but in most cases, they are partially protected by the larger space of the bay in which they were built. Because of steep slopes right next to the waterfront, further port expansions are difficult to engineer, although they are generally quite large. Passes through steep hillsides are crucial for the development of port city territories on parts of the Mediterranean. Sometimes port developers sited ports in less favourable areas and protected more exposed sites with new construction. Holyhead Port, on the Atlantic, for example, is built on an exposed waterfront. Similarly, the ports in Dover, Calais, Zeebrugge, Dunkirk, Hartlepool, Frederikshaven and Hirtshals are the most exposed port locations along the North Sea; and here too protective constructions secure port operations from wind, sea and swell. The port city territories vary widely, ranging from densely populated industrial cities near Zeebrugge to the non-metropolitan region of Hartlepool.

Port Functions

Port authorities across Europe decide which functions will be performed in the port based on strategic considerations, including national preferences. The choice of such a function has multiple effects on the nearby port city and port city territory, offering different types of jobs and producing diverse environmental impacts. Sometimes shipping companies, which are global actors, also make decisions about the functions of ports or terminals within them, which are previously agreed upon with national authorities. The organization of these terminals determines the role and function of the port.[6] Containers are sent across rail and road infrastructure to numerous destinations scattered throughout the vast port city territory, while oil refineries, chemical companies, and other oil businesses are usually co-located with a terminal facility or near the port, as seen in Algeciras. In other cases, as in Trieste with the Transalpine Pipeline, the oil is destined for liquid hinterland flows. In the majority of the cases, European ports, such as Rotterdam, prepare master plans for such port planning and expansion, which include development visions for port functions, infrastructure, and other facilities and capacities, usually with a planning horizon of 10 to 30 years. The type of goods handled by ports has an impact on urban and territorial development. In ports where multiple types of cargos are handled, the environmental impact of transport and transhipment accumulates, often with a negative effect on sustainable development.

Ports sometimes have only one terminal or handle only one type of cargo, such as the Butinge oil terminal in the Baltic Sea, in operation since 1999. It was planned, designed and implemented by the US multinational engineering and construction firm Fluor Corporation as part of the only Mažeikiai oil refinery in the Baltic States. These monofunctional ports most often handle bulk or liquid cargoes, via specialized quays. The passenger port is one kind of monofunctional port (or sometimes a terminal within a port) where passengers can board and disembark from watercraft. In contrast, other major ports have numerous terminals to handle, store, and process cargo, such as Algeciras, Livorno and Genoa in the Mediterranean, Belfast, Southampton and Las Palmas in the North Atlantic Ocean waters; Dover, Rotterdam and Zeebrugge in the North Sea; and Rostock, Tallinn and Swinoujscie in the Baltic Sea. These polyfunctional ports handle a variety of specialized and general cargoes, such as containers, bulk, cars and liquids. Some do not only handle cargo, but also host other activities such as fishing, ferries, cruises and marinas; others cater to leisure vessels and yet others handle a significant amount of commercial traffic.

In European port city territories, some ports are military—the port of Toulon, for example, is the principal base of the French navy—which has its own challenges for the surrounding areas in terms of safety and security. And some commercial ports have terminals dedicated to military functions. In case of armed conflict, these ports have a plan for the whole port to support deployment of material and troops. Such ports have a double strategic role: their day-to-day commercial functions continue to be important in wartime, as their routine enables them to minimize disruption to trade, and when the war is over, these ports can quickly transform infrastructure and facilities from a wartime footing back to commercial work. Diversification of ports and terminals is an important prerequisite for the successful import/export of combat-ready equipment.[7] Such port cities and port city territories are of a strategic importance and can be targets of military operations, just like the port itself.

Port Governance

There is no such thing as a standard governance of port city territories; in fact, no two ports operate in exactly the same way. This variety of governance models and ownership structures is an

7 Lt. Col. J.D. Tillman and Maj. A.M. Karlewicz, 'Port Diversification and Strengthening: Sustainment Relies on U.S. Military's Ship-to-Shore Capacity in Europe' (2021). Also online. Available HTTPS: https://www.army.mil/article/252652/port_diversification_and_strengthening_sustainment_relies_on_u_s_militarys_ship_to_shore_capacity_in_europe.

important feature of the European port system and has major impact on the port city territory. The World Bank's 2007 Port Reform Toolkit defines four port governance models (the Service Port, the Tool Port, the Landlord Port and the Fully Privatized Port) that summarize how ports are organized, structured and managed. These models differ in the services provided by the public sector, the private sector or mixed-ownership providers. Their orientation (local, regional or global) is also taken into account, as well as who owns the superstructure and capital assets, and who provides port workers and management. The vast majority of European port authorities are publicly owned and, for that reason, tend to engage closely with the nearby city and territory.

The following examples show the diverse ways in which port governance influences port city territory relationships. In Portugal, the public sector (the government or port authority) is usually responsible for constructing and dredging the port, as well as for ensuring land access to the port.[8] In Lisbon, dredging affects the sensitive environmental systems in the Tagus estuary, but the interests of the port, the city and the port city territory collide. This impasse can only be resolved through a joint approach, so in order to balance the quality of the estuary and the quality of life of the people living there, cooperation has been sought with other organizations and communities in the port city territory. In Spain, the State Port Authority, under the Spanish Ministry of Economic Promotion, is responsible for managing the Spanish port system. The planning, design and construction of ports are subject to the provisions of the 1998 'Strategic Framework of the State Ports System' and are the responsibility of the Ministry of Public Affairs in cooperation with the port authorities.[9] Each Spanish port operates as an 'Advanced Landlord Port', a market-oriented model that brings in capital from the private sector and thereby reduces the public fiscal burden. Each port manages its entire port cluster, meaning the port land and the surrounding port water. It also plans and leases port space and infrastructure to private operating companies. In Italy, reform in 2016 restructured, streamlined and simplified port authorities,[10] merging 24 existing port authorities and other smaller ports into 15 Port System Authorities (PSAs). The central government decides on finances, while the PSAs coordinate and plan ports logistics and expansion. Changing the governance system also changed the port city territory, because the reform addressed inefficiencies related to hinterland connections. The 15 PSAs assumed the duties and powers of traditional port authorities, but with a broader geographic scope, as within the region of Apulia: Bari and Brindisi formed a single PSA with a couple of minor ports. Finally, the major French port authorities consist of advisory and decision-making bodies in accordance with the provisions of the French Port Reform Act of 2008. Consequently, the Port of

Le Havre, the 'Grand Port Maritime', is a public body that manages both the port functions and the development of the port area. Port authorities are full owners of their domains, but their objective is still to develop and expand the port area in accordance with the interests of local stakeholders and authorities, and in coordination with other ports on the same coast or waterway in the port city territory.[11]

Ports and Planning Culture
Port development is in line with local and national planning cultures, which define, for example, the participation of stakeholders in planning processes, the identification of planning challenges, the interpretation of planning tasks, or the application of planning procedures and rules. The degree of consensus and compromise between the wide range of stakeholders in the port city territory—the level of collaboration among city planning departments, residents, local administration, private companies, non-governmental local associations, educational institutions and regional governments—is also a result of such a planning culture. Yet stakeholders have come into conflict over issues like urban development and environmental protection. The absence of governance at the port city territory level is a key challenge here. Port authorities can help bridge different styles of planning (or planning cultures) in the port city and port city territory to contribute not only to the success of the port, but also to urban and spatial planning. Our work points to areas where experienced planners think port authorities are more likely to seek port development alternatives, particularly because of the sensitivity of Natura2000 protected areas along the ports and in the hinterland, as can be found in Huelva and Le Havre, for instance.

Planning culture also plays an important role in the social and cultural engagement of port city territories with their neighbouring areas. The European Sea Ports Organization (ESPO) holds that social integration, or bringing social groups together by preventing segregation between them, is one of the main tasks of port authorities in the twenty-first century. Social integration includes creating supportive and transparent planning and spatial planning processes that foster and maintain public participation in decision-making, better communication in all planning areas, the participation of all sectors, and, ultimately, consensus between public and private interests. In line with that premise, the organization has awarded its ESPO Award since 2009 'to promote innovative projects by port authorities that improve the social integration of ports, particularly with the city or wider community in which they are located'.[12] It is not surprising that all the winners of ESPO Awards are among the leading ports on the *Port City Atlas* list.

---

11 A. Serry and L. Loubet, 'Comparative analysis of port governance and cooperation between actors in European port-cities', World of Shipping Portugal, An International Research Conference on Maritime Affairs, 21–22 November 2019, Carcavelos, Portugal.

12 'ESPO Award'. Online. Available HTTPS: https://www.espo.be/news/seven-ports-in-the-running-for-the-espo-award-2022.

Conclusions

Our maps identify key elements in the complex relationship between the functioning and planning of the selected ports and their role in the European port city territories. The mapping also shows the relationship between the port area, the urban area and the landscape as they negotiate many current challenges, including the climate crisis and trouble in the contact areas between ports and their surroundings. Port planning policy responses to these challenges can vary widely—by port, port city, port city territory and EU member state—even when all countries agree on common objectives. These situations offer the opportunity to find and develop innovative urban planning solutions,[13] including balanced and sustainable development, or to implement already established advanced urban planning solutions. Port city territory development therefore makes an important contribution to the development of the discipline of urban planning in general.

Mapping

4 Exploring Europe through the Mapping of Coastal Areas and Seaports: a Comprehensive Approach

Abstract
Scholars and professionals have recently started to pay more attention to maritime perspectives on Europe. This renewed engagement with the continent's coastal areas harks back to centuries of sea-based European development and global engagement. This is an important turn both in terms of Europe's global economic competition and for the continent's sustainable development. Comprehensive European policies are urgently needed to address these dual challenges, facilitating the decision-making and development of European ports as important economic players that can work together when faced with new competitors, for example in the context of the Chinese Belt and Road development. Policies are also needed to address the economic, social and ecological impact of ports on their neighbouring cities and territories.

The port city territories we mapped are all part of the same political entities, the European Union (EU) and European Free Trade Association (EFTA), with shared European legislation, regulation and history. We define Europe on the basis of the spatial coverage of European Commission data, including all 27 EU member states, plus Norway as member of EFTA and the United Kingdom as a former member of the EU. The Spanish islands of Las Palmas and Tenerife are included analytically, as they are located in the North Atlantic Ocean, but we do not show them on the maps due to scale and page size. As we are looking inland from the perspective of the European seas, we did not include overseas territories. The European scale allows us to see major differences in the length of sea borders per country (notably, island nations have longer sea borders), the number of seas accessed (consider how many seas France and Spain touch), and in the number of major port city territories (particularly high in Italy).

Our sea-based approach links this atlas to a growing number of maritime and marine studies that go beyond a long-standing

Carola Hein, Yvonne van Mil, Lucija Ažman-Momirski

focus on land-based reflections that considers the sea a barrier. New fields of international historical investigation include investigations of seascapes focused on maritime histories cultures and exchanges,[1] and studies that pay new attention to ships and other types of sea machines, exploring these marine technologies in relation to architecture over time.[2] Other historical studies explore Europe's role in the maritime world, the role of traders and shippers in exchanging goods,[3] Europe and the sea,[4] and European trading networks that connected diverse geographical and cultural spaces.[5] Our own work has engaged with the sea-based approaches notably through the study of the urbanization of the sea[6] in line with Neil Brenner and Christian Schmid's concept of planetary or extended urbanization,[7] and explorations of the sea as a blank place to be reclaimed for comprehensive spatial development.[8] Using geospatial mapping and visualization, we aim to overcome approaches that stay within the borders of a nation-state or language region.

European coastal areas are not only highly recognizable, they are also key to European history. European port city territories are heritage landscapes: over centuries, they have attracted travellers from sea and land, hosted ports and settlements, and brought trade and prosperity to rural areas. The Greek and Roman Empires depended on maritime transport, as did the Venetians and the Dutch. Shipping was central to European colonialism, and the architecture and urban design of European seaports have shaped the European imagination. In the nineteenth century, European seaport cities started to thrive as hubs of petroleum storage and refining, eventually fuelling the growth of industrial ports, metropolises and territories, and of new mobilities between them. In turn, the growth of nation states and later European unification fostered the mobility of goods, people and ideas, with seaport city territories as key nodes of arrival and departure between sea and land. The scale of port city territories increased as petroleum-fuelled engines shortened workers' travel times, allowed people to live further away from their workplaces, and made it possible for individuals and companies to transport goods faster and over longer distances. Seaport cities became hubs for infrastructural innovation once railways and canals (such as the New Waterway in Rotterdam) connected ports to their fore- and hinterlands. Cross-oceanic connections were at the heart of global flows; the British Empire and the transfer of planning ideas via maritime colonialism to other parts of the world are key examples. Cities around the world looked at London as a model of a capital city and an exemplary seaport. New metropolises emerged as private and public investments rapidly expanded ports; these were often so-called second cities,[9] like Rotterdam, Hamburg, Antwerp and Dunkirk, that tried to keep up with their rapidly growing territories.

European coastal ports, cities and port city territories rapidly expanded in the 1960s, a result of decolonization and Europe's loss of access to colonial port infrastructure, the rapid growth of car use and urbanization, and shipping containerization. In particular, containerization and the accompanying automation rendered traditional workforces and warehouses obsolete. Only a few workers were needed to handle containers, and the containers themselves could be stored on large open areas accessible by rail and road. Globalization, increased transportation speed, new high-speed road and rail infrastructure, and more consumption all fuelled private and public investment and planning of larger port areas and of deep-sea ports, with automated terminals for transhipment where possible. In fact, ports no longer had to be in cities, and urban and port planning spatially disconnected as well. Inland intermodal terminals, so called dry ports, emerged as storage and distribution centres for cargo. Private companies and public institutions sited such hubs on cheaper land outside of major metropolises; this extended the port city territory along major highways and railway infrastructure into the landscape and to smaller settlements. At sea, new infrastructure—windmills, drilling platforms, and waiting spots for ships—has also expanded the range of ports and the port city territory on sea and land.

With the creation of the European communities and later the European Union, policymakers focused on European cohesion by forging internal connections, such as border-crossing road and rail infrastructure throughout Europe. Yet EU ports and cities have often competed with one another in line with EU policy and often lack the power to withstand the consolidated interventions of actors from outside Europe. The impact of the Chinese Belt and Road Initiative exemplifies the urgency of this issue: when the state-owned China COSCO shipping company purchased rights to operate in European ports such as Piraeus, local protests and conflicts ensued.[10] Citizens fought the construction of six new cruise ship piers which threatened to bring pollution and environmental damage to heavily populated areas and heritage sites, destroy a popular local beach, and create heavily polluted mud, harmful to public health. Advanced attention to European waters, coasts and port city territories can facilitate European cohesion and help model new governance at the territorial scale—in turn, a coherent port policy would help ports, cities and territories make coherent decisions in line with European values.

At the scale of 1:27,000,000, as used in this section, one centimetre on the map corresponds to 27 kilometres on the ground, making the morphology of Europe clearly visible: coastlines, mountainous areas, major rivers and bodies of water. This scale helps us see how port city territories are related to their geographical, topographical and political context, including European networks

10 Contested Ports. Online. Available HTTPS: https://www.contestedports.com/piraeus-greece/.

of trade, the location of military ports or of capital cities. The presence of political functions, for example, can go hand in hand with the existence of a military port or certain political interests, which can hinder free trade that is so important for port cities. The maps make spatial and functional patterns visible, including for example relationships between neighbouring ports, dynamics between military ports and capital cities, and political relationships between ports and national capital functions that result of geographical, locational and historic factors. For example, the maps show that only 12 per cent of the largest port cities in terms of throughput are also capital cities, and most of them are in the Baltic Sea. Some countries on the Mediterranean have coastal capital cities in port city territories, either because they are small, such as Latvia with the port city and capital Riga, or because they have long maritime borders, such as Italy. Many port city territories on the Baltic Sea are also capitals, including Helsinki, Tallinn, Stockholm, Riga, Oslo and Copenhagen. For the large countries of Scandinavia, the reason for maritime capitals may be historical proximity to the heart of Europe and population density.

Exploring Europe from a sea-based perspective with an eye towards port city territories, the maps also reveal useful information about industrial development, including environmental and health issues, and potential challenges. For example, we can see on the maps that numerous protected Natura2000 areas—a large coordinated network of protected breeding and resting sites for endangered species that covers 18 per cent of the EU's land and 8 per cent of its marine territories[11]—lie in the vicinity of port city territories. Clearly ports, which are densely built-up areas with intense traffic, need to develop sustainable environmental practices to further protect and preserve these unique natural sites. Mapping on the European scale also helps us see the probable impact of maritime traffic and maritime spatial development on the health of people on European coasts and in port city territories. They show, for example, that the great number of ships in the English Channel and around Gibraltar overlaps with air pollution corridors; that is, we can see where and why air pollution affects some port city territories more than others. Finally, the maps show that numerous European historic landscapes and heritage sites are located in coastal areas and are therefore under threat of sea-level rise, unstable weather, and other climate change related water threats. Our atlas can help planners develop shared responses to these and other threats.

Ranking European Ports by Type of Throughput

Mapping ports based on their throughput of goods or passengers in relation to their vessel density produces two different patterns on the map (pages 68–69). Ports have multiple types of throughput and can appear in both cargo and passenger-based rankings. Cargo ports are scattered all over the European coastline, while passenger ports are concentrated on island regions. Cargo ports are gateways for global flows of containers and bulk goods, and vessels docking at these ports often travel long distances. Passenger ports serve as a base for ferries (travel) and cruise ships (holidays); these vessels travel short distances, often as scheduled services. The function of the ports also determines their relation to the city and territory. Cargo ports are largely automated nowadays and can be located outside the city, often in the less densely built territory and closer to the hinterland dryports and logistics centres. Passenger ports remain more connected to urban areas.

1   Natural Earth.
2   EEA EuroGeographics EuroDEM, 2022.
3   EMODnet Human Activities, Vessel Density Map 2019.
4   Eurostat/Natural Earth.
5   Eurostat Maritime transport data, 2019.

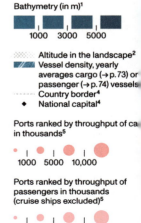

Bathymetry (in m)[1]

1000   3000   5000

Altitude in the landscape[2]
Vessel density, yearly averages cargo (→ p. 73) or passenger (→ p. 74) vessels[3]
Country border[4]
♦   National capital[4]

Ports ranked by throughput of cargo in thousands[5]

1000   5000   10,000

Ports ranked by throughput of passengers in thousands (cruise ships excluded)[5]

200   500   1000

0   250 km

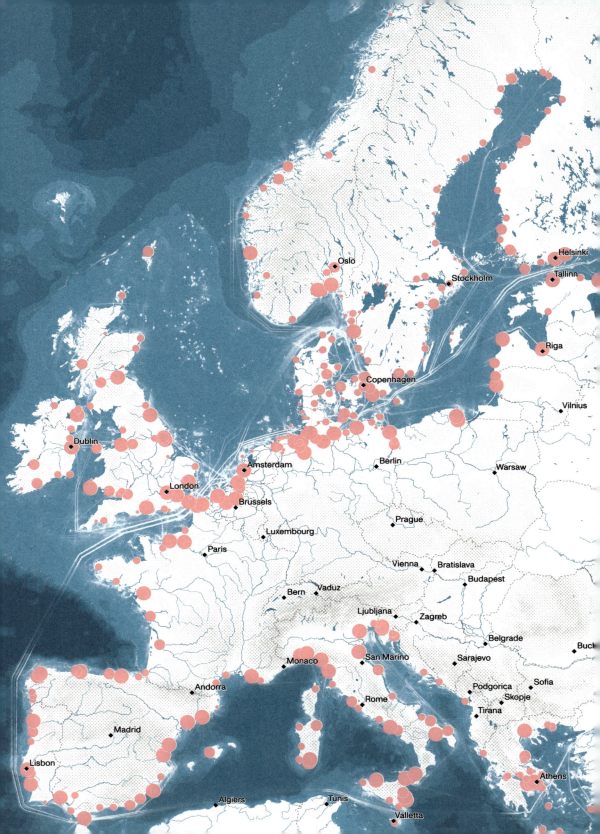

5 Looking at Europe through the Lens of its Four Maritime Waters: (Re)connecting Nations

Abstract
Looking at Europe from the seas allows us to study how people have adapted the spatial configuration of their port city territories to the characteristics of their neighbouring sea or seas. Starting with the four maritime waters—the Mediterranean, North and Baltic Sea and the Atlantic—that surround Europe on three sides, the maps show distinctive characteristics of sea and land, including the morphology and bathymetry of each sea. They identify maritime patterns, including shipping routes, oil platforms, wind farms on the seas and Natura2000 areas; they also identify land-based conditions, including topography along the coastlines, national borders, and regional and urban data entities (NUTS). The sea-based approach allows us to discern similarities and dissimilarities in port city territory development on a single sea and among seas.

European development is heavily influenced by its four waters, each with its own character: the Mediterranean in the south, the North and Baltic Sea in the northwest, and in the west the North-Western and South-Western Waters, here called the Atlantic. We focus here on the four major seas that surround the European continent, the outlines of which are defined on the basis of the European Regional Advisory Councils of Emodnet.[1] The Norwegian and Barents Seas are not included in the maps as they do not border EU countries. Each of the four maritime waters includes several smaller seas, such as the Adriatic Sea as part of the Mediterranean and the Gulf of Bothnia of the Baltic Sea; each has its own character and challenges while connecting the different nations of Europe.

These seas are hubs of regional exchange and shared development. Yet, few publications speak to the potential of exploration through the lens of a specific sea. The French historian Fernand Braudel's masterly book *The Mediterranean*[2] has modelled a sea-based approach to studying larger territories. In *The Edge of the World: How the North Sea Made Us Who We Are*, British novelist

[1] Emodnet, 'European Atlas of the Seas' (2014). Online. Available HTTPS: https://ec.europa.eu/maritimeaffairs/atlas/maritime_atlas/#lang=EN;p=w;bkgd=5;theme=2:0.7 5;c=1224514.3987259883,6446 275.841017013;z=4.

[2] F. Braudel, *The Mediterranean and the Mediterranean World in the Age of Philip* Second edition (Fontana, Collins: University of California, 1975).

Carola Hein, Yvonne van Mil, Lucija Ažman-Momirski

and journalist Michael Pye[3] points out that the world looks different when the sea is perceived as facilitating movement: land becomes a barrier and the sea the bearer of trade and prosperity. We have started to challenge this approach: exchange across the North Sea is the focus of a recent article by Yvonne van Mil and Reinout Rutte.[4] In the *Urbanisation of the Sea*, Nancy Couling and Carola Hein[5] demonstrate how spatial development in and on water shapes port city territories. For centuries, people and goods have flowed through and around these seas, linking port city territories. In each of the seas, seaports have been key gates from and to Europe in war and peace, as numerous heritage sites attest. Having a location by the sea can also mean access to the resources and raw materials available in the sea, including oil, gas, and fish. Indeed, for port city territories, the maritime foreland is as important as the hinterland. Maritime zones, established through international conventions, allow coastal states to use such resources and maintain political harmony in international waters.

The unique features of the four seas warrant shared analysis as they shape development of the European Union and the European continent. The Baltic Sea is a semi-enclosed, relatively shallow sea basin that can only be entered through the Kattegat and Skagerrak straits, along which lie major port cities such as Copenhagen, Malmo and Helsingborg. In addition to nine EU Member States, the Baltic Sea borders Russian territory and provides shipping access to the two major Russian port cities of Kaliningrad and St. Petersburg. The Baltic Sea serves a range of functions, including shipping, fishing, wind farms and mineral extraction. The coastline is characterized by large gorges and smaller bays in the south, and archipelagos and islands in the north. Historically, port cities such as the Hanseatic cities collaborated across the North and Baltic seas and even set up shared fleets and protection. Today, collaboration continues, but its various functions also increasingly compete for limited space.

The North Sea—bordered by the five EU countries of North-West Europe, Norway and Great Britain—connects to the Atlantic Ocean via the English Channel and the Norwegian Sea and gives ships access to two of the world's largest ports: Rotterdam and Hamburg. The North Sea is relatively shallow and has a wide variety of marine landscapes, including fjords, estuaries, sandbanks, bays and intertidal mudflats. It has been the point of origin for colonial empires, notably the British and the Dutch. Throughout history, it has been one of the busiest European seas, with extensive shipping, fishing, energy production, aggregate extraction, defence and recreation; it also has the world's largest agglomeration of drilling rigs. It is precisely all these spatial claims on the sea that threaten its rich and complex biological systems, with important areas for marine birds, fish and mammals.

The European (North-East) Atlantic is generally characterized in the north by relatively shallow water and a gently sloping flat landscape. Along the coastline there are several estuaries and estuarine systems. The southern part, on the other hand, is characterized by a steep and deep coastline and a mountainous landscape. Fishing has long been a key industry here, while coastal tourism and shipping are of great importance to all EU member states bordering this area. The Gibraltar Strait and the English Channel are major shipping gateways connecting Europe with the wider world. Port city territories such as Dublin and Lisbon have been shaped by global (including colonial) connections across this sea; after the discovery of the Americas, New World gold coming through Sevilla and Cadiz propelled the growth of Spanish cities.

The Mediterranean Sea is an almost-enclosed sea basin that can be reached from the west via the Strait of Gibraltar, passing the ports of Algeciras and Ceuta; from the south-east via the Suez Canal; and via the Bosporus by Istanbul from the Black Sea. It is part of one of the most important maritime corridors in the world, the gateway to Africa for EU countries and non-EU countries alike. The coastline of the Mediterranean Sea is characterized by its depth, together with a mountainous landscape above the water and a multitude of small islands off the coast, especially along Croatia. The Mediterranean Sea was at the heart of several empires: heritage sites still speak to the presence of the Greeks, who created new colonies whenever Athens became too crowded; Venice (and Genova) ruled the trade with Asia for many centuries. Today, this millennial heritage attracts cruise tourists, while refugees from Africa and the Middle East brave the sea to reach the safety of the European Union.

The morphology of each sea and its surrounding lands—water depths, mountains, plateaus and plains, bays and islands along the coastline—greatly influences its respective port city territories and nations: it determines what port infrastructure suits shipping; whether the location best suits military uses, fishing or transhipment; what infrastructure can connect the port to the hinterland. A bay or estuary protects the port from physical risks like wind and tides, offering ships a calm environment for loading and unloading. It also creates a permanent problem of siltation, requiring continuous dredging. A mountainous coastline can mean a less populated hinterland or poorer connection to the hinterland. Islands influence the foreland by protecting the coast from wind and tides, but they also limit the accessibility of the port for large ships, and ports located on an island may be at a disadvantage from a smaller hinterland or poor connection with the mainland.

In this section, we show seaport territories at the scale of 15,000,000 (which means that one centimetre on the map corresponds to 15 kilometres on the ground), distinguishing the different seas with different shades of blue. Their spatial characteristics, such as the shape of the coastline and islands and peninsulas, are represented on the maps on the basis of the morphology of water and land, the depth and profile of the seabed (bathymetry) and unique maritime landscapes (Natura2000 areas). The importance of shipping routes is shown by vessel density (at European and sea level) and ferry lines (at territorial level). Maritime borders and borders of administrative entities (defined at European level in NUTS) show the political situation and therewith indicate the multiplicity of international, national, regional and local regulations, interests and policies in which the port city territories are placed.

This atlas allows readers to compare port city territories and thus to address questions about the role of coastal topographies in the development of major port city territories. For example, one can posit that flat sandy territories in the North Sea have facilitated the growth of Hamburg, Rotterdam and Antwerp, while mountainous areas confine Genova, Rijeka and Toulon. Other questions can be asked about opportunities for stakeholder collaborations or, on the contrary, competing economic interests of ports sharing their position on the international transport network and hinterland.

Europe through its Four Waters

The west coast of Europe is surrounded by water: the Baltic Sea, the North Sea, the Mediterranean Sea and the Atlantic. Each maritime water has its own unique character, shaped by its geographical landscape and maritime history. They provide a common, sheltered base for port cities to emerge and develop in. The map shows that we selected our 100 port city territories based on the ranking of the largest European ports in terms of passenger and cargo throughput and the population density of local administrative areas (LAU). Although the selected ports are all leading ports in Europe, the individual differences in volume of transit are significant, both within a maritime water and between maritime waters. This becomes clear when studying the list of selected ports attached to the maps of the four maritime waters (p. 81, 133, 185, 236–237). Although almost all port cities are located in densely populated areas, the combination of maps and data also makes it clear that high population density is not necessarily a prerequisite for high throughput.

1 EMODnet Human Activities: Regional Advisory Councils, 2014.
2 EEA EuroGeographics EuroDEM, 2022.
3 Based on Eurogeographics, (2020). EuroGlobalMap. Version 2020 Eurogeographics. Retrieved from https://eurogeographics.org/maps-for-europe/open-data.
4 Eurostat NUTS 1 data.
5 Eurostat Maritime transport data, 2019.
6 Natural Earth.
7 Eurostat, GISCO LAU, 2019.

6 Examining 100 European Port City Territories through Maps and Infographics: (Re)conceptualizing Water-Land Intersections

Abstract

We have mapped and depicted all 100 European port city territories in a comparative and uniform manner, which allow us to identify, compare and examine their water-land intersections. The chapter describes in detail the methodology used to select the top 100 European port city territories. Our maps show selected ports with adjacent cities and the port city territories, integrating their maritime and land part. Infographic information additionally further illustrates key geographic, port, port city and port city territory data. This work lays the foundation for reconceptualizing the water and land of European port city territories, both in academic research and in future development and planning.

Port city territories sit at the intersection of sea and land, and the distinctive characters of each intersection of land and water in a given port city territory determines their ecosystem. Uniform mapping and infographics information allow us to identify and compare these water-land intersections.

When selecting the top 100 seaport city territories, we considered ports as key signifiers in the transmission of people and goods from sea to land and land to sea. Starting from maritime flows, we identified leading ports first, then looked at each port's adjacent city or cities and port city territory. To identify ports, we used existing statistics. Eurostat categorizes the main ports according to the Directive 2009/42/EC as ports handling more than 1 million tonnes of goods or 200,000 passengers annually.[1] If we were to limit ourselves only to these figures, the Mediterranean ports would dominate the top 100 of European ports, with 38 cargo ports and 52 passenger ports. But these criteria do not provide the comprehensive overview of sea and land, of port, city and territory that we sought. The focus on ports alone does not provide insights into relation with the urban and rural development near the port or the people inhabiting port city territories. The inclusion

1 Eurostat, 'Glossary:Main ports' (2022). Online. Available HTTPS: https://ec.europa.eu/eurostat/statistics-explained/index.php?title=Glossary:Main_ports.

Carola Hein, Yvonne van Mil, Lucija Ažman-Momirski

of a population density factor in the list of the top 100 ports in Europe not only increased the number of cargo ports in the North Sea from 25 to 32 and in the Baltic Sea from 18 to 22, but also increased the number of passenger ports in the Mediterranean from 52 to 59.

To identify the leading port city territories, we used port functions (cargo and passenger ports) to rank the top 25 ports for each of the four maritime waters (Mediterranean, Baltic, North Sea and Western Waters). Taking into account the total gross weight of cargo and the total number of passengers in combination with the number of people living in the urban area resulted in our selection of leading 100 European ports.[2] More specifically, the main ports were ranked by combining four indicators from Eurostat (2019). Indicator 1 presents the absolute values of cargo, which is the gross weight of goods handled (unloaded and loaded) in the port. Indicator 2 provides the number of passengers who embarked and disembarked in the port. Indicator 3 and 4 are the total tonnage of the throughput in the port and the total numbers of passengers, divided by the number of people living in NUTS 3 where the port is located. NUTS 3 is a subdivision of the European territory into metropolitan areas and other areas with a population between 150,000 and 800,000 people.

We used the indicators at both the level of the EU and of the four maritime waters. All eight data points for each port were given weights: We gave Indicator 1 and 2 for EU and for each water a heavier weight underlining our focus on ports and their functions, than Indicator 3 and 4 for EU and for each water. The sum of all eight values gave a final score or final ranking of leading 25 ports in each of the four maritime waters. Only a handful of ports received the highest final score: two in Western waters—Belfast and Southampton; one port in the North Sea—Dover; and two in the Baltic Sea—Rostock and Tallinn. No ports in the Mediterranean ranked this high. In the selection process, we saw that ports fell into three groups within the 25 selected ports for each water: ports important for both cargo and passenger traffic; ports where cargo traffic is the main focus; and ports we included to correct for selection error or because we thought they were too important to leave out even though the methodology did not select them. We included the port of Rijeka, for example, because in the past, it was one of the ten busiest European ports: on the eve of the First World War the port recorded 2,1 million tons of traffic,[3] and it still is the largest and most important seaport in Croatia because of a cargo throughput of 13.6 million tonnes (2020). To examine and select port city territories from the sea meant that we needed a methodology to help understand sea-land transfers. To do this, and to depict each port city territory comparatively uniformly, we chose a scale of 1:450,000, which means that 1 centimetre on the map corresponds to 450 metres on the ground. This view, the most detailed in this atlas, shows the port, the city, their maritime foreland and their terrestrial hinterland of the 25 port city territories of the Mediterranean, Baltic, North Sea and Western Waters. Some maps (and thus port city territories) contain two or more important ports or port cities, as for example Gdansk and Gdynia in the Baltic Sea; while some ports and cities need two maps to fully represent all of the port city territory, as for example London in the North Sea. This scale also allows us to show sea and land elements, including sea depth, administrative borders, transport networks, and the relief of the terrain. The maps furthermore depict concentrations of primary (agriculture and forestry), secondary (industry), tertiary (services and transport) and quaternary (health, education, administration) socio-economic activity in port city territories. Maps display some of these activities as infrastructural and socio-cultural functions: information on the locations of, for example, hospitals, universities and city government headquarters shows their proximity to the port.

An infographic page accompanies each map, with the name of the selected port and its nationality code in the header. In the footer, there is a schematic cross-section of the port on the seaward and landward sides. Four uneven areas on the page display: the name of the water and associated coast category defined by ESPO;[4] detailed information about the port (such as data on ships, terminals, number of passengers, cargo types); information on the port city (such as percentage of built-up area, industrial area, port area, the number of people living in the area); and information on the port city territory (such as data on geography, demography).

This state-of-the-art identification allows scholars and professionals to reconceptualize water-land intersections both in interpretation and in future development and planning. They can see, for example, whether there is room for ports to move into adjacent vacant land and areas of the city, or whether expansion will encroach on ecologically valuable areas. They can also use the maps to see whether port areas are located near or co-located with other industrial areas where stakeholders might develop spontaneous or planned forms of circular economy (a production and consumption model that extends the life cycle of products). These are all urban and spatial planning issues, the resolution of which can bring positive attention and recognition to the water-land intersections of the European port city territories in the context of port planning.

We can see from the maps that the character of the water side of European port city territories varies greatly: from large snake-shaped rivers in Hamburg, Bremen and London, where the predominant port city territory is land, to seas around islands like Las Palmas, Santa Cruz de Tenerife or Rønne, where other land is barely in sight. In the former case, the water element is highly subordinate to a terrestrial landscape within the port city territory; in the latter

[4] ESPO, 'ESPO Port Performance Dashboard' (2013). Online. Available PDF: https://www.espo.be/media/espopublications/espo_dashboard_2013%20final.pdf.

case, the sea is the overwhelming and central feature of the port city territory. Such different geomorphological baselines lead to completely different development and planning of port city territories, and they shape the quality of life throughout the port city territory. In turn, these territories are key to European development, though port, urban and spatial planners do not yet approach them as one spatial unit.

Baltic Sea Map and Statistics

ID	Port name	🛢️[1]	🚢[2]
HEL	Helsingborg, SE	8,839	7,153
HLS	Helsingør, DK	5,052	7,105
CPH	Københavns, DK	6,659	1,213
TRG	Trelleborg, SE	11,798	1,814
MMA	Malmø, SE	7,813	329
RNN	Rønne, SE	1,393	1,860
STO	Stockholm, SE	4,726	8,349
LLA	Luleå, SE	7,355	0
TKU	Turku, FI	2,134	3,137
NLI	Naantali, FI	7,589	194
HEL	Helsinki, FI	14,370	11,619
SKV	Sköldvik, FI	25,198	
SLM	Sillamäe, EE	10,492	
TLL	Tallinn, EE	19,636	9,961
RIX	Riga, LV	30,628	799
VNT	Ventspils, LV	19,600	232
LPX	Liepaja, LV	7,025	40
KLJ	Klaipeda, LT	42,705	343
BOT	Butinge, LT	9,542	0
GDN	Gdansk, PL	45,520	289
GDY	Gdynia, PL	20,551	791
SZZ	Szczecin, PL	9,583	6
SWI	Swinoujscie, PL	15,937	1,170
RSK	Rostock, DE	19,993	3,394
RDF	Rødby, DK	8,394	0
PJT	Puttgarden, DE	5,375	6,007
LBX	Lübeck, DE	16,022	458
KEL	Kiel, DE	4,819	2,331
FRC	Fredericia, DK	6,869	0
AAR	Århus, DK	8,617	3,385
SST	Statoil-Havnen, DK	7,900	0
SJO	Sjaellands Odde, DK		3,493

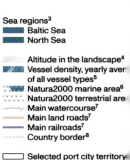

Sea regions[3]
- Baltic Sea
- North Sea

- Altitude in the landscape[4]
- Vessel density, yearly average of all vessel types[5]
- Natura2000 marine area[6]
- Natura2000 terrestrial area
- Main watercourse[7]
- Main land roads[7]
- Main railroads[7]
- Country border[8]

- Selected port city territory
- Selected port based on tonnage of cargo handled
- Selected port based on number of passengers har
- Main port outside the EU
- National capital[10]

Population density LAU (in inhabitants per km²)[11]

300 600

0 100 km

1. Total tonnage of cargo in thousands and in relation to the other selected European ports. Eurostat, 2019.
2. Total number of passengers in thousands and in relation to other selected European ports. Eurostat, 2019.
3. EMODnet Human Activities: Regional Advisory Councils, 2014.
4. EEA EuroGeographics EuroDEM, 2022.
5. EMODnet Human Activities, Vessel Density Map 2019.
6. ———, Environment, Natura2000, 2015.
7. Based on Eurogeographics, (2020). EuroGlobalMap. Version 2020 Eurogeographics. Retrieved from https://eurogeographics.org/maps-for-europe/open-data.
8. Eurostat NUTS 1 data.
9. Eurostat Maritime transport data, 2019.
10. Natural Earth.
11. Eurostat, GISCO LAU, 2019.

HEL # Helsingborg, SE
HLS # Helsingør, DK

≈ Øresund
≈ Øresund

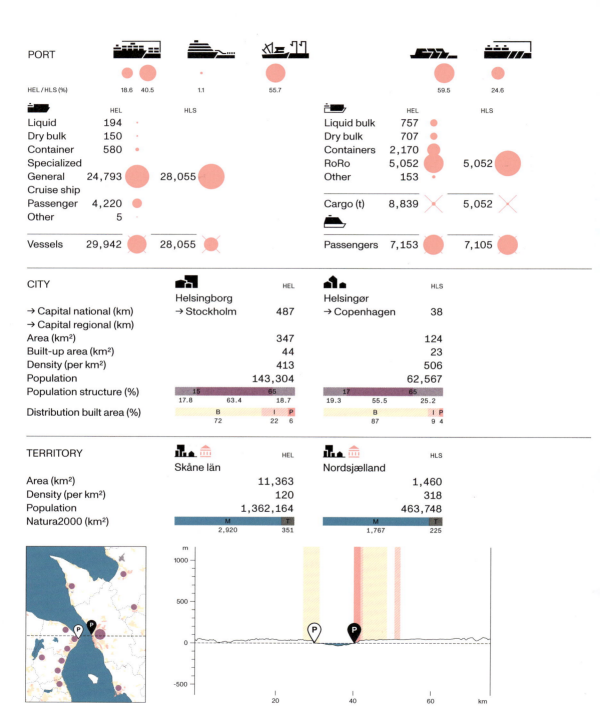

PORT

HEL / HLS (%)   18.6   40.5   1.1   55.7   59.5   24.6

	HEL	HLS			HEL	HLS
Liquid	194			Liquid bulk	757	
Dry bulk	150			Dry bulk	707	
Container	580			Containers	2,170	
Specialized				RoRo	5,052	5,052
General	24,793	28,055		Other	153	
Cruise ship						
Passenger	4,220			Cargo (t)	8,839	5,052
Other	5					
Vessels	29,942	28,055		Passengers	7,153	7,105

CITY

	Helsingborg	HEL	Helsingør	HLS
→ Capital national (km)	→ Stockholm	487	→ Copenhagen	38
→ Capital regional (km)				
Area (km²)		347		124
Built-up area (km²)		44		23
Density (per km²)		413		506
Population		143,304		62,567
Population structure (%)	17.8 / 63.4 / 18.7		19.3 / 55.5 / 25.2	
Distribution built area (%)	B 72 / I 22 / P 6		B 87 / I 9 / P 4	

TERRITORY

	Skåne län	HEL	Nordsjælland	HLS
Area (km²)		11,363		1,460
Density (per km²)		120		318
Population		1,362,164		463,748
Natura2000 (km²)	M 2,920 / T 351		M 1,767 / T 225	

82   Port City Atlas   Baltic Sea

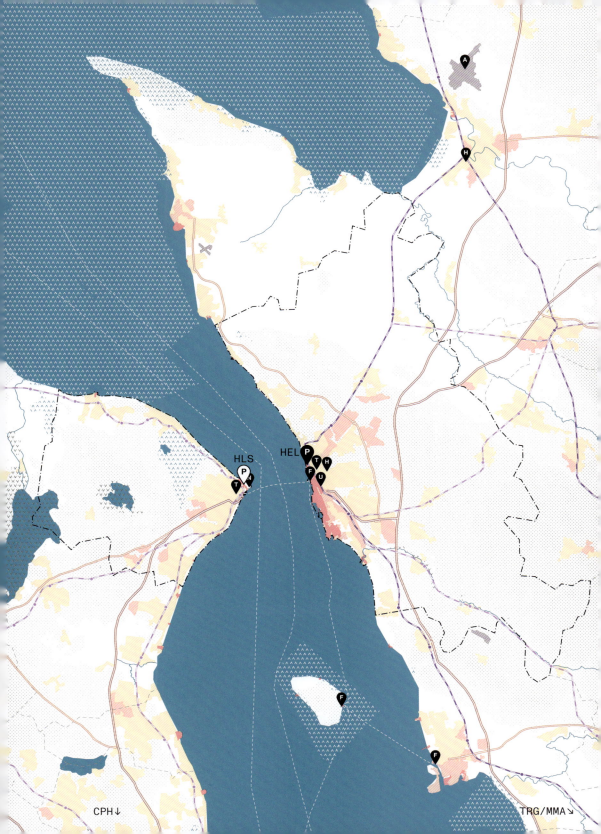

CPH # Københavns, DK

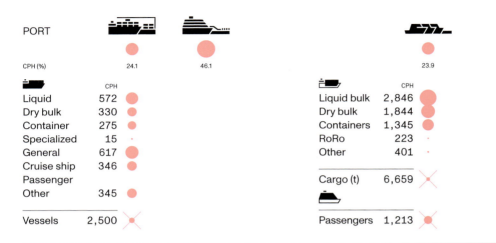

PORT

CPH (%) 24.1 46.1 23.9 5.9

	CPH			CPH
Liquid	572		Liquid bulk	2,846
Dry bulk	330		Dry bulk	1,844
Container	275		Containers	1,345
Specialized	15		RoRo	223
General	617		Other	401
Cruise ship	346			
Passenger			Cargo (t)	6,659
Other	345			
Vessels	2,500		Passengers	1,213

CITY

	CPH
København	
→ Capital national (km)	→ Copenhagen 0
→ Capital regional (km)	
Area (km²)	460
Built-up area (km²)	259
Density (per km²)	6,141
Population	559,440
Population structure (%)	15 / 74.2 / 65 — 15.4 / 10.4
Distribution built area (%)	B 79 / A 4 / I 12 / P 5

TERRITORY

	CPH
Byen København	
Area (km²)	185
Density (per km²)	4,241
Population	784,618
Natura2000 (km²)	M 1,065

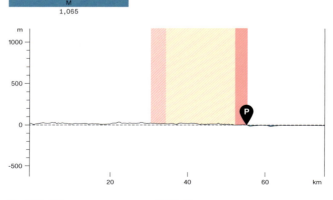

84 Port City Atlas Baltic Sea

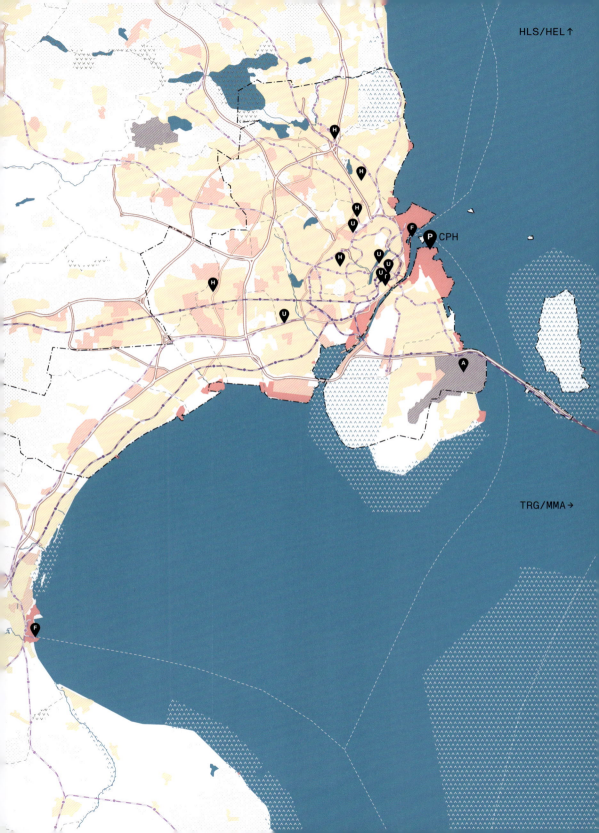

TRG
MMA

Trelleborg, SE
Malmø, SE

 Baltic Sea
 Øresund

PORT

TRG / MMA (%) 100 100

	TRG	MMA
Liquid	13	451
Dry bulk	5	54
Container		49
Specialized		241
General	5,412	2,062
Cruise ship		
Passenger		
Other	2	17
Vessels	5,432	2,874

	TRG	MMA
Liquid bulk	44	2,253
Dry bulk	39	578
Containers		183
RoRo	11,715	4,298
Other		501
Cargo (t)	11,798	7,813
Passengers	1,814	329

CITY

Trelleborg (TRG) / Malmö (MMA)

	TRG	MMA
→ Capital national (km) → Stockholm	512	529
→ Capital regional (km)		
Area (km²)	344	159
Built-up area (km²)	19	67
Density (per km²)	131	2,105
Population	44,902	333,633
Population structure (%)	17 / 65 — 21.4 / 57.1 / 21.5	15 / 65 — 18.4 / 66.3 / 15.2
Distribution built area (%)	B 84 / I 15 / P 1	B 70 / I 16 / P 13

TERRITORY

Skåne län / Skåne län

	TRG	MMA
Area (km²)	11,363	11,363
Density (per km²)	120	120
Population	1,362,164	1,362,164
Natura2000 (km²)	M 2,920 / T 351	M 2,920 / T 351

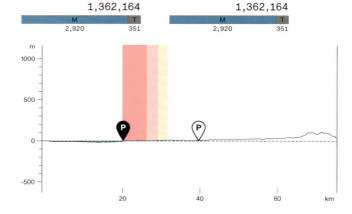

86 Port City Atlas Baltic Sea

RNN # Rønne, DK  Baltic Sea

PORT

RNN (%) 33.0 8.5 40.3 18.2

	RNN			RNN
Liquid	20		Liquid bulk	68
Dry bulk	158		Dry bulk	688
Container			Containers	
Specialized	583		RoRo	607
General	2,399		Other	30
Cruise ship			Cargo (t)	1,393
Passenger				
Other	46		Passengers	1,860
Vessels	3,206			

CITY

Bornholm   RNN

→ Capital national (km)
→ Capital regional (km)   → Copenhagen   150
Area (km²)   590
Built-up area (km²)   25
Density (per km²)   67
Population   39,572
Population structure (%)   17 / 65   16.9 / 53.3 / 29.8
Distribution built area (%)   B 79   A 9 I 7 P 5

TERRITORY

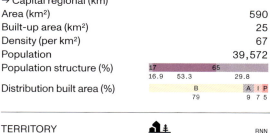

Bornholm   RNN

Area (km²)   592
Density (per km²)   67
Population   39,662
Natura2000 (km²)   M 45   T 61

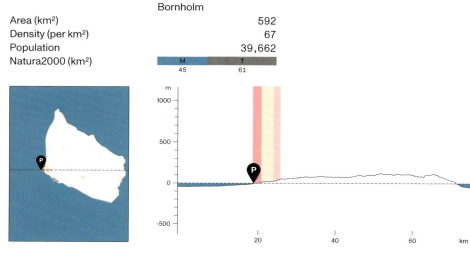

88   Port City Atlas   Baltic Sea

STO

Stockholm, SE

Riddarfjärden

PORT

STO (%)
6.2   32.7   52.8   8.3

	STO	
Liquid	93	
Dry bulk	540	
Container	160	
Specialized		
General	3,211	
Cruise ship		
Passenger	322	
Other	305	

| Vessels | 4,631 | |

	STO	
Liquid bulk	349	
Dry bulk	921	
Containers	420	
RoRo	2,451	
Other	585	

| Cargo (t) | 4,726 | |

| Passengers | 8,349 | |

CITY

→ Capital national (km)
→ Capital regional (km)
Area (km²)
Built-up area (km²)
Density (per km²)
Population
Population structure (%)
Distribution built area (%)

Stockholm   STO
→ Stockholm   0
             1,458
             407
             651
             949,761

15 65
18.5   66.3   15.0

B   A I P
86   1 12 1

TERRITORY

Area (km²)
Density (per km²)
Population
Natura2000 (km²)

Stockholms län   STO
                  7,073
                  331
                  2,344,124

M   T
612   46

m
1000

500

0

-500

         20   40   60   km

90   Port City Atlas   Baltic Sea

LLA # Luleå, SE 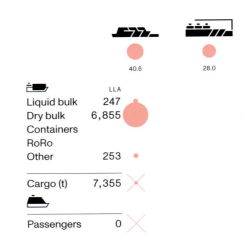 Lule River

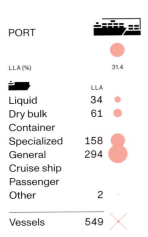

PORT

LLA (%) 31.4 40.6 28.0

	LLA			LLA	
Liquid	34		Liquid bulk	247	
Dry bulk	61		Dry bulk	6,855	
Container			Containers		
Specialized	158		RoRo		
General	294		Other	253	
Cruise ship					
Passenger			Cargo (t)	7,355	✕
Other	2				
Vessels	549	✕	Passengers	0	✕

CITY

Luleå LLA
→ Capital national (km) → Stockholm 729
→ Capital regional (km)
Area (km²) 2,255
Built-up area (km²) 50
Density (per km²) 35
Population 77,832
Population structure (%) 17 / 65
18.8 60.2 21.0
Distribution built area (%) B A I P
64 6 29 1

TERRITORY

Norrbottens län LLA
Area (km²) 105,908
Density (per km²) 2
Population 250,497
Natura2000 (km²) M T
1,270 27,458

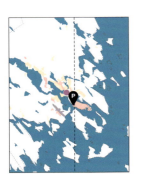

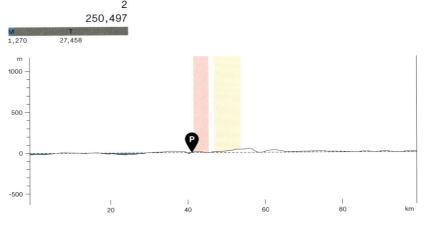

92 Port City Atlas Baltic Sea

TKU
NLI

Turku, FI
Naantali, FI

River Aura
Archipelago Sea

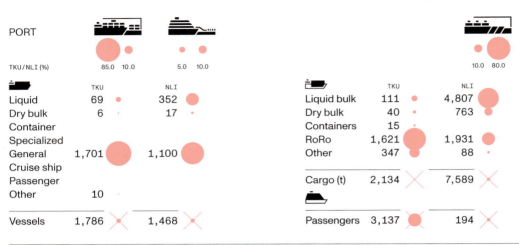

PORT						
TKU/NLI (%)	85.0	10.0	5.0	10.0	10.0	80.0

	TKU	NLI		TKU	NLI
Liquid	69	352	Liquid bulk	111	4,807
Dry bulk	6	17	Dry bulk	40	763
Container			Containers	15	
Specialized			RoRo	1,621	1,931
General	1,701	1,100	Other	347	88
Cruise ship					
Passenger			Cargo (t)	2,134	7,589
Other	10				
Vessels	1,786	1,468	Passengers	3,137	194

CITY	TKU	NLI
	Turku	Naantali / Nådendal
→ Capital national (km)	→ Helsinki 154	→ Helsinki 164
→ Capital regional (km)		
Area (km²)	246	295
Built-up area (km²)	73	20
Density (per km²)	776	65
Population	191,331	19,245
Population structure (%)	12.8 66.7 20.5	18.0 54.9 27.1
Distribution built area (%)	B 72 A 3 I 19 P 6	B 80 I 18 P 2

TERRITORY	TKU	NLI
	Varsinais-Suomi	Varsinais-Suomi
Area (km²)	10,598	10,598
Density (per km²)	45	45
Population	478,582	478,582
Natura2000 (km²)	M 3,639 T 223	M 3,639 T 223

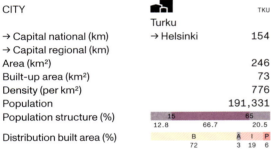

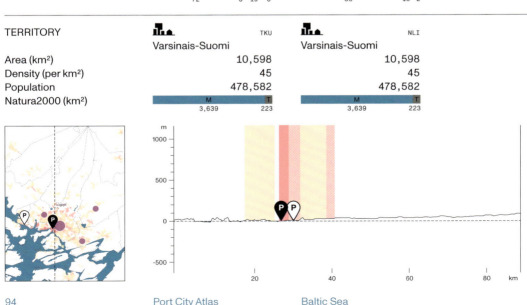

94 Port City Atlas Baltic Sea

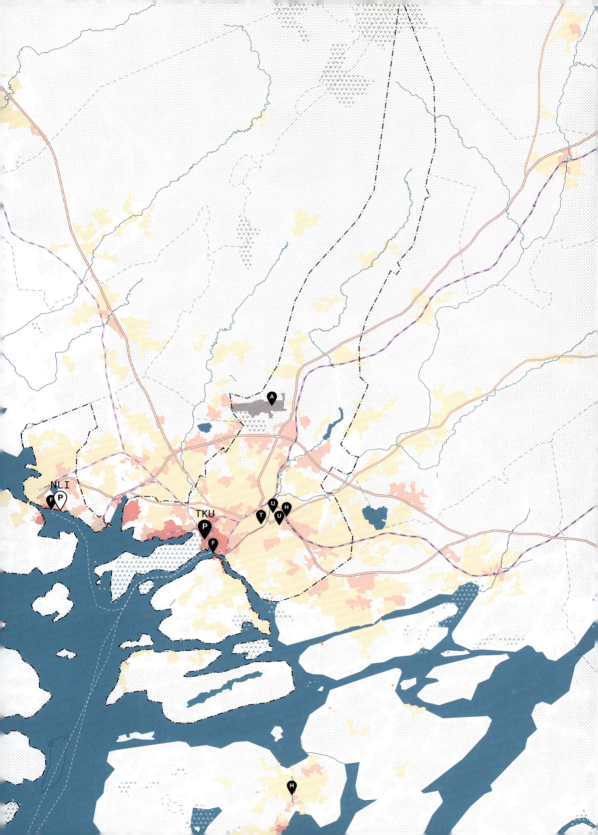

HEL

Helsinki, FI

 Gulf of Finland

PORT

HEL (%)   28.7   71.1   0.1

	HEL
Liquid	62
Dry bulk	68
Container	705
Specialized	
General	6,867
Cruise ship	
Passenger	628
Other	
Vessels	8,035

	HEL
Liquid bulk	138
Dry bulk	1,544
Containers	3,719
RoRo	8,017
Other	952
Cargo (t)	14,370
Passengers	11,619

CITY

Helsinki Greater city   HEL
→ Helsinki   0

→ Capital national (km)
→ Capital regional (km)
Area (km²)   779
Built-up area (km²)   364
Density (per km²)   1,482
Population   1,154,967
Population structure (%)   15 / 65   16.3   67.8   15.9
Distribution built area (%)   B 76   A 4   I 19   P 1

TERRITORY

Helsinki-Uusimaa   HEL

Area (km²)   9,420
Density (per km²)   177
Population   1,671,024
Natura2000 (km²)   M 3,925   T 245

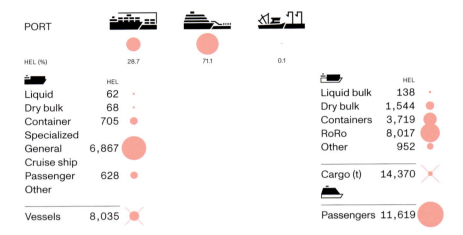

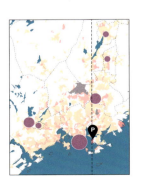

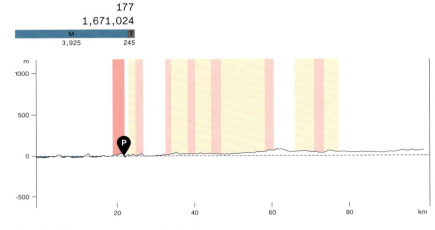

96   Port City Atlas   Baltic Sea

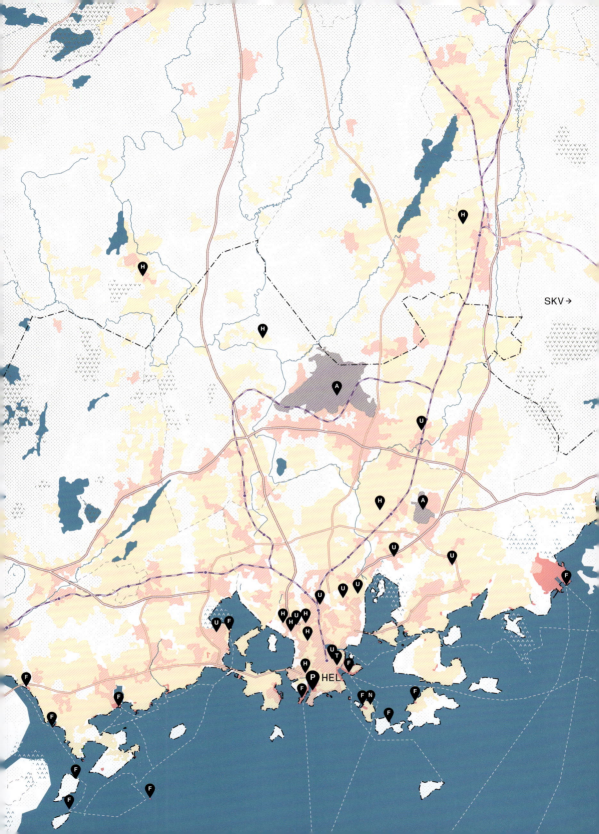

SKV # Sköldvik, FI    Svartbäckfjärden

PORT

SKV (%)

	SKV
Liquid	1,251
Dry bulk	
Container	
Specialized	
General	
Cruise ship	
Passenger	
Other	2
Vessels	1,253

67.4   32.6

	SKV
Liquid bulk	25,160
Dry bulk	
Containers	
RoRo	
Other	38
Cargo (t)	25,198
Passengers	

CITY

Porvoo

	SKV
→ Capital national (km)	
→ Capital regional (km)	→ Helsinki 38
Area (km²)	646
Built-up area (km²)	39
Density (per km²)	78
Population	50,262
Population structure (%)	17 / 65 — 20.4 / 57.5 / 22.2
Distribution built area (%)	B 73 / I 26 / P 1

TERRITORY

Helsinki-Uusimaa

	SKV
Area (km²)	9,420
Density (per km²)	177
Population	1,671,024
Natura2000 (km²)	M 3,925 / T 245

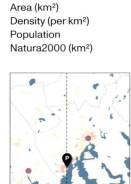
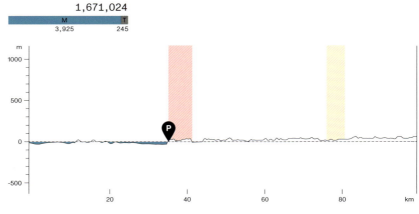

98 Port City Atlas Baltic Sea

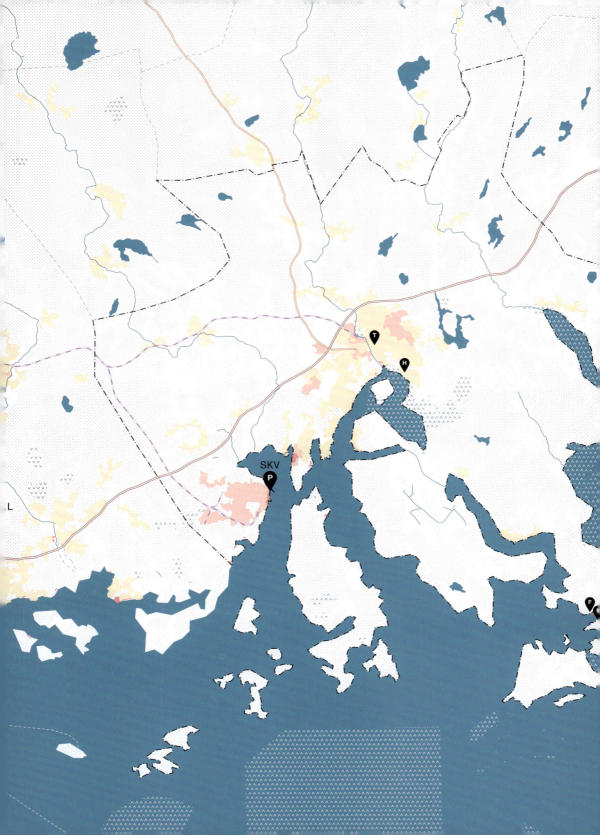

SLM # Sillamäe, EE Narva Bay

PORT

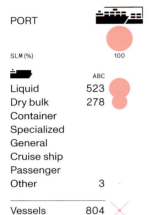

SLM (%) 100

	ABC			SLM
Liquid	523		Liquid bulk	7,712
Dry bulk	278		Dry bulk	2,465
Container			Containers	130
Specialized			RoRo	
General			Other	185
Cruise ship				
Passenger			Cargo (t)	10,492
Other	3			
Vessels	804		Passengers	

CITY

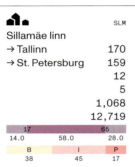

Sillamäe linn SLM

→ Capital national (km)	→ Tallinn	170
→ Capital regional (km)	→ St. Petersburg	159
Area (km²)		12
Built-up area (km²)		5
Density (per km²)		1,068
Population		12,719
Population structure (%)	14.0 / 58.0 / 28.0	17 / 65
Distribution built area (%)	B 38 / I 45 / P 17	

TERRITORY

Kirde-Eesti SLM

Area (km²)	3,457
Density (per km²)	629
Population	140,506
Natura2000 (km²)	M 99 / T 911

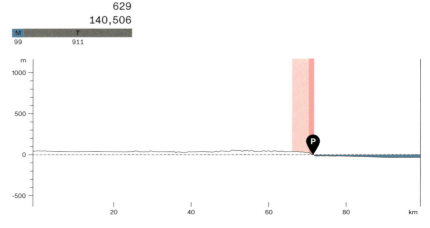

100 Port City Atlas Baltic Sea

TLL # Tallinn, EE ⛴ Tallinn Bay

PORT

TLL (%) 50.5 20.1 29.4

	TLL			TLL
Liquid	397		Liquid bulk	7,368
Dry bulk	111		Dry bulk	4,516
Container	342		Containers	1,834
Specialized			RoRo	5,365
General	6,561		Other	553
Cruise ship	361			
Passenger			Cargo (t)	19,636
Other	20			
Vessels	7,792		Passengers	9,961

CITY

	TLL
Tallinn	
→ Capital national (km)	→ Tallinn 0
→ Capital regional (km)	
Area (km²)	159
Built-up area (km²)	91
Density (per km²)	2,728
Population	434,562
Population structure (%)	15 / 65
	16.0 / 65.6 / 18.4
Distribution built area (%)	B / A / I / P
	71 / 2 / 25 / 2

TERRITORY

Põhja-Eesti TLL

Area (km²)	4,328
Density (per km²)	139
Population	599,478
Natura2000 (km²)	M 1,104 / T 1,218

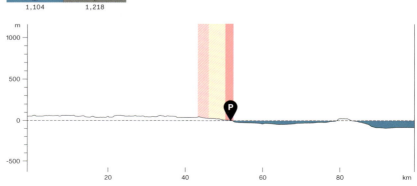

102 Port City Atlas Baltic Sea

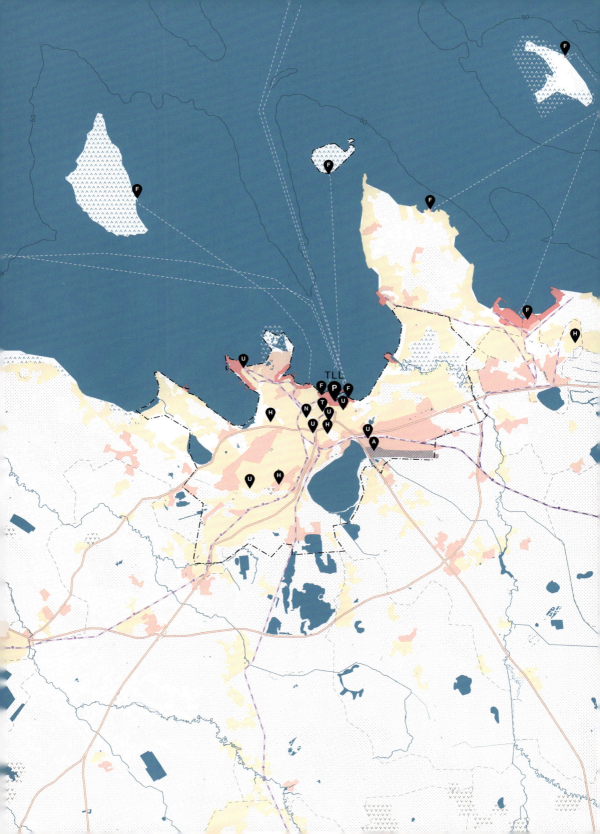

RIX # Riga, LV  Gulf of Riga

PORT

RIX (%)

	RIX	
Liquid	373	
Dry bulk	1,941	
Container	536	
Specialized	28	
General	12	
Cruise ship	81	
Passenger	359	
Other	33	
Vessels	3,363	✕

100

	RIX	
Liquid bulk	3,748	
Dry bulk	20,103	
Containers	3,851	
RoRo	143	
Other	2,783	
Cargo (t)	30,628	✕
Passengers	799	✕

CITY

Rīga | RIX

→ Capital national (km)	→ Rīga	0
→ Capital regional (km)		
Area (km²)		304
Built-up area (km²)		144
Density (per km²)		2,059
Population		626,147
Population structure (%)	15.4 / 64.1 / 20.6	
Distribution built area (%)	B 58 / A 1 / I 34 / P 7	

TERRITORY

Rīga | RIX

Area (km²)	304
Density (per km²)	2,081
Population	632,614
Natura2000 (km²)	M 443 / T 9

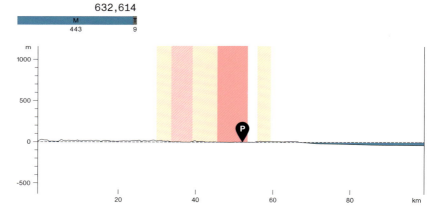

104 | Port City Atlas | Baltic Sea

VNT # Ventspils, LV  Baltic Sea

PORT

VNT (%) 100

	VNT			VNT
Liquid	456		Liquid bulk	10,231
Dry bulk	442		Dry bulk	7,438
Container			Containers	
Specialized			RoRo	1,302
General			Other	626
Cruise ship				
Passenger	602		Cargo (t)	19,600
Other	8			
Vessels	1,508		Passengers	232

CITY

Ventspils — VNT

→ Capital national (km) → Riga 161
→ Capital regional (km)
Area (km²) 58
Built-up area (km²) 19
Density (per km²) 593
Population 34,377
Population structure (%) 15.2 | 61.4 | 23.4
Distribution built area (%) B 53 | Ã 1 | I 29 | P 17

TERRITORY

Kurzeme — VNT

Area (km²) 13,604
Density (per km²) 18
Population 240,113
Natura2000 (km²) M 3,837 | T 853

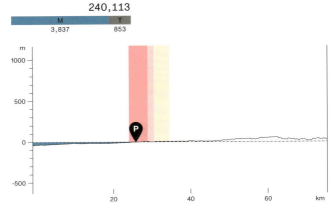

106 Port City Atlas Baltic Sea

LPX   # Liepaja, LV    Baltic Sea

PORT

LPX (%)   100

	LPX		LPX
Liquid	163	Liquid bulk	566
Dry bulk	1,124	Dry bulk	5,489
Container	8	Containers	36
Specialized		RoRo	471
General		Other	463
Cruise ship			
Passenger	254	Cargo (t)	7,025
Other	8		
Vessels	1,557	Passengers	40

CITY

Liepāja   LPX

→ Capital national (km)   → Vilnius   339
→ Capital regional (km)   → Kaliningrad   206
Area (km²)   61
Built-up area (km²)   26
Density (per km²)   1,124
Population   68,569
Population structure (%)   15   65
                          17.2 61.5 21.3
Distribution built area (%) B   I   P
                            46   45   9

TERRITORY

Kurzeme   LPX

Area (km²)   13,604
Density (per km²)   18
Population   240,113
Natura2000 (km²)   M   T
                         3,837   853

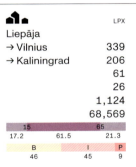

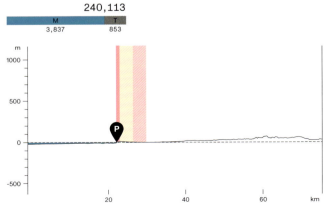

108   Port City Atlas   Baltic Sea

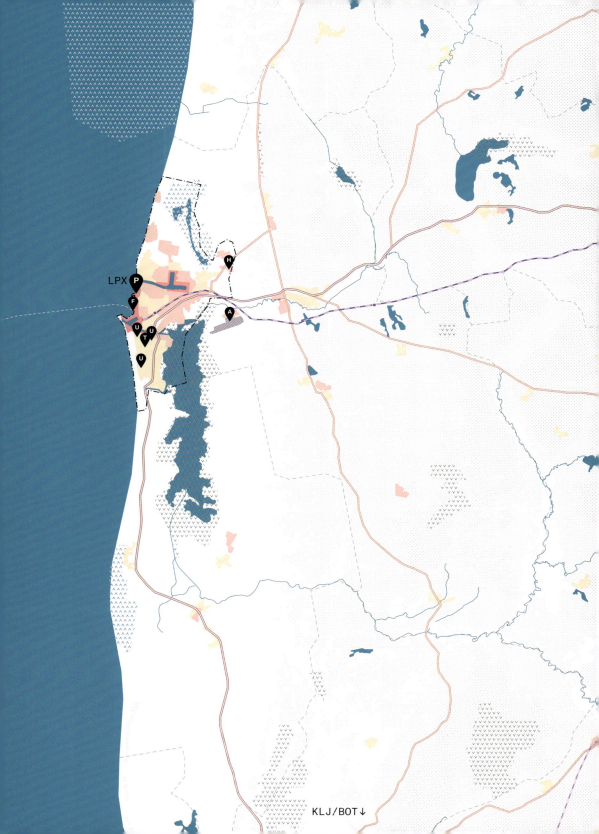

KLJ
BOT

Klaipeda, LT
Butinge, LT

Baltic Sea
Baltic Sea

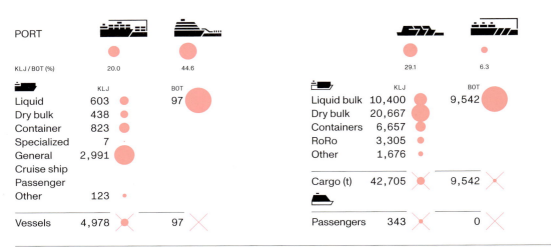

PORT

KLJ / BOT (%) 20.0 44.6 29.1 6.3

	KLJ	BOT		KLJ	BOT
Liquid	603	97	Liquid bulk	10,400	9,542
Dry bulk	438		Dry bulk	20,667	
Container	823		Containers	6,657	
Specialized	7		RoRo	3,305	
General	2,991		Other	1,676	
Cruise ship					
Passenger			Cargo (t)	42,705	9,542
Other	123				
Vessels	4,978	97	Passengers	343	0

CITY

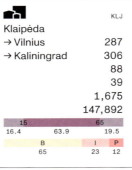
Klaipėda KLJ
Palanga City Municipality BOT

	KLJ	BOT
→ Capital national (km)	→ Vilnius 287	→ Vilnius 117
→ Capital regional (km)	→ Kaliningrad 306	→ Kaliningrad 152
Area (km²)	88	79
Built-up area (km²)	39	12
Density (per km²)	1,675	199
Population	147,892	15,664
Population structure (%)	16.4 / 63.9 / 19.5	
Distribution built area (%)	B 65 / I 23 / P 12	B 70 / A 15 / I 15

TERRITORY

Klaipėdos apskritis KLJ
Klaipėdos apskritis BOT

	KLJ	BOT
Area (km²)	4,819	4,819
Density (per km²)	66	66
Population	317,722	317,722
Natura2000 (km²)	M 2,455 / T 410	M 2,455 / T 410

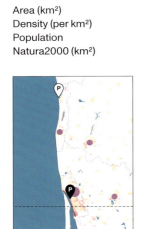
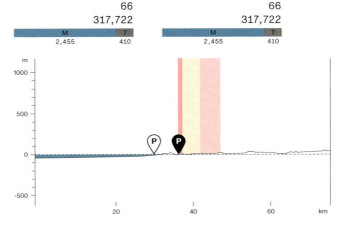

Port City Atlas Baltic Sea

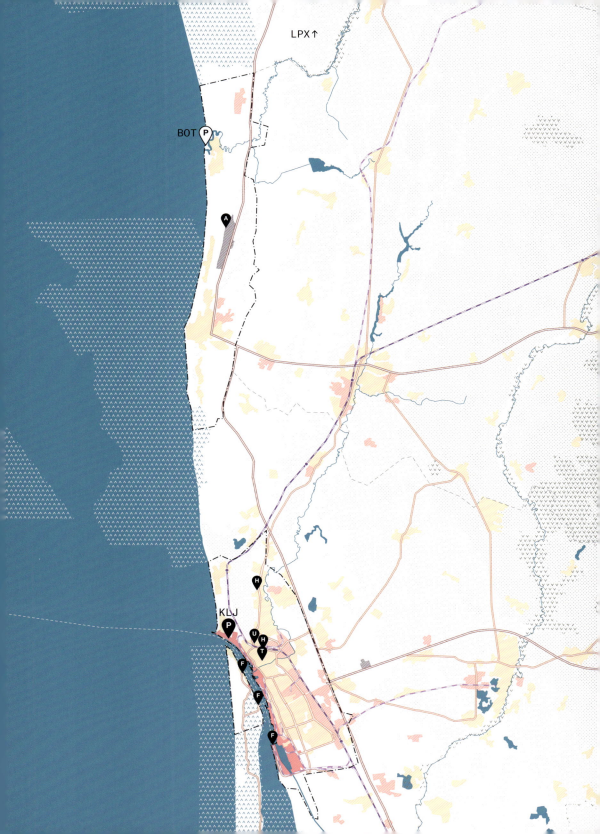

GDN
GDY

Gdansk, PL
Gdynia, PL

≋ Gdansk Bay
⇩ Gdansk Bay

PORT

GDN / GDY (%)   20.7   66.4   76.5 24.0   2.8 0.2   9.3

	GDN	GDY
Liquid	763	303
Dry bulk	276	263
Container	663	1,074
Specialized	114	26
General	1,213	1,873
Cruise ship		
Passenger		472
Other	715	73
Vessels	3,738	4,084

	GDN	GDY
Liquid bulk	18,000	2,500
Dry bulk	10,952	7,355
Containers	15,358	7,153
RoRo	394	2,298
Other	816	1,245
Cargo (t)	45,520	20,551
Passengers	289	791

CITY

	M. Gdańsk (GDN)	M. Gdynia (GDY)
→ Capital national (km) → Warsaw	284	303
→ Capital regional (km) → Kaliningrad	126	128
Area (km²)	262	135
Built-up area (km²)	98	42
Density (per km²)	1,783	1,823
Population	466,631	246,309
Population structure (%)	15.2 / 64.8 / 20.1	13.8 / 64.8 / 21.4
Distribution built area (%)	B 69 / Â 2 / I 23 / P 6	B 75 / Â 1 / I 14 / P 10

TERRITORY

	Trójmiejski (GDN)	Trójmiejski (GDY)
Area (km²)	416	416
Density (per km²)	1,795	1,795
Population	745,972	745,972
Natura2000 (km²)	M 1,330 / T 108	M 1,330 / T 108

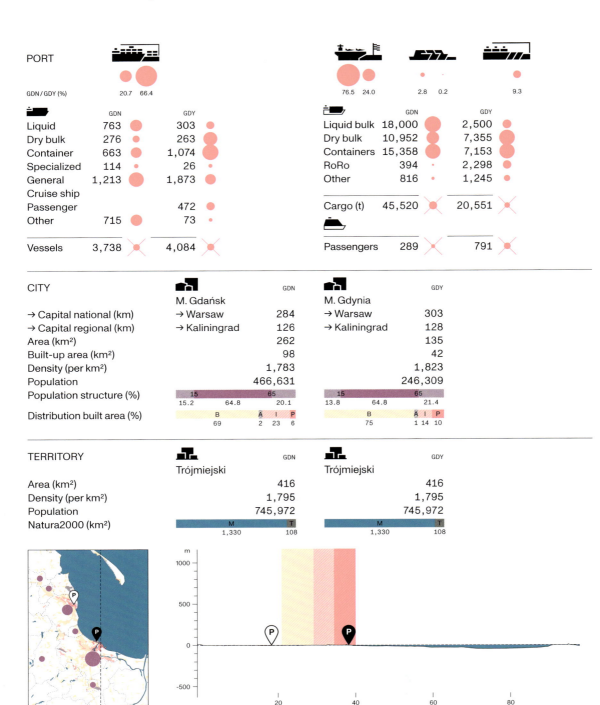

112   Port City Atlas   Baltic Sea

SZZ # Szczecin, PL  River Oder

PORT

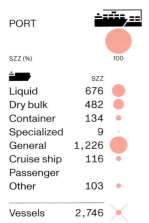

SZZ (%)   100

	SZZ
Liquid	676
Dry bulk	482
Container	134
Specialized	9
General	1,226
Cruise ship	116
Passenger	
Other	103
Vessels	2,746

	SZZ
Liquid bulk	1,418
Dry bulk	4,999
Containers	555
RoRo	7
Other	2,604
Cargo (t)	9,583
Passengers	6

CITY

Miasto Szczecin   SZZ

→ Capital national (km) → Warsaw	454
→ Capital regional (km) → Hamburg	303
Area (km²)	301
Built-up area (km²)	78
Density (per km²)	1,339
Population	402,465

Population structure (%)   15 65
13.6   65.9   20.5

Distribution built area (%)   B 72   I 20   P 8

TERRITORY

Miasto Szczecin   SZZ

Area (km²)	300
Density (per km²)	1,335
Population	400,859
Natura2000 (km²)	M 2,127 T 401

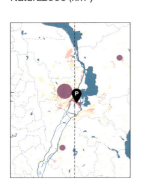

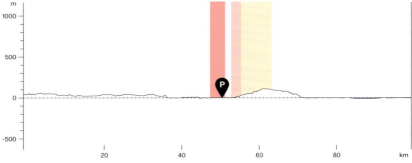

114   Port City Atlas   Baltic Sea

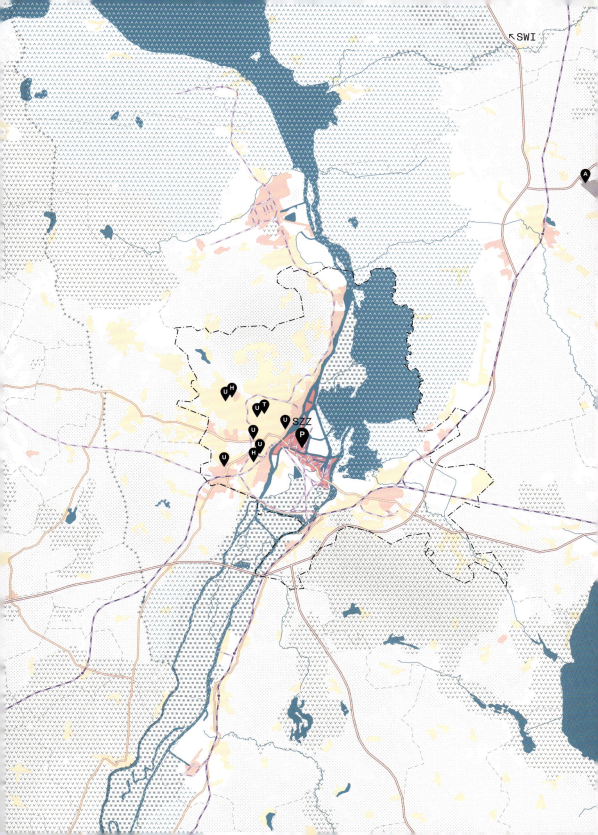

SWI

Swinoujscie, PL

 Swine

PORT

SWI (%)

	SWI
Liquid	585
Dry bulk	111
Container	17
Specialized	
General	4,034
Cruise ship	47
Passenger	1,357
Other	1
Vessels	6,152

41.6

7.9   50.4

	SWI
Liquid bulk	4,830
Dry bulk	4,442
Containers	19
RoRo	6,227
Other	419
Cargo (t)	15,937
Passengers	1,170

CITY

Świnoujście   SWI

→ Capital national (km) → Warsaw	489
→ Capital regional (km) → Hamburg	284
Area (km²)	101
Built-up area (km²)	12
Density (per km²)	404
Population	40,910
Population structure (%)	17 / 14.6 / 62.9 / 65 / 22.6
Distribution built area (%)	B 65 / I 5 / P 30

TERRITORY

Szczeciński   SWI

Area (km²)	7,441
Density (per km²)	68
Population	506,021
Natura2000 (km²)	M 6,636 / T 2,032

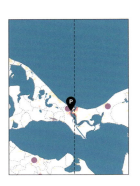

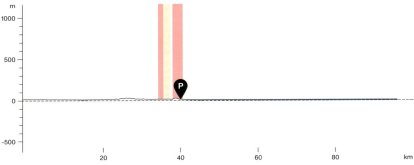

116   Port City Atlas   Baltic Sea

RSK   # Rostock, DE    Unterwarnow

PORT

RSK (%)   0.7   55.3   4.3   39.7

	RSK			RSK
Liquid	256		Liquid bulk	3,816
Dry bulk	48		Dry bulk	6,289
Container	5		Containers	22
Specialized	9		RoRo	7,987
General	6,660		Other	1,819
Cruise ship				
Passenger			Cargo (t)	19,993
Other	217			
Vessels	7,195		Passengers	3,394

CITY

		RSK
	Rostock	
→ Capital national (km)	→ Berlin	195
→ Capital regional (km)	→ Hamburg	154
Area (km²)		169
Built-up area (km²)		51
Density (per km²)		1,233
Population		208,886
Population structure (%)	12.0 / 64.5 / 23.6	
Distribution built area (%)	B 63 / I 30 / P 7	

TERRITORY

		RSK
	Rostock, Kreisfreie Stadt	
Area (km²)		169
Density (per km²)		1,234
Population		208,886
Natura2000 (km²)	M 2,125 / T 136	

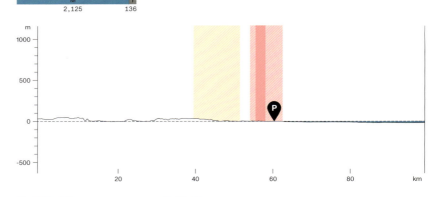

118   Port City Atlas   Baltic Sea

ROF **Rødby, DK**
PUT **Puttgarden, DE**

≡ ⊍ Fehmarnbelt
≡ ⊍ Fehmarnbelt

PORT

ROF / PUT (%)   12.3   0.2   87.7   99.8

	ROF	PUT		ROF	PUT
Liquid			Liquid bulk		
Dry bulk			Dry bulk		
Container			Containers		
Specialized			RoRo	8,394	5,375
General	17,378	17,378	Other		
Cruise ship			Cargo (t)	8,394	5,375
Passenger					
Other					
Vessels	17,378	17,378	Passengers	0	6,007

CITY   ROF   PUT
                            Lolland   Fehmarn, Stadt
→ Capital national (km)   → Copenhagen   142   → Berlin   264
→ Capital regional (km)   → Hamburg   134
Area (km²)   724   182
Built-up area (km²)   23   6
Density (per km²)   46   69
Population   41,615   12,592
Population structure (%)   17   65   17   65
                            15.2 51.2   33.6   13.6 58.1   28.3
Distribution built area (%)   B   A I P   B   I P
                                  83   1 14 2   85   8 7

TERRITORY   ROF   PUT
                            Vest- og Sydsjælland   Ostholstein
Area (km²)   6,507   1,386
Density (per km²)   90   145
Population   587,379   200,581
Natura2000 (km²)   M   T   M   T
                                7,884   188   2,808   180

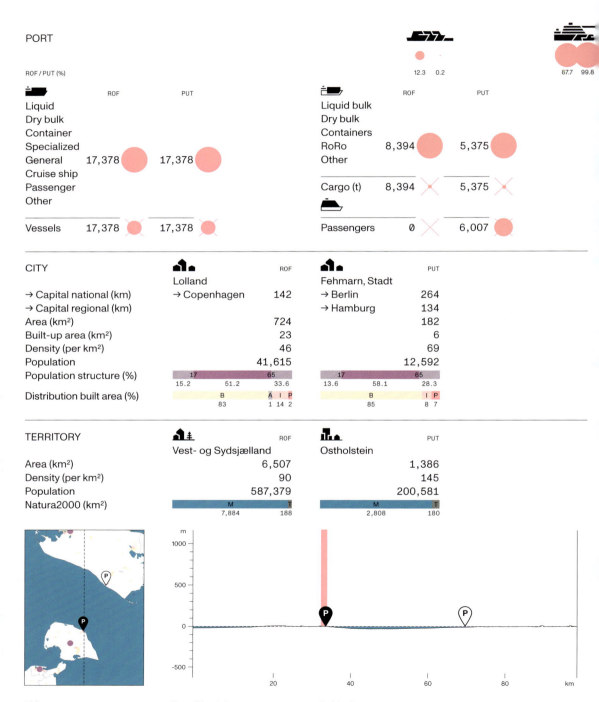

120   Port City Atlas   Baltic Sea

LBC

Lübeck, DE

 Trave

PORT

LBC (%)

	LBC			LBC
Liquid	6		Liquid bulk	29
Dry bulk	29		Dry bulk	984
Container	167		Containers	1,827
Specialized			RoRo	12,717
General	3,883		Other	465
Cruise ship				
Passenger			Cargo (t)	16,022
Other	14			
Vessels	4,099		Passengers	458

98.0   2.0

CITY

	LBC
Lübeck	
→ Capital national (km) → Berlin	237
→ Capital regional (km) → Hamburg	57
Area (km²)	212
Built-up area (km²)	66
Density (per km²)	1,025
Population	217,198
Population structure (%)	12.5 64.2 23.2
Distribution built area (%)	B 75 A 2 I 19 P 4

15 65

TERRITORY

Lübeck, Kreisfreie Stadt   LBC

Area (km²)	212
Density (per km²)	1,025
Population	217,198
Natura2000 (km²)	M 604 1 19

122   Port City Atlas   Baltic Sea

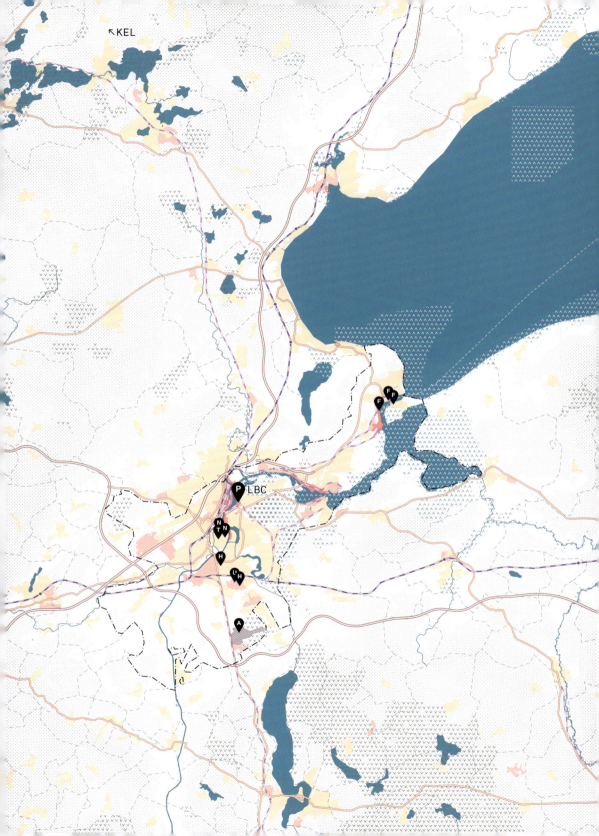

KEL | # Kiel, DE | | 📧 Kiel Fjord

PORT

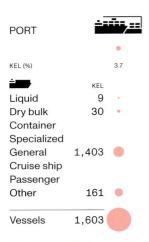
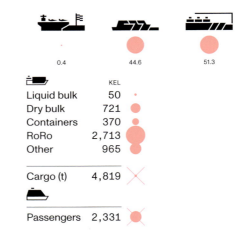

| KEL (%) | 3.7 | | 0.4 | 44.6 | 51.3 |

	KEL			KEL	
Liquid	9		Liquid bulk	50	
Dry bulk	30		Dry bulk	721	
Container			Containers	370	
Specialized			RoRo	2,713	
General	1,403		Other	965	
Cruise ship					
Passenger			Cargo (t)	4,819	✗
Other	161				
Vessels	1,603		Passengers	2,331	✗

CITY

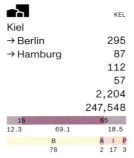

		KEL
	Kiel	
→ Capital national (km)	→ Berlin	295
→ Capital regional (km)	→ Hamburg	87
Area (km²)		112
Built-up area (km²)		57
Density (per km²)		2,204
Population		247,548
Population structure (%)	12.3 69.1 18.5	15 · 65
Distribution built area (%)	B 78 · A 2 · I 17 · P 3	

TERRITORY

		KEL
	Kiel, Kreisfreie Stadt	
Area (km²)		113
Density (per km²)		2,186
Population		247,548
Natura2000 (km²)	M 981 · T 25	

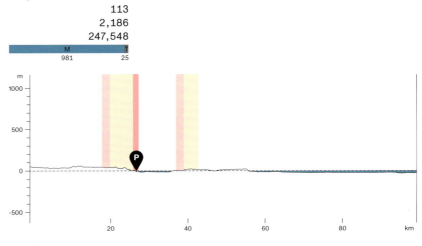

124 | Port City Atlas | Baltic Sea

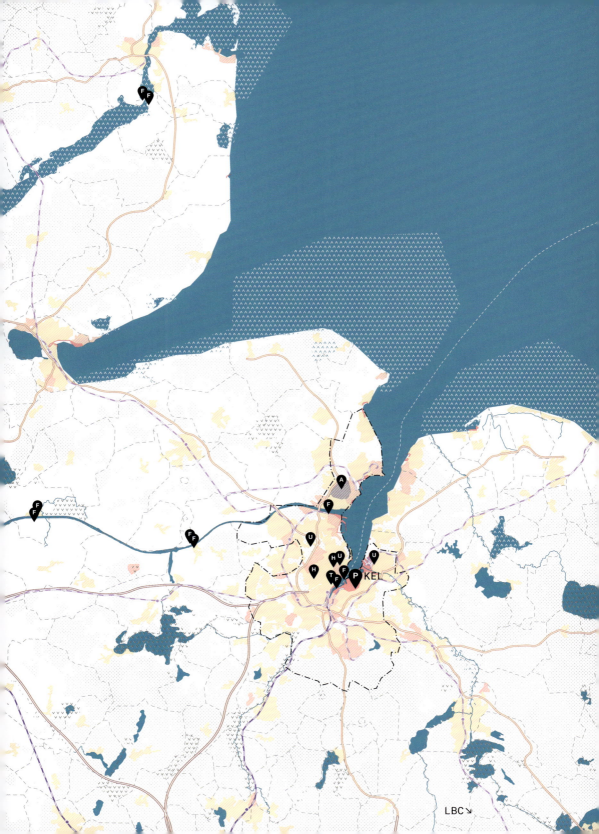

FRC

Fredericia, DK

 U Kattegat

PORT

FRC (%)

	FRC	
Liquid	353	
Dry bulk	30	
Container	211	
Specialized	87	
General	280	
Cruise ship		
Passenger		
Other	21	
Vessels	982	✕

100

	FRC	
Liquid bulk	4,846	
Dry bulk	950	
Containers	694	
RoRo	327	
Other	52	
Cargo (t)	6,869	✕
Passengers	0	✕

CITY

Fredericia — FRC

→ Capital national (km)	→ Copenhagen	178
→ Capital regional (km)	→ Hamburg	224
Area (km²)		135
Built-up area (km²)		28
Density (per km²)		380
Population		51,427
Population structure (%)	17 / 19.5 / 58.8 / 21.7 / 65	
Distribution built area (%)	B 73 / I 24 / P 3	

TERRITORY

Sydjylland — FRC

Area (km²)	8,661
Density (per km²)	84
Population	724,867
Natura2000 (km²)	M 8,796 / T 234

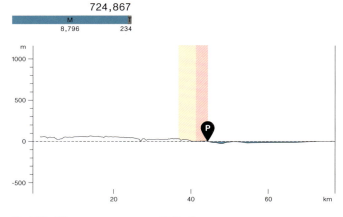

126 Port City Atlas Baltic Sea

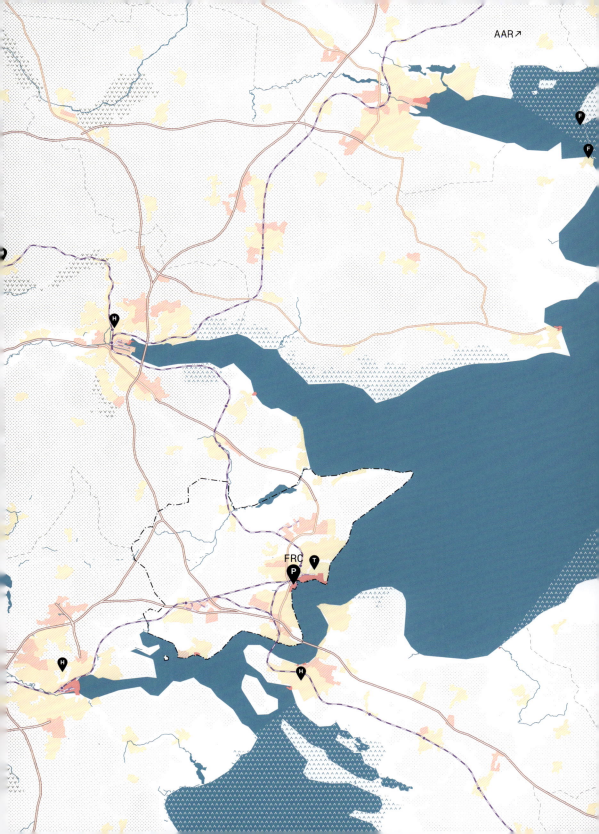

AAR Århus, DK  Aarhus Bay

PORT

AAR (%) 22.7   77.3

	AAR			AAR
Liquid	332		Liquid bulk	1,435
Dry bulk	667		Dry bulk	3,010
Container	788		Containers	3,808
Specialized	34		RoRo	345
General	3,849		Other	19
Cruise ship				
Passenger			Cargo (t)	8,617
Other	35			
Vessels	5,705		Passengers	3,385

CITY

Århus

→ Capital national (km)   → Copenhagen   154
→ Capital regional (km)
Area (km²)   473
Built-up area (km²)   105
Density (per km²)   675
Population   319,094
Population structure (%)   15   65
                           16.1 70.5 13.5
Distribution built area (%)   B   I   P
                               83   10 7

TERRITORY

Østjylland   AAR

Area (km²)   5,929
Density (per km²)   150
Population   890,567
Natura2000 (km²)   M   T
                   4,567   261

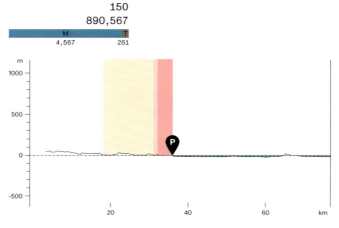

128 Port City Atlas Baltic Sea

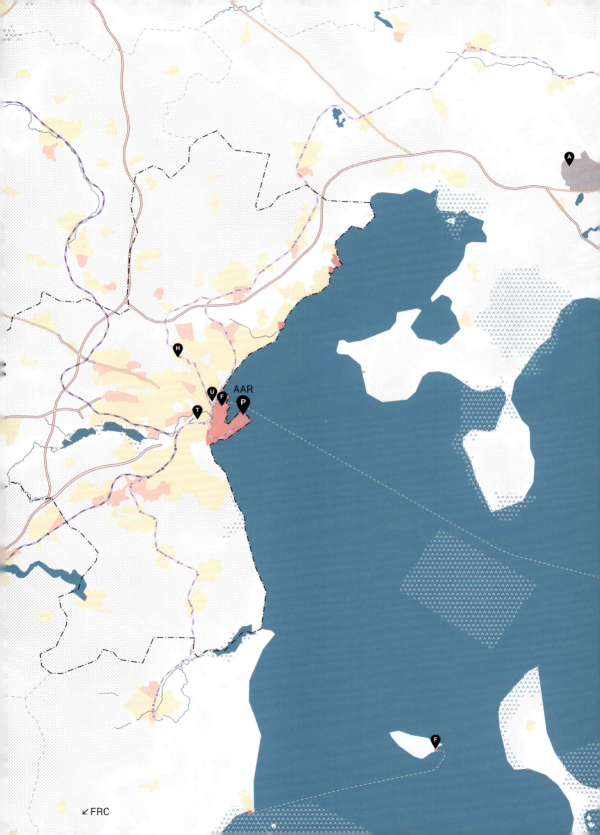

SST Statoil-Havnen, DK
SJO Sjaellands Odde, DK

 Sejerø Bay
 Kalundborg Fjord

PORT

SST / SJO (%)   96.6   100   3.4

	SST	SJO		SST	SJO
Liquid	492		Liquid bulk	7,900	
Dry bulk			Dry bulk		
Container			Containers		
Specialized			RoRo		
General		3,821	Other		
Cruise ship					
Passenger			Cargo (t)	7,900	0
Other					
Vessels	492	3,821	Passengers		3,493

CITY

	SST	SJO
	Kalundborg	Sjaellands Odde
→ Capital national (km)	→ Copenhagen 92	→ Copenhagen 85
→ Capital regional (km)		
Area (km²)	607	359
Built-up area (km²)	30	10
Density (per km²)	80	92
Population	48,681	33,122
Population structure (%)	18.4 / 56.4 / 25.2 (17 / 65)	15.3 / 52.5 / 32.2 (17 / 65)
Distribution built area (%)	B 66 / I 13 / P 21	B 93 / I 6 / P 1

TERRITORY

	SST	SJO
	Vest- og Sydsjælland	Vest- og Sydsjælland
Area (km²)	6,507	6,507
Density (per km²)	90	90
Population	587,379	587,379
Natura2000 (km²)	M 7,884 / T 188	M 7,884 / T 188

130   Port City Atlas   Baltic Sea

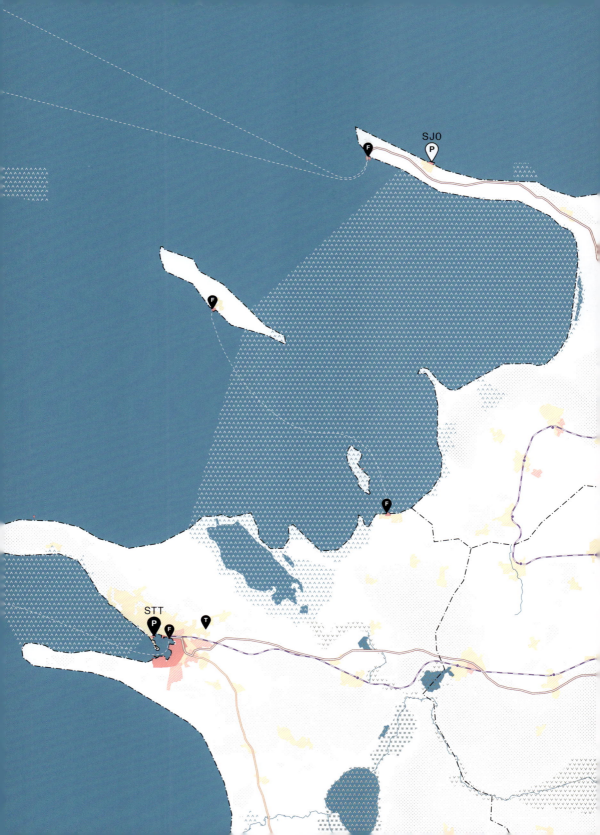

North Sea Map and Statistics

ID	Port name	🚢[1]	🛳[2]
AAL	Aalborg, DK	2,994	0
FDH	Frederikshavn, DK	2,568	1,960
HIR	Hirtshals, DK	1,948	2,541
EJB	Esbjerg, DK	4,310	1,824
BRB	Brunsbüttel, DE	10,131	0
HAM	Hamburg, DE	117,154	847
BRE	Bremen, DE	12,123	2
WVN	Wilhelmshaven, DE	28,869	13
BRV	Bremerhaven, DE	47,586	248
DZL	Delfzijl, NL	6,063	26
EME	Emden, DE	4,428	1,137
AMS	Amsterdam, NL	103,911	614
RTM	Rotterdam, NL	439,631	1,333
ANR	Antwerp, BE	214,025	61
GNE	Ghent, BE	33,336	4
ZEE	Zeebrugge, BE	28,993	1,022
DKK	Dunkirk, FR	42,555	2,330
DVR	Dover, UK	23,432	11,025
CQF	Calais, FR	18,099	8,478
MED	Medway, UK	13,137	0
LON	London, UK	54,034	112
FXT	Felixstowe, UK	25,344	9
HRW	Harwich, UK	4,275	692
IPS	Ipswich, UK	2,367	0
IMM	Immingham, UK	54,084	95
HUL	Hull, UK	9927	827
MME	Tees & Hartlepool, UK	28,154	2
TYN	Tyne, UK	4,679	670
FOR	Forth (Edinburgh), UK	25,221	25
BGO	Bergen, NO	44,174	169
TON	Tønsberg, NO	10,709	0
OSL	Oslo, NO	6,039	2,362
GOT	Göteborg, SE	38,890	1,675

Sea regions[3]
- Atlantic
- Baltic Sea
- North Sea

- Altitude in the landscape[4]
- Vessel density, yearly average of all vessel types[5]
- Natura2000 marine area[6]
- Natura2000 terrestrial area
- Main watercourse[7]
- Main land roads[7]
- Main railroads[7]
- Country border[8]

- Selected port city territory
- Selected port based on tonnage of cargo handled
- Selected port based on number of passengers har
- Main port outside the EU
- National capital[10]

Population density LAU (in inhabitants per km²)[11]

300 600

1 Total tonnage of cargo in thousands and in relation to the other selected European ports. Eurostat, 2019.
2 Total number of passengers in thousands and in relation to other selected European ports. Eurostat, 2019.
3 EMODnet Human Activities: Regional Advisory Councils, 2014.
4 EEA EuroGeographics EuroDEM, 2022.
5 EMODnet Human Activities, Vessel Density Map 2019.
6 ———, Environment, Natura2000, 2015.
7 Based on Eurogeographics, (2020). EuroGlobalMap. Version 2020 Eurogeographics. Retrieved from https://eurogeographics.org/maps-for-europe/open-data.
8 Eurostat NUTS 1 data.
9 Eurostat Maritime transport data, 2019.
10 Natural Earth.
11 Eurostat, GISCO LAU, 2019.

AAL # Aalborg, DK  Limfjord

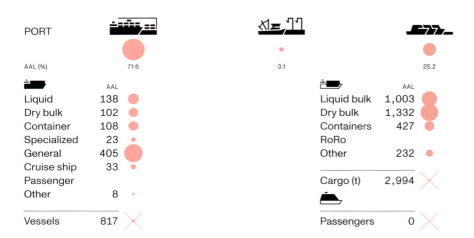

PORT		AAL
AAL (%)		71.6 / 3.1 / 25.2
Liquid	138	
Dry bulk	102	
Container	108	
Specialized	23	
General	405	
Cruise ship	33	
Passenger		
Other	8	
Vessels	817	
Liquid bulk	1,003	
Dry bulk	1,332	
Containers	427	
RoRo		
Other	232	
Cargo (t)	2,994	
Passengers	0	

CITY

Aalborg — AAL
→ Capital national (km) → Copenhagen 222
→ Capital regional (km)
Area (km²) 1,142
Built-up area (km²) 99
Density (per km²) 178
Population 203,448
Population structure (%) 15.9 / 67.3 / 16.9
Distribution built area (%) B 76 / A 10 / I 12 / P 2

TERRITORY

Nordjylland — AAL
Area (km²) 7,944
Density (per km²) 74
Population 589,755
Natura2000 (km²) M 7,642 / T 252

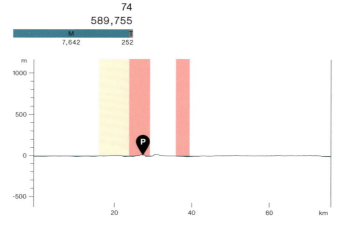

134 Port City Atlas North Sea

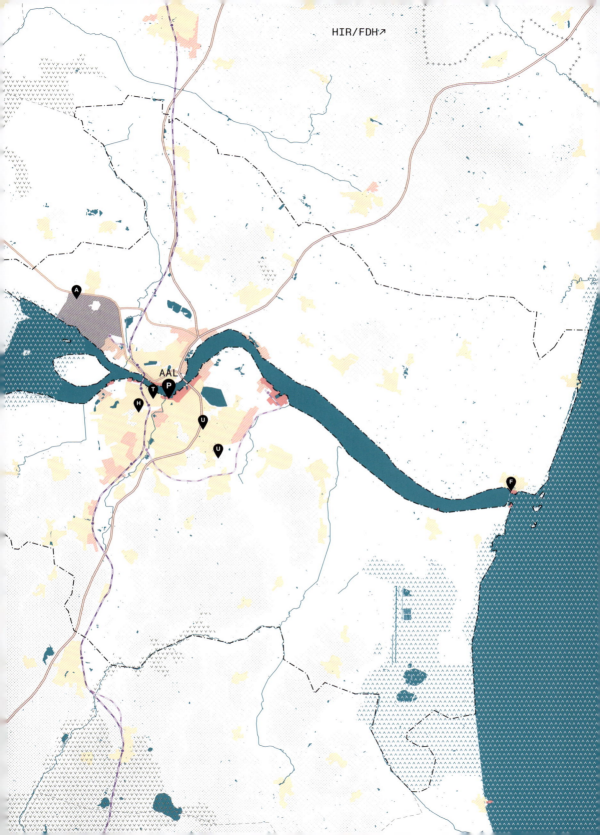

FDH
HIR

Frederikshavn, DK
Hirtshals, DK

Skaggerak

Skaggerak

PORT							
FDH/HIR (%)	64.0	100			36.0		
	FDH	HIR			FDH	HIR	
Liquid	14	67		Liquid bulk	70	69	
Dry bulk	94			Dry bulk	291	4	
Container				Containers			
Specialized				RoRo	2,146	1,704	
General	3,769	2,293		Other	61	171	
Cruise ship							
Passenger				Cargo (t)	2,568	1,948	
Other							
Vessels	3,877	2,360		Passengers	1,960	2,541	

CITY		FDH		HIR
	Frederikshavn		Hjørring	
→ Capital national (km)	→ Copenhagen	229	→ Copenhagen	267
→ Capital regional (km)				
Area (km²)		652		929
Built-up area (km²)		34		31
Density (per km²)		92		70
Population		59,987		64,665
Population structure (%)	17.2 / 55.0 / 27.8		19.0 / 56.1 / 24.9	
Distribution built area (%)	B 86 / I 6 / P 8		B 82 / A 1 / I 15 / P 2	

TERRITORY		FDH		HIR
	Nordjylland		Nordjylland	
Area (km²)		7,944		7,944
Density (per km²)		74		74
Population		589,755		589,755
Natura2000 (km²)	M 7,642 / T 252		M 7,642 / T 252	

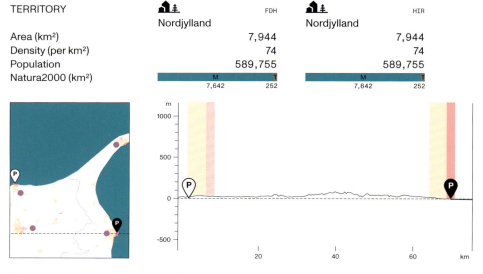

136   Port City Atlas   North Sea

EJB # Esbjerg, DK  Vesebanke

PORT

EJB (%)

	EJB			EJB
Liquid	140	Liquid bulk	540
Dry bulk	14	Dry bulk	1,119
Container	33	Containers	209
Specialized	685	RoRo	1,789
General	17,124	Other	653
Cruise ship			
Passenger		Cargo (t)	4,310
Other	10		
Vessels	18,006	Passengers	1,824

100

CITY

Esbjerg | EJB
→ Capital national (km) | → Copenhagen | 262
→ Capital regional (km) | → Hamburg | 239
Area (km²) | | 759
Built-up area (km²) | | 59
Density (per km²) | | 152
Population | | 115,652
Population structure (%) | 17 / 65 / 23.1 / 55.3 / 21.6
Distribution built area (%) | B 79 / A 1 / I 15 / P 5

TERRITORY

Sydjylland | EJB
Area (km²) | 8,661
Density (per km²) | 84
Population | 724,867
Natura2000 (km²) | M 8,796 / T 234

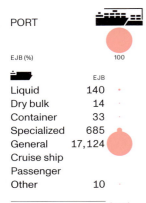
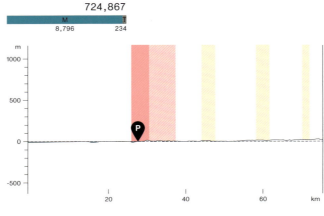

138 | Port City Atlas | North Sea

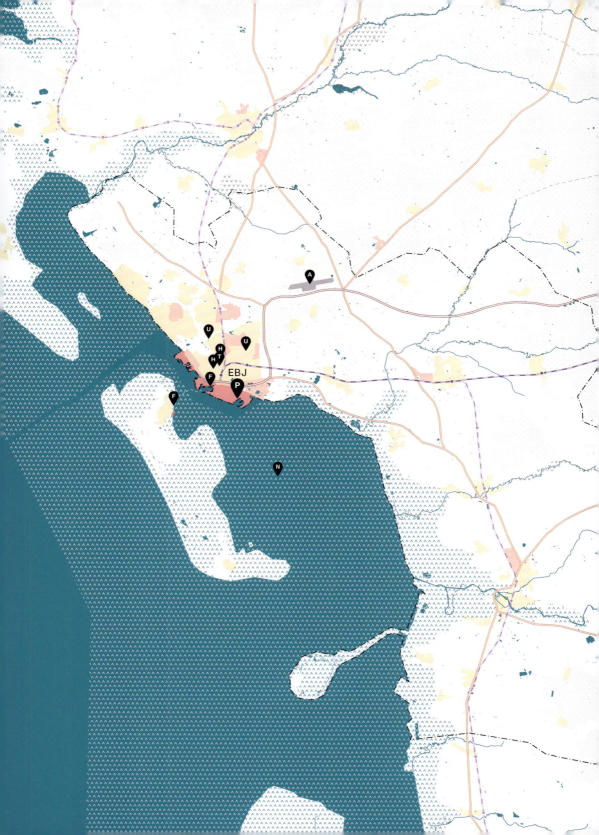

BRB # Brunsbüttel, DE   Elbe

PORT

BRB (%) 100

	BRB			BRB
Liquid	158		Liquid bulk	6,128
Dry bulk	102		Dry bulk	3,980
Container			Containers	
Specialized			RoRo	
General	62		Other	23
Cruise ship				
Passenger			Cargo (t)	10,131
Other				
Vessels	322		Passengers	0

CITY

Brunsbüttel, Stadt — BRB

→ Capital national (km) → Berlin	323
→ Capital regional (km) → Hamburg	68
Area (km²)	49
Built-up area (km²)	13
Density (per km²)	255
Population	12,554
Population structure (%)	17 / 15.5 / 58.0 / 65 / 26.4
Distribution built area (%)	B 48 / I 10 / P 42

TERRITORY

Dithmarschen — BRB

Area (km²)	1,442
Density (per km²)	92
Population	133,210
Natura2000 (km²)	M 9,764 / T 201

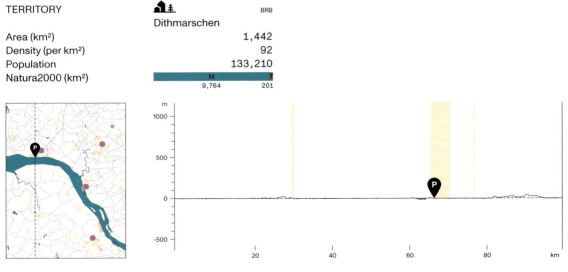

140 — Port City Atlas — North Sea

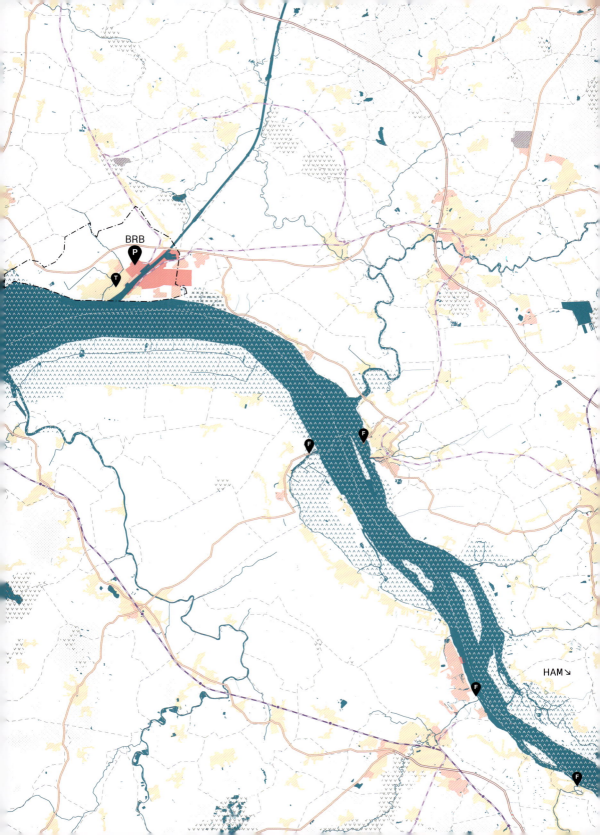

HAM
Hamburg, DE
 Elbe

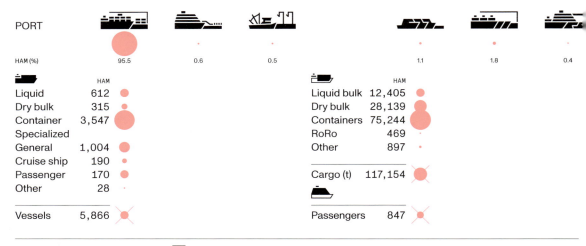

PORT							
HAM (%)	95.5	0.6	0.5		1.1	1.8	0.4

	HAM			HAM
Liquid	612		Liquid bulk	12,405
Dry bulk	315		Dry bulk	28,139
Container	3,547		Containers	75,244
Specialized			RoRo	469
General	1,004		Other	897
Cruise ship	190			
Passenger	170		Cargo (t)	117,154
Other	28			
Vessels	5,866		Passengers	847

CITY

		HAM
	Hamburg	
→ Capital national (km)	→ Berlin	257
→ Capital regional (km)		
Area (km²)		739
Built-up area (km²)		377
Density (per km²)		2,491
Population		1,841,179
Population structure (%)	14.0 / 67.7 / 18.4	
Distribution built area (%)	B 78 / A 3 / I 14 / P 5	

TERRITORY

		HAM
	Hamburg	
Area (km²)		753
Density (per km²)		2,446
Population		1,841,179
Natura2000 (km²)	M 10,055 / T 91	

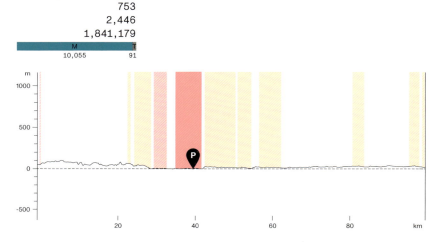

142   Port City Atlas   North Sea

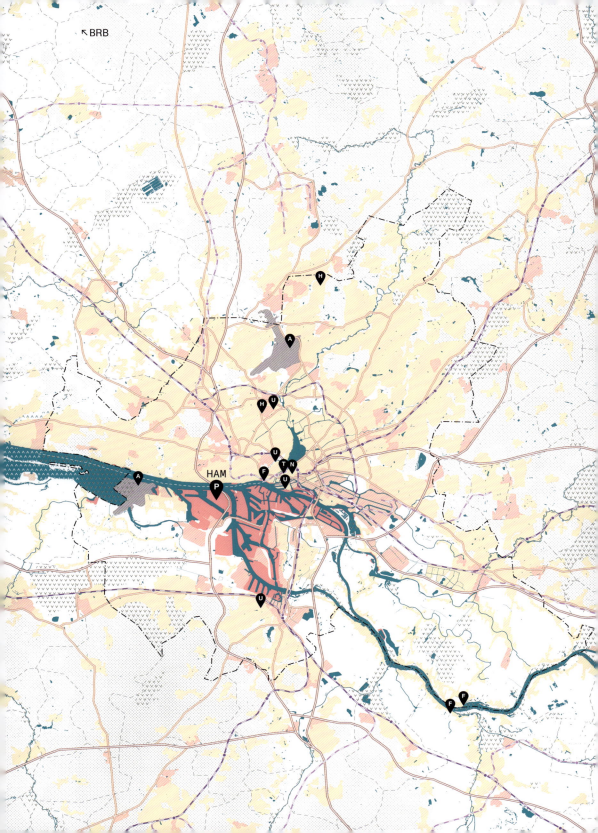

BRE # Bremen, DE Wezer

PORT

BRE (%) 100

	BRE			BRE
Liquid	104		Liquid bulk	1,719
Dry bulk	173		Dry bulk	6,824
Container	13		Containers	21
Specialized	7		RoRo	35
General	557		Other	3,524
Cruise ship				
Passenger			Cargo (t)	12,123
Other				
Vessels	838		Passengers	2

CITY

Bremen BRE

→ Capital national (km) → Berlin	320
→ Capital regional (km) → Hamburg	95
Area (km²)	326
Built-up area (km²)	153
Density (per km²)	1,748
Population	569,352
Population structure (%)	15 / 65
	13.1 / 65.9 / 21.0
Distribution built area (%)	B 66 / A 2 / I 24 / P 8

TERRITORY

Bremen, Kreisfreie Stadt BRE

Area (km²)	326
Density (per km²)	1,749
Population	569,352
Natura2000 (km²)	M 6,198 / T 146

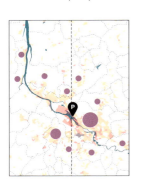

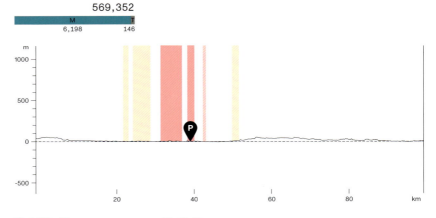

144 · Port City Atlas · North Sea

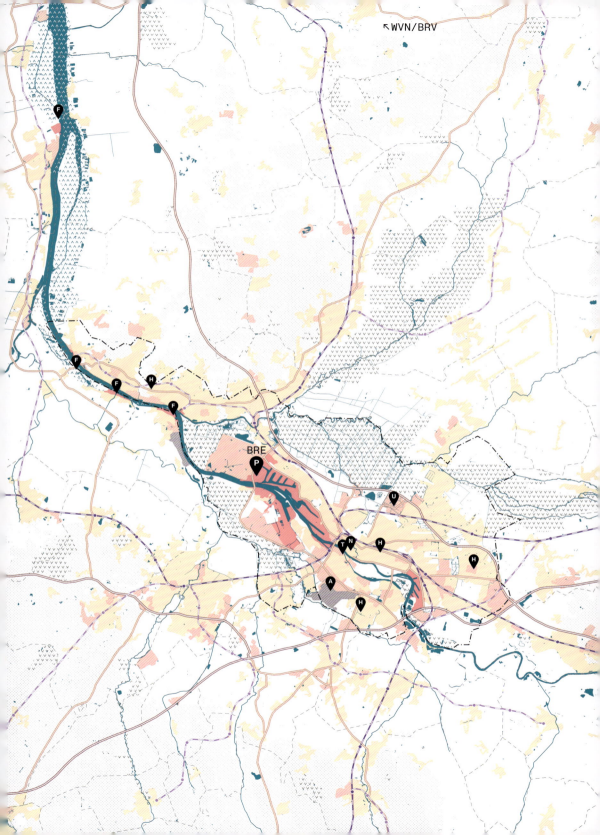

WVN # Wilhelmshaven, DE
BRV # Bremerhaven, DE

Jadeboezem
Jadeboezem

PORT

| WVN/BRV (%) | 51.9 / 98.9 | 0.4 | 35.3 | 0.7 | 12.8 |

	WVN	BRV			WVN	BRV
Liquid	498	349		Liquid bulk	20,154	388
Dry bulk	76	20		Dry bulk	2,943	216
Container	408	2,749		Containers	5,771	42,068
Specialized				RoRo		4,440
General	16	226		Other	1	474
Cruise ship		132				
Passenger				Cargo (t)	28,869	47,586
Other	99	956				
Vessels	1,097	4,432		Passengers	13	248

CITY

	Wilhelmshaven (WVN)	Bremerhaven (BRV)
→ Capital national (km)	→ Berlin 396	→ Berlin 344
→ Capital regional (km)	→ Hamburg 121	→ Hamburg 94
Area (km²)	108	77
Built-up area (km²)	36	38
Density (per km²)	709	1,482
Population	76,278	113,634
Population structure (%)	11.8 / 61.9 / 26.2 (15 / 65)	14.4 / 63.9 / 21.8 (15 / 65)
Distribution built area (%)	B 55 / I 35 / P 10	B 66 / A 2 / I 30 / P 2

TERRITORY

	Wilhelm., Kreisfreie Stadt (WVN)	Bremerh., Kreisfreie Stadt (BRV)
Area (km²)	107	94
Density (per km²)	711	1,211
Population	76,278	113,634
Natura2000 (km²)	M 6,111	M 6,198 / T 4

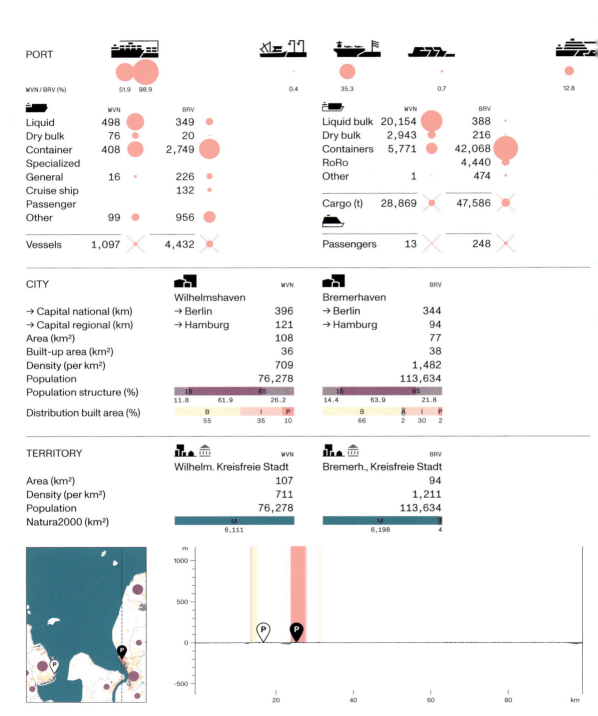

146 Port City Atlas North Sea

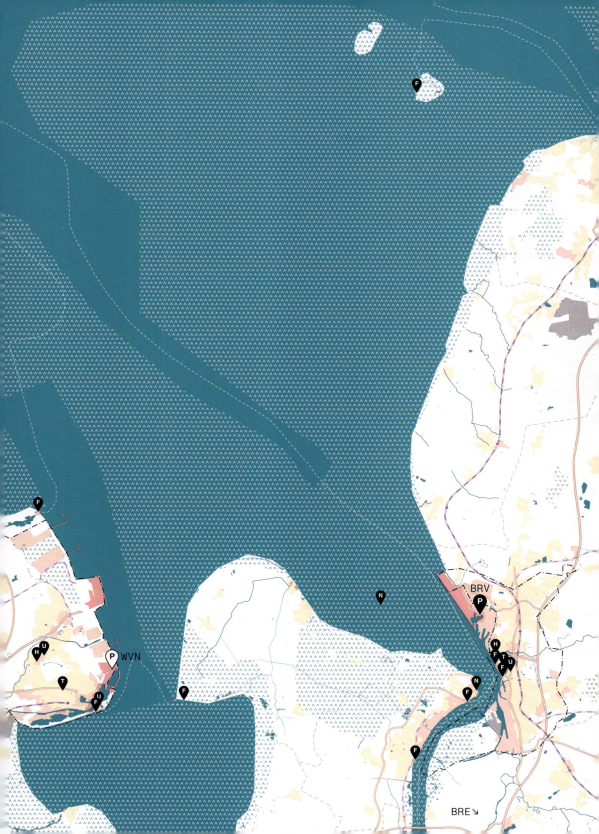

DZL
EME

Delfzijl, NL
Emden, DE

 Eems
 Eems

PORT

DZL / EME (%)   100   100

	DZL	EME
Liquid	144	96
Dry bulk	124	16
Container		
Specialized	25	
General	1,592	1,074
Cruise ship		
Passenger		730
Other	60	373
Vessels	1,945	2,289

	DZL	EME
Liquid bulk	457	752
Dry bulk	4,370	751
Containers	76	11
RoRo	22	2,271
Other	1,138	643
Cargo (t)	6,063	4,428
Passengers	26	1,137

CITY

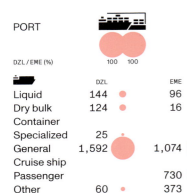

	DZL	EME
	Delfzijl	Emden, Stadt
→ Capital national (km)	→ Amsterdam 287	→ Berlin 708
→ Capital regional (km)	→ Hamburg 34	→ Hamburg 31
Area (km²)	136	111
Built-up area (km²)	16	26
Density (per km²)	181	451
Population	24,716	50,195

Population structure (%)
17 / 65
14.7 62.2 23.1
16.7 61.6 21.7

Distribution built area (%)
B 65 I 30 P 5
B 53 A 1 I 30 P 16

TERRITORY

	DZL	EME
	Delfzijl and surroundings	Emden, Kreisfreie Stadt
Area (km²)	273	112
Density (per km²)	169	449
Population	46,051	50,195
Natura2000 (km²)	M 9,335	M 9,360 / 59

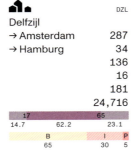
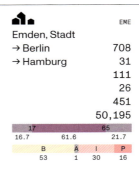
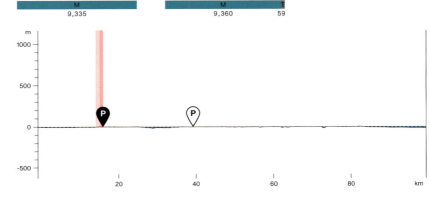

148   Port City Atlas   North Sea

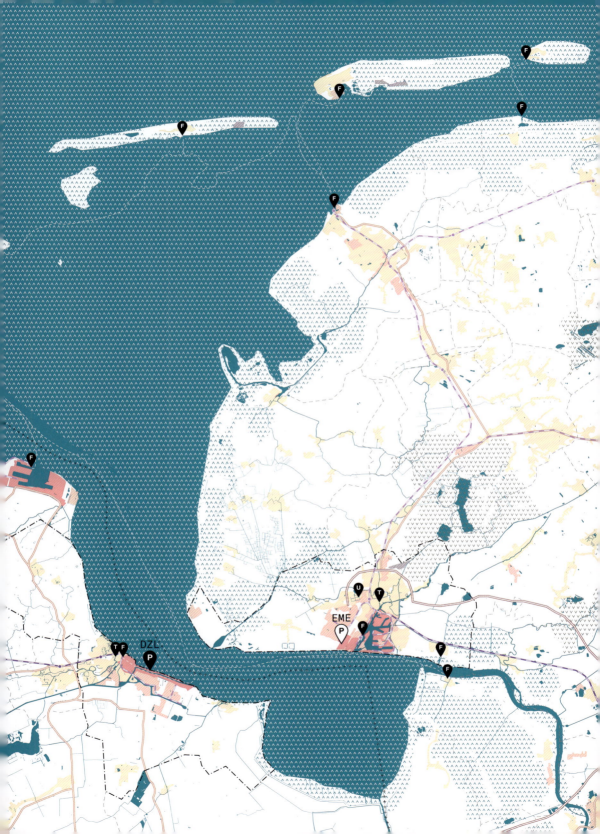

AMS # Amsterdam, NL  North Sea Canal

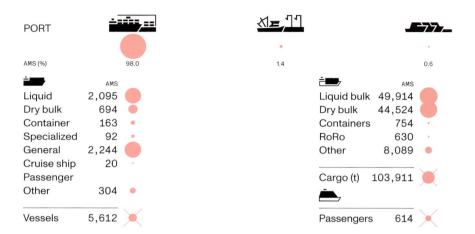

PORT

AMS (%) 98.0   1.4   0.6

	AMS
Liquid	2,095
Dry bulk	694
Container	163
Specialized	92
General	2,244
Cruise ship	20
Passenger	
Other	304
Vessels	5,612

	AMS
Liquid bulk	49,914
Dry bulk	44,524
Containers	754
RoRo	630
Other	8,089
Cargo (t)	103,911
Passengers	614

CITY

Greater Amsterdam AMS

	AMS
→ Capital national (km)	
→ Capital regional (km)	→ Amsterdam 0
Area (km²)	303
Built-up area (km²)	135
Density (per km²)	3,286
Population	996,915
Population structure (%)	14.9 71.7 13.3
Distribution built area (%)	B 74 I 13 P 13

TERRITORY

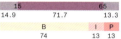

Groot-Amsterdam AMS

	AMS
Area (km²)	875
Density (per km²)	1,567
Population	1,370,657
Natura2000 (km²)	M 165 T 777

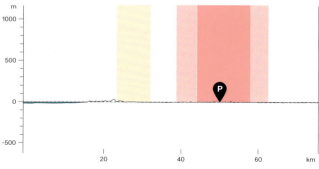

150 Port City Atlas North Sea

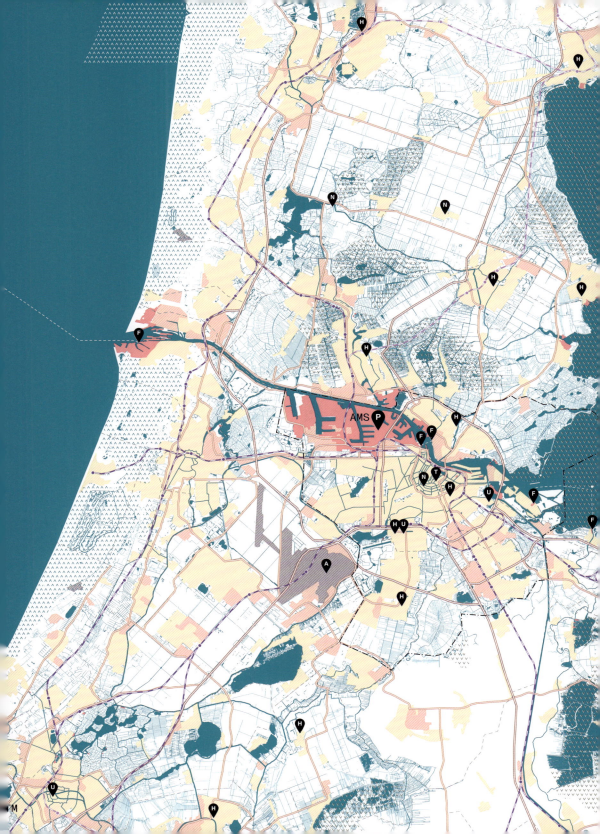

RTM # Rotterdam, NL  New Waterway

PORT

RTM (%)	58.2			41.8
	RTM			RTM
Liquid	7,050		Liquid bulk	207,366
Dry bulk	939		Dry bulk	70,612
Container	5,474		Containers	127,901
Specialized	197		RoRo	12,039
General	5,162		Other	21,713
Cruise ship				
Passenger			Cargo (t)	439,631
Other	43			
Vessels	18,865		Passengers	1,333

CITY

			RTM
	Greater Rotterdam		
→ Capital national (km)	→ Amsterdam		58
→ Capital regional (km)	→ Antwerp		75
Area (km²)			563
Built-up area (km²)			283
Density (per km²)			2,191
Population			1,232,747
Population structure (%)	16.3	66.2	17.5
Distribution built area (%)	B 60	A I 1 12	P 27

TERRITORY

		RTM
	Groot-Rijnmond	
Area (km²)		1,498
Density (per km²)		963
Population		1,441,452
Natura2000 (km²)	M 1,866	T 20

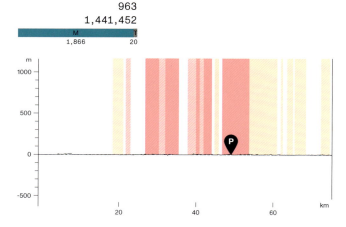

152 Port City Atlas North Sea

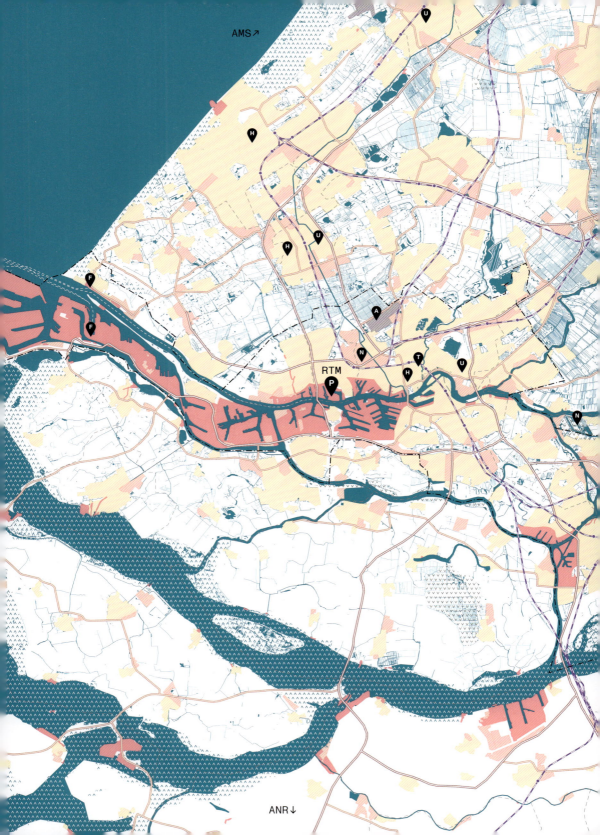

ANR # Antwerp, BE   Scheldt

PORT

	ANR
ANR (%)	100
Liquid	5,419
Dry bulk	14
Container	4,616
Specialized	1,246
General	3,134
Cruise ship	
Passenger	41
Other	93
Vessels	14,563

	ANR
Liquid bulk	71,089
Dry bulk	13,727
Containers	114,573
RoRo	6,351
Other	8,285
Cargo (t)	214,025
Passengers	61

CITY

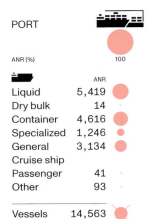

Antwerpen — ANR
→ Capital national (km) → Brussels 45
→ Capital regional (km) → Rotterdam 75
Area (km²) 204
Built-up area (km²) 108
Density (per km²) 2,580
Population 526,439
Population structure (%) 19.5 / 64.0 / 16.5 (15 / 65)
Distribution built area (%) B 54 / A 1 / I 15 / P 30

TERRITORY

Arr. Antwerpen — ANR
Area (km²) 1,003
Density (per km²) 1,050
Population 1,053,033
Natura2000 (km²) M 1,437 / T 257

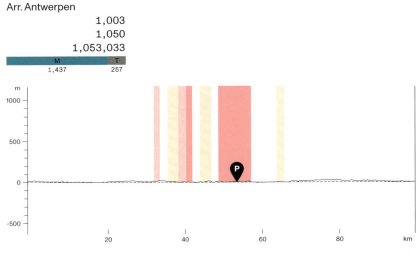

154 — Port City Atlas — North Sea

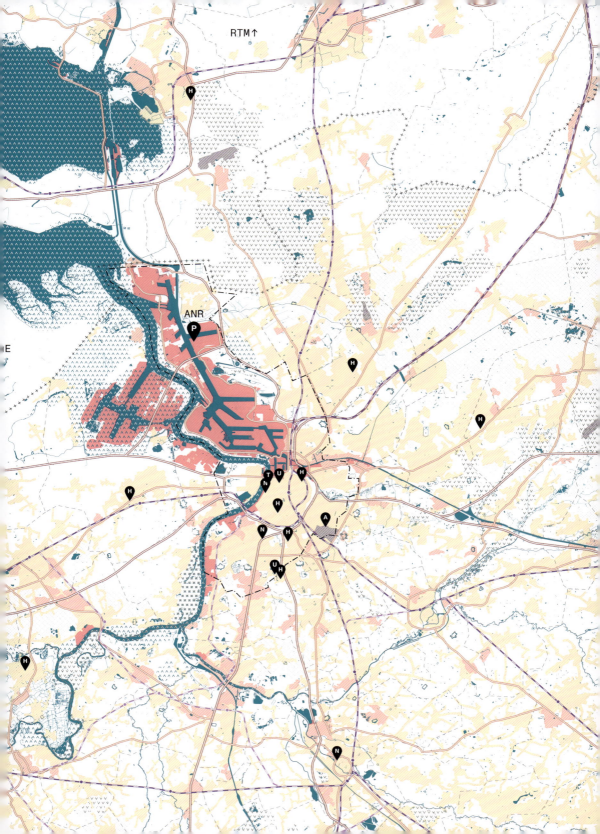

GNE | # Ghent, BE | Ghent–Terneuze Canal

PORT

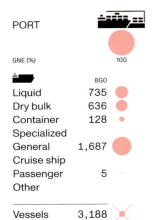

GNE (%) 100

	BGO
Liquid	735
Dry bulk	636
Container	128
Specialized	
General	1,687
Cruise ship	
Passenger	5
Other	
Vessels	3,188

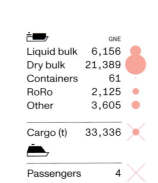

	GNE
Liquid bulk	6,156
Dry bulk	21,389
Containers	61
RoRo	2,125
Other	3,605
Cargo (t)	33,336
Passengers	4

CITY

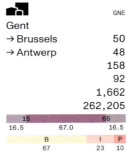

Gent — GNE

→ Capital national (km) → Brussels	50
→ Capital regional (km) → Antwerp	48
Area (km²)	158
Built-up area (km²)	92
Density (per km²)	1,662
Population	262,205

Population structure (%): 16.5 / 67.0 / 16.5

Distribution built area (%): B 67 | I 23 | P 10

TERRITORY

Arr. Gent — GNE

Area (km²)	950
Density (per km²)	591
Population	560,690
Natura2000 (km²)	M 1,155 / T 76

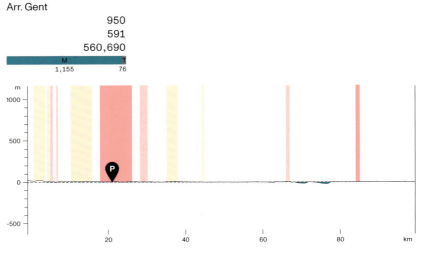

156 — Port City Atlas — North Sea

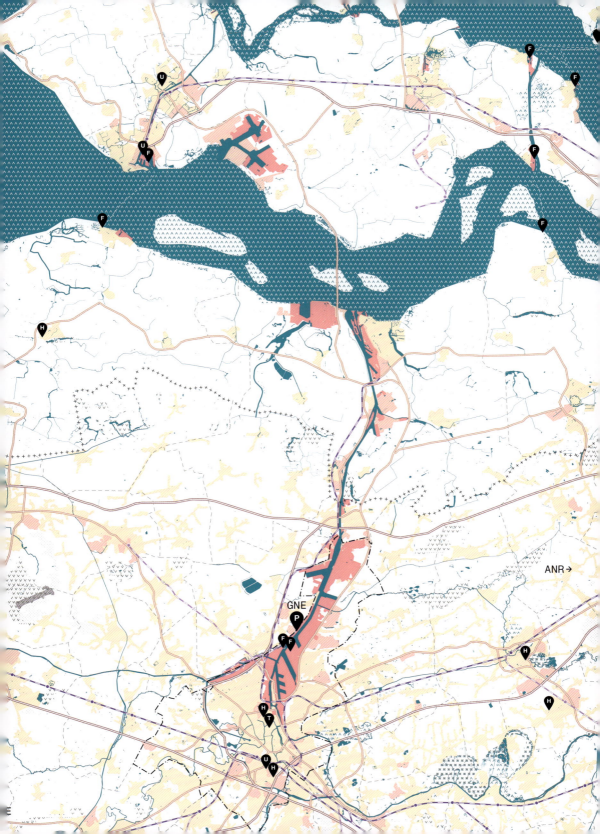

ZEE

Zeebrugge, BE

 North Sea

PORT

ZEE (%) 100

	ZEE			ZEE
Liquid	1,032		Liquid bulk	9,319
Dry bulk			Dry bulk	1,326
Container	495		Containers	3,091
Specialized	4,751		RoRo	14,361
General	346		Other	896
Cruise ship	149			
Passenger			Cargo (t)	28,993
Other	953			
Vessels	7,726		Passengers	1,022

CITY

Brugge ZEE

→ Capital national (km)	→ Brussels	100
→ Capital regional (km)	→ Antwerp	84
Area (km²)		139
Built-up area (km²)		55
Density (per km²)		56
Population		7,768
Population structure (%)	15 / 65	
	13.7 / 63.0 / 23.4	
Distribution built area (%)	B 64 / I 14 / P 22	

TERRITORY

Arr. Brugge ZEE

Area (km²)	666
Density (per km²)	424
Population	282,520
Natura2000 (km²)	M 1,893 / T 31

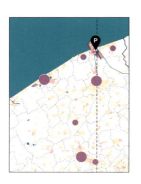

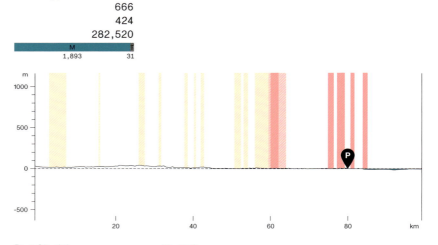

158   Port City Atlas   North Sea

DKK # Dunkerque, FR  North Sea

PORT

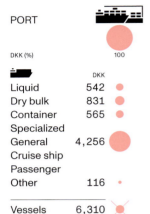

DKK (%)   100

	DKK	
Liquid	542	
Dry bulk	831	
Container	565	
Specialized		
General	4,256	
Cruise ship		
Passenger		
Other	116	
Vessels	6,310	

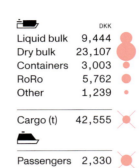

	DKK	
Liquid bulk	9,444	
Dry bulk	23,107	
Containers	3,003	
RoRo	5,762	
Other	1,239	
Cargo (t)	42,555	
Passengers	2,330	

CITY

City of Dunkerque   DKK

		DKK
→ Capital national (km)	→ Paris	241
→ Capital regional (km)	→ Lille	75
Area (km²)		77
Built-up area (km²)		51
Density (per km²)		1,763
Population		135,715

Population structure (%)   18.2 | 62.8 | 19.1   (15 / 65)

Distribution built area (%)   B 50 | I 37 | P 13

TERRITORY

Nord   DKK

	DKK
Area (km²)	5,742
Density (per km²)	454
Population	2,608,346
Natura2000 (km²)	M 1,858 / T 291

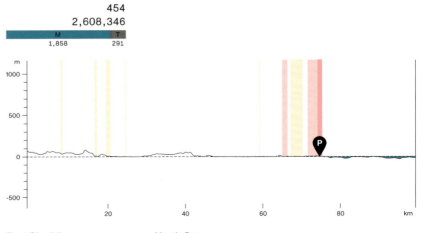

160   Port City Atlas   North Sea

DVR
CQF

Dover, UK
Calais, FR

 Strait of Dover
 Strait of Dover

PORT

DVR/CQF (%)   19.2   80.8   71.2   28.8

	DVR	CQF		DVR	CQF
Liquid	45		Liquid bulk		140
Dry bulk		190	Dry bulk		324
Container			Containers	146	
Specialized			RoRo	22,997	17,590
General	17,193	13,187	Other	248	45
Cruise ship	131				
Passenger			Cargo (t)	23,432	18,099
Other	1	63			
Vessels	17,370	13,440	Passengers	11,025	8,478

CITY

	Dover DVR	City of Calais CQF
→ Capital national (km)	→ London 108	→ Paris 238
→ Capital regional (km)		→ Lille 95
Area (km²)	316	33
Built-up area (km²)	29	21
Density (per km²)	367	2,235
Population	115,803	73,911
Population structure (%)	17 / 19.6 56.6 23.8 65	15 / 19.2 65.0 15.7 65
Distribution built area (%)	B 81 I 14 P 5	P 9 B 71 I 20

TERRITORY

	East Kent DVR	Pas-de-Calais CQF
Area (km²)	1,084	6,695
Density (per km²)	496	218
Population	538,428	1,462,720
Natura2000 (km²)	M 4,373 T 16	M 2,603 T 58

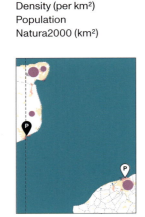

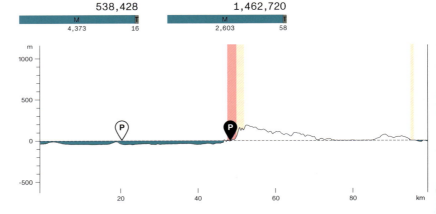

162   Port City Atlas   North Sea

MED | # Medway, UK |

PORT

MED (%) 54.8 | 45.2

	MED			MED
Liquid	125		Liquid bulk	6,673
Dry bulk	167		Dry bulk	3,650
Container	258		Containers	711
Specialized	301		RoRo	717
General	885		Other	1,386
Cruise ship				
Passenger			Cargo (t)	13,137
Other	184			
			Passengers	0
Vessels	1,920			

CITY

		MED
	Medway	
→ Capital national (km)	→ London	47
→ Capital regional (km)		
Area (km²)		193
Built-up area (km²)		62
Density (per km²)		1,442
Population		277,736
Population structure (%)	19.6 64.6 15.8	15 / 65
Distribution built area (%)	B 75 / A 1 / I 20 / P 4	

TERRITORY

		MED
	Medway	
Area (km²)		192
Density (per km²)		1,460
Population		280,894
Natura2000 (km²)	M 3,156 / 3	

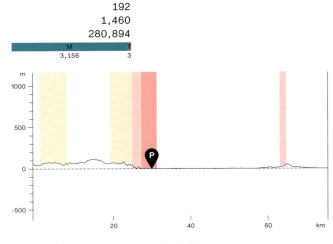

164 | Port City Atlas | North Sea

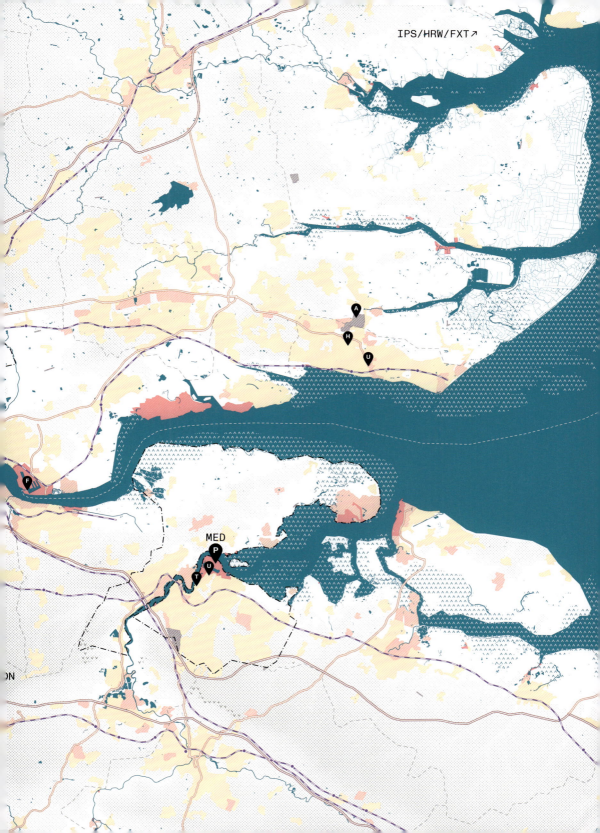

LON # London, UK  Thames

PORT

LON (%)

	LON			LON
Liquid	1,145		Liquid bulk	14,561
Dry bulk	198		Dry bulk	15,141
Container	2,068		Containers	14,891
Specialized	94		RoRo	7,708
General	3,533		Other	1,733
Cruise ship	82		Cargo (t)	54,034
Passenger				
Other	1,284		Passengers	112
Vessels	8,404			

2.7   97.3

CITY

London → London 0

	LON
→ Capital national (km)	
→ Capital regional (km)	
Area (km²)	1,576
Built-up area (km²)	1,091
Density (per km²)	5,627
Population	8,866,541
Population structure (%)	15 / 65 — 19.5 / 68.5 / 11.8
Distribution built area (%)	B 91 / A 1 / I 8

TERRITORY

Camden & City of London LON

Area (km²)	25
Density (per km²)	10,943
Population	270,016
Natura2000 (km²)	0

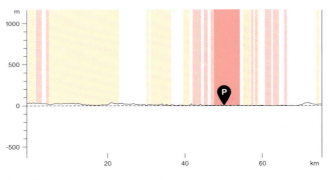

166   Port City Atlas   North Sea

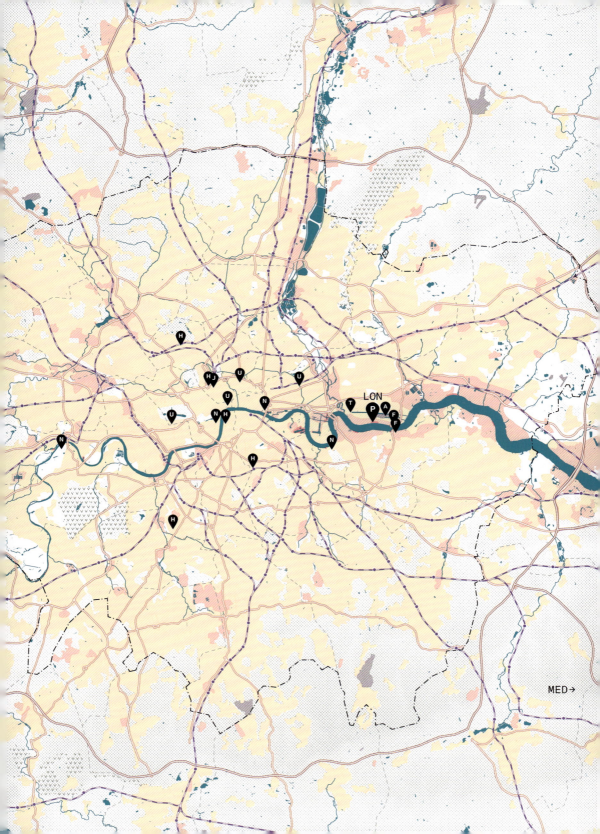

FXT	**Felixstowe, UK**	North Sea
HRW	**Harwich, UK**	Stour
IPS	**Ipswich, UK**	River Orwell

PORT

FXT / HRW / IPS (%)   99.1   100   63.6   0.3   36.4   0.6

	FXT	HRW	IPS		FXT	HRW	IPS
Liquid	11	109	22	Liquid bulk	45	338	112
Dry bulk			11	Dry bulk		40	2,045
Container	1,108			Containers	21,714	93	
Specialized				RoRo	3,582	3,663	
General	822	1,302	500	Other	3	141	210
Cruise ship							
Passenger				Cargo (t)	25,344	4,275	2,367
Other	1	13	19				
Vessels	1,942	1,424	552	Passengers	9	692	0

CITY

	FXT	HRW	IPS
	Suffolk Coastal	Tendring	Ipswich
→ Capital national (km)	→ London 109	→ London 105	→ London 107
→ Capital regional (km)			
Area (km²)	896	341	40
Built-up area (km²)	42	37	31
Density (per km²)	144	424	3,491
Population	129,016	144,705	138,006
Population structure (%)	17.4 52.7 29.9	21.6 53.9 24.5	19.2 64.4 16.3
Distribution built area (%)	B 71 A 16 I 8 P 5	B 86 A 1 I 12 P 1	B 82 I 16 P 2

TERRITORY

	FXT	HRW	IPS
	Suffolk	Essex Haven Gateway	Suffolk
Area (km²)	3,807	1,284	3,807
Density (per km²)	200	384	200
Population	760,472	492,514	760,472
Natura2000 (km²)	M 5,809 T 454	M 3,241 T 7	M 5,809 T 454

168   Port City Atlas   North Sea

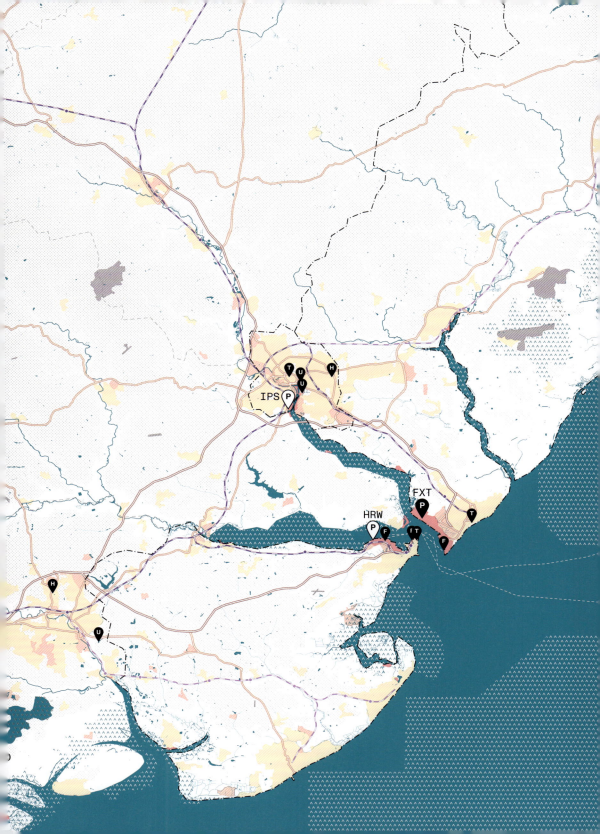

IMM
HUL

Immingham, UK
Hull, UK

🚢 📄 Humber
🚢 📄 Humber

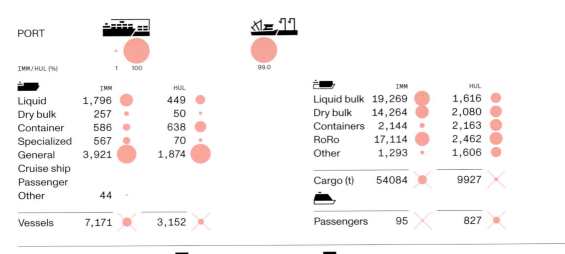

PORT

IMM/HUL (%)   1   100   99.0

	IMM	HUL			IMM	HUL
Liquid	1,796	449		Liquid bulk	19,269	1,616
Dry bulk	257	50		Dry bulk	14,264	2,080
Container	586	638		Containers	2,144	2,163
Specialized	567	70		RoRo	17,114	2,462
General	3,921	1,874		Other	1,293	1,606
Cruise ship						
Passenger				Cargo (t)	54084	9927
Other	44					
Vessels	7,171	3,152		Passengers	95	827

CITY

	IMM	HUL
	North East Lincolnshire	Kingston upon Hull, City of
→ Capital national (km) → London	237	→ London 247
→ Capital regional (km) → Manchester	139	→ Manchester 130
Area (km²)	192	72
Built-up area (km²)	81	48
Density (per km²)	832	3,632
Population	159,824	260,659
Population structure (%)	15 65	15 65
	18.2 62.8 19.1	18.9 66.2 14.9
Distribution built area (%)	B I P	B I P
	84 9 7	75 16 9

TERRITORY

	IMM	HUL
	North and North East Lincolnshire	Kingston upon Hull, City of
Area (km²)	72	5,742
Density (per km²)	3,636	454
Population	261,149	2,608,346
Natura2000 (km²)	M 2,234	M T 1,858 291

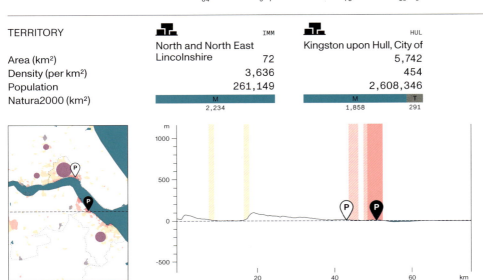

170 Port City Atlas North Sea

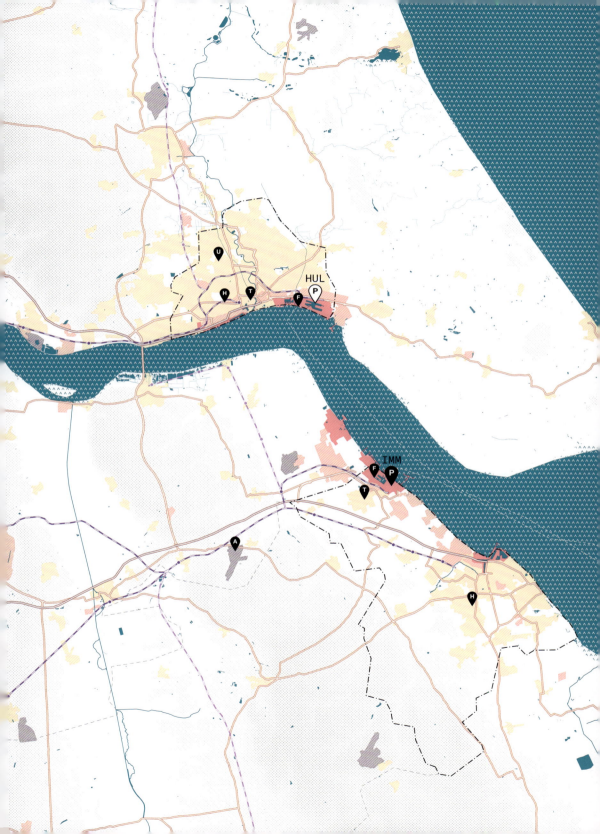

MME # Tees & Hartlepool, UK
TYN Tyne, UK

 Tees, Hartepool
 Tyne

PORT

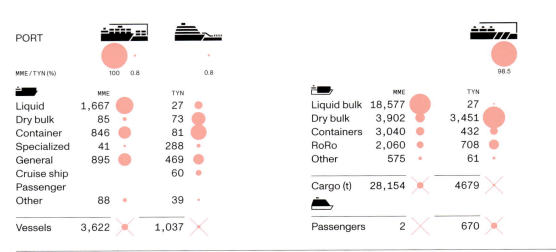

MME / TYN (%)   100   0.8   0.8   98.5

	MME	TYN
Liquid	1,667	27
Dry bulk	85	73
Container	846	81
Specialized	41	288
General	895	469
Cruise ship		60
Passenger		
Other	88	39
Vessels	3,622	1,037

	MME	TYN
Liquid bulk	18,577	27
Dry bulk	3,902	3,451
Containers	3,040	432
RoRo	2,060	708
Other	575	61
Cargo (t)	28,154	4679
Passengers	2	670

CITY

	Hartlepool (MME)	Tyneside conurbation (TYN)
→ Capital national (km) → London	352	
→ Capital regional (km) → Edinburgh	144	
Area (km²)	94	405
Built-up area (km²)	27	194
Density (per km²)	985	2,110
Population	93,019	855,622
Population structure (%)	18.0 / 62.9 / 19.1	16.6 / 65.4 / 17.9
Distribution built area (%)	B 69 / I 10 / P 21	B 86 / A 1 / I 12 / P 1

TERRITORY

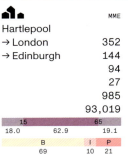
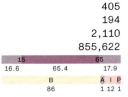

	Hart. & Stockton-on-Tees (MME)	Tyneside (TYN)
Area (km²)	300	405
Density (per km²)	970	2,118
Population	290,998	858,694
Natura2000 (km²)	M 912	M 901

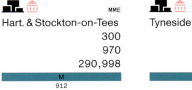
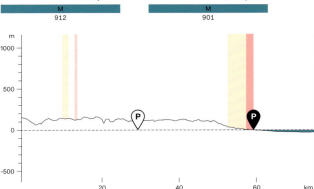

172   Port City Atlas   North Sea

FOR # Forth (Edinburgh), UK Forth

PORT

	FOR			FOR
FOR (%)	14.3			85.7
Liquid	969		Liquid bulk	21,201
Dry bulk	23		Dry bulk	1,355
Container	334		Containers	2,432
Specialized			RoRo	
General	385		Other	233
Cruise ship				
Passenger			Cargo (t)	25,221
Other	69			
Vessels	1,780		Passengers	25

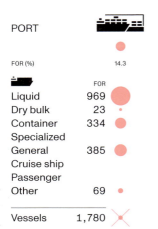
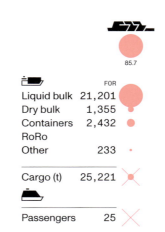

CITY

		FOR
	City of Edinburgh	
→ Capital national (km)	→ London	545
→ Capital regional (km)	→ Manchester	294
Area (km²)		263
Built-up area (km²)		104
Density (per km²)		1,959
Population		515,855
Population structure (%)	14.4 / 70.6 / 15.1	
Distribution built area (%)	B 82 / A 4 I 11 P 3	

TERRITORY

		FOR
	Edinburgh, City of	
Area (km²)		263
Density (per km²)		1,976
Population		520,483
Natura2000 (km²)	M 161	

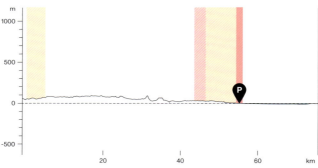

174 Port City Atlas North Sea

BGO

Bergen, NO

PORT

BGO (%) 3.1   74.6   22.3

	BGO			BGO
Liquid	1,934		Liquid bulk	40,523
Dry bulk	550		Dry bulk	2,297
Container	328		Containers	212
Specialized	239		RoRo	168
General	3,514		Other	974
Cruise ship				
Passenger			Cargo (t)	44,174
Other	2,868			
			Passengers	169
Vessels	9,433			

CITY

Bergen | BGO
→ Capital national (km) | → Oslo | 306
→ Capital regional (km)
Area (km²) | 465
Built-up area (km²) | 98
Density (per km²) | 577
Population | 267,950
Population structure (%) | 18.0 67.6 14.1
Distribution built area (%) | B 90 A I P 4 5 1

TERRITORY

Vestland | BGO
Area (km²) | 33,808
Density (per km²) | 19
Population | 636,531
Natura2000 (km²) | M 3,081

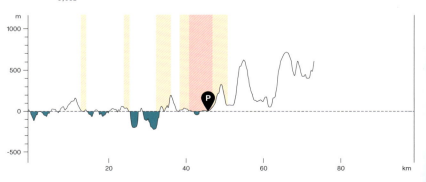

176 Port City Atlas North Sea

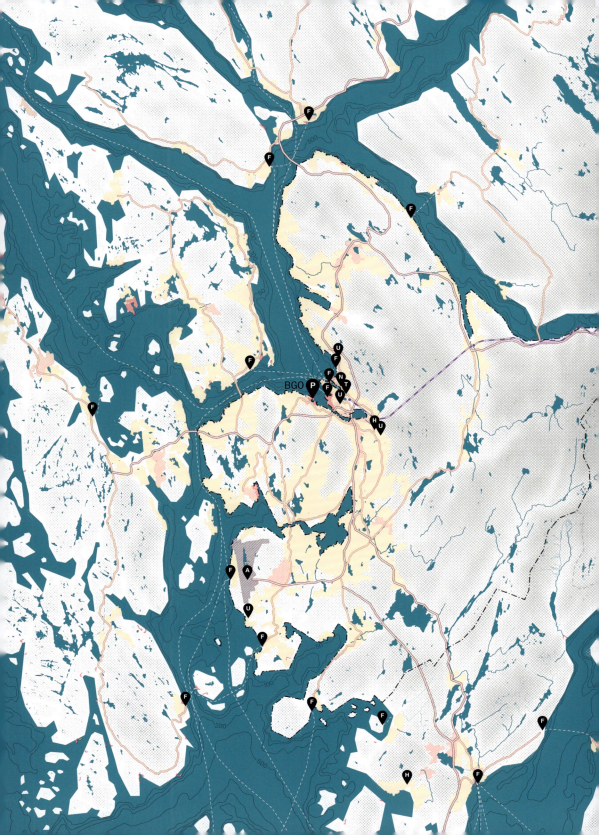

TON # Tønsberg, NO 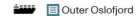 Outer Oslofjord

PORT

TON (%)

  TON
Liquid   659
Dry bulk   9
Container
Specialized
General   176
Cruise ship
Passenger
Other   3

Vessels   847

100

TON
Liquid bulk   10,660
Dry bulk   49
Containers
RoRo
Other

Cargo (t)   10,709

Passengers   0

CITY

Tønsberg   TON
→ Capital national (km)   → Oslo   66
→ Capital regional (km)
Area (km²)   110
Built-up area (km²)   21
Density (per km²)   409
Population   44,922
Population structure (%)   15   65
                         20.1   61.1   18.8
Distribution built area (%)   B   I P
                                85   14 1

TERRITORY

Vestfold og Telemark   TON
Area (km²)   17,449
Density (per km²)   24
Population   419,316
Natura2000 (km²)   M   T
                        7,884   188

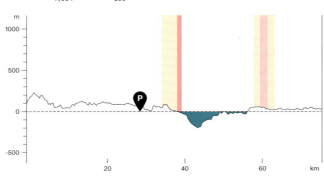

178   Port City Atlas   North Sea

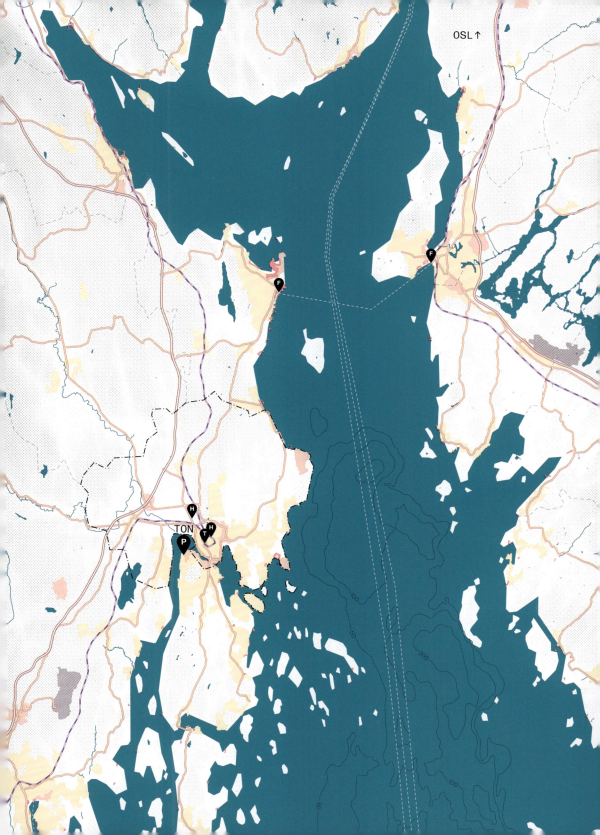

OSL # Oslo, NO  Inner Oslofjord

PORT

OSL (%)

8.3 1.2 90.5

	OSL	
Liquid	260	
Dry bulk	55	
Container	545	
Specialized	79	
General	1,079	
Cruise ship		
Passenger		
Other	59	
Vessels	2,077	

	OSL	
Liquid bulk	2,020	
Dry bulk	1,587	
Containers	1,479	
RoRo	702	
Other	251	
Cargo (t)	6,039	
Passengers	2,362	

CITY

Oslo OSL

→ Capital national (km) → Oslo 0
→ Capital regional (km)
Area (km²) 454
Built-up area (km²) 104
Density (per km²) 1,374
Population 623,966
Population structure (%) 15 / 65
 17.3 71.0 11.9
Distribution built area (%) B
 87 12 1

TERRITORY

Oslo OSL

Area (km²) 455
Density (per km²) 1,525
Population 693,494
Natura2000 (km²) 0

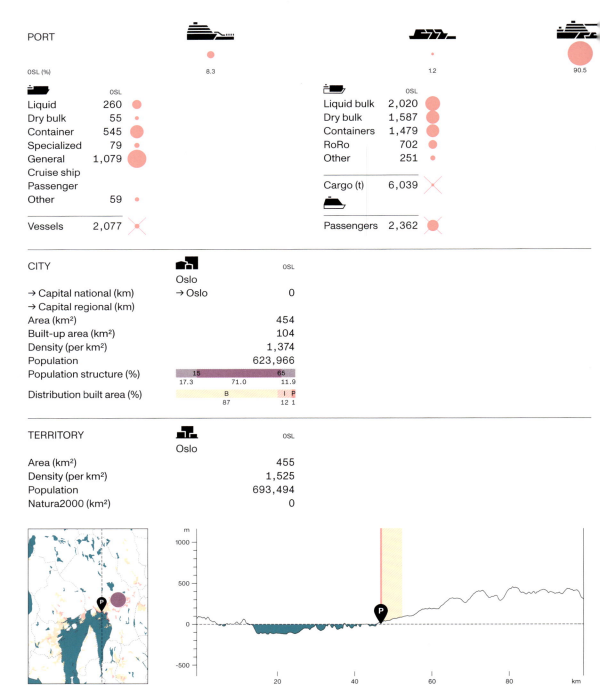

180 Port City Atlas North Sea

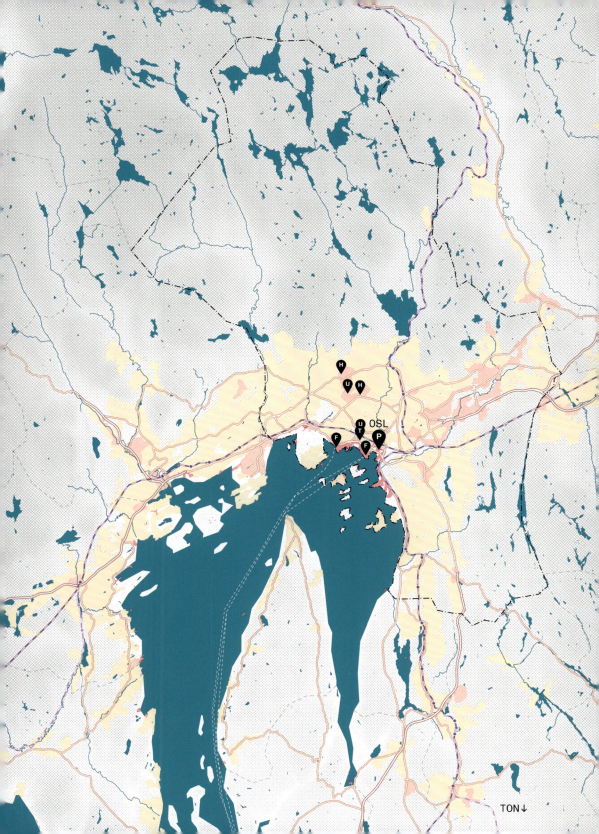

GOT

Göteborg, SE

 Göta river

PORT

GOT (%)   75.1   24.9

	GOT		GOT
Liquid		Liquid bulk	22,311
Dry bulk	1,027	Dry bulk	57
Container	990	Containers	7,109
Specialized	151	RoRo	8,988
General	3,786	Other	425
Cruise ship			
Passenger		Cargo (t)	38,890
Other	60		
Vessels	6,014	Passengers	1,675

CITY

Greater Göteborg — GOT

→ Capital national (km)
→ Capital regional (km)   → Aalborg   143km
Area (km²)   515
Built-up area (km²)   157
Density (per km²)   1,095
Population   564,039
Population structure (%)   16.9   67.8   15.4
                               15   65
Distribution built area (%)   B 74   A 1 I 22 P 3

TERRITORY

Västra Götalands län — GOT

Area (km²)   28,859
Density (per km²)   59
Population   1,709,814
Natura2000 (km²)   M 1,248   T 1,474

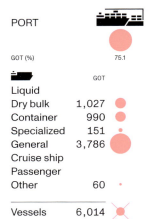

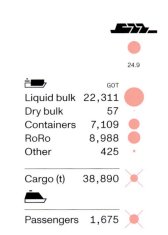

182   Port City Atlas   North Sea

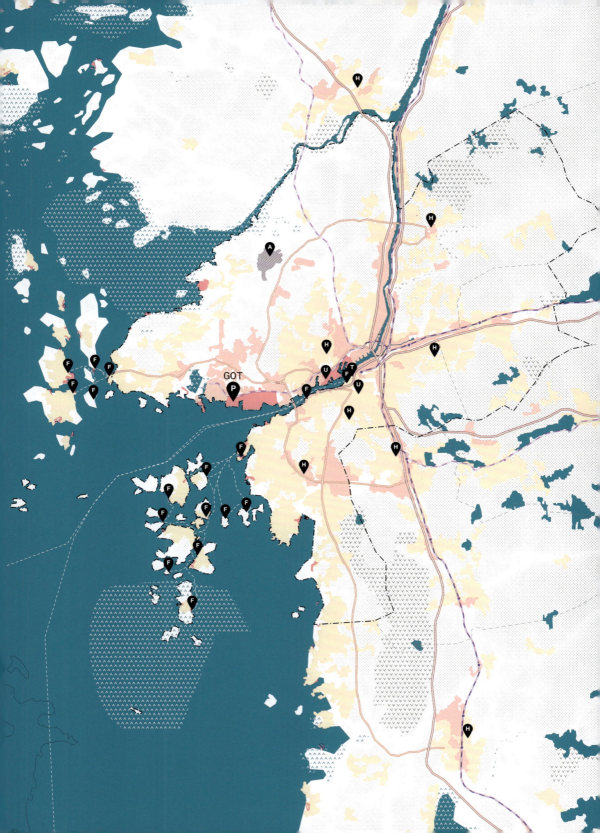

Atlantic Map and Statistics

ID	Port name	[1]	[2]
CYP	Clydeport (Glasgow), UK	8,801	0
CYN	Cairnryan, UK	2,705	1,770
BEL	Belfast, UK	18,515	1,626
LAR	Larne, UK	2,767	467
DUB	Dublin, IE	26,332	1,991
LMK	Limerick, IE	9,622	2
ORK	Cork, IE	8,706	114
HYM	Heysham, UK	4,538	284
LIV	Liverpool, UK	34,314	694
HLY	Holyhead, UK	5,324	1,886
MLF	Milford Haven, UK	34,952	327
BRS	Bristol, UK	8,190	0
SOU	Southampton, UK	33,151	1,807
PME	Portsmouth, UK	3,620	1,754
LEH	Le Havre, FR	60,173	172
NTE	Nantes Saint-Nazaire, FR	30,155	0
LRH	La Rochelle, FR	9,763	0
BOD	Bordeaux, FR	6,499	1
BIO	Bilbao, ES	33,881	107
GIJ	Gijón, ES	17,220	0
LCG	La Coruña, ES	13,584	1
FRO	Ferrol, ES	11,154	0
LEI	Leixões (Porto), PT	17,924	1
LIS	Lisboa, PT	10,465	73
SET	Setúbal, PT	6,735	0
HUV	Huelva, ES	33,255	43
LPA	Las Palmas, ES	19,850	1,994
SCT	Santa Cruz de Tenerife, ES	9,788	5,615
CAD	Cádiz, ES	4,015	25

Sea regions[3]
- Atlantic
- Mediterranean Sea
- North Sea

Altitude in the landscape[4]
Vessel density, yearly average of all vessel types[5]
Natura2000 marine area[6]
Natura2000 terrestrial area
Main watercourse[7]
Main land roads[7]
Main railroads[7]
Country border[8]

Selected port city territory
Selected port based on tonnage of cargo handled[9]
Selected port based on number of passengers han...
Main port outside the EU
National capital[10]

Population density LAU (in inhabitants per km²)[11]

300   600

1   Total tonnage of cargo in thousands and in relation to the other selected European ports. Eurostat, 2019.
2   Total number of passengers in thousands and in relation to the other selected European ports. Eurostat, 2019.
3   EMODnet Human Activities: Regional Advisory Councils, 2014.
4   EEA EuroGeographics EuroDEM, 2022.
5   EMODnet Human Activities, Vessel Density Map 2019.
6   ———, Environment, Natura2000 2015.
7   Based on Eurogeographics, (2020). EuroGlobalMap. Version 2020 Eurogeographics. Retrieved from https://eurogeographics.org/maps-for-europe/open-data.
8   Eurostat NUTS 1 data.
9   Eurostat Maritime transport data, 2019.
10 Natural Earth.
11 Eurostat, GISCO LAU, 2019.

184   Port City Atlas   Atlantic

0   100 km

CYP   # Clydeport (Glasgow), UK    Clyde River

PORT

CYP (%) — 100

	CYP
Liquid	206
Dry bulk	46
Container	201
Specialized	
General	273
Cruise ship	82
Passenger	
Other	32
Vessels	809

	CYP
Liquid bulk	7,211
Dry bulk	813
Containers	598
RoRo	
Other	179
Cargo (t)	8,801
Passengers	0

CITY

Greater Glasgow

	CYP
→ Capital national (km)	
→ Capital regional (km)	
→ Dublin	308
→ Edinburgh	70
Area (km²)	786
Built-up area (km²)	278
Density (per km²)	1,278
Population	1,004,220

Population structure (%) 15.8 | 68.3 | 15.9

Distribution built area (%) B 82 | A 1 | I 17

TERRITORY

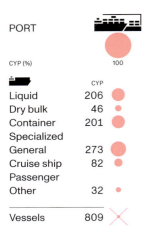

Glasgow City

	CYP
Area (km²)	175
Density (per km²)	3,586
Population	627,479
Natura2000 (km²)	

M 18 | T 90

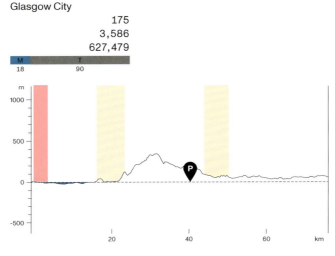

186   Port City Atlas   Atlantic

CYN

Cairnryan, UK

 Loch Ryan

PORT

87.5   7.3   5.3

CYN (%)

 CYN
Liquid
Dry bulk
Container
Specialized
General   2,245
Cruise ship
Passenger
Other   1

Vessels   2,246

Liquid bulk   CYN
Dry bulk
Containers
RoRo   2,705
Other

Cargo (t)   2,705

Passengers   1,770

CITY

 CYN
Dumfries and Galloway

→ Capital national (km)   → London   504
→ Capital regional (km)   → Edinburgh   166
Area (km²)   6,447
Built-up area (km²)   5
Density (per km²)   23
Population   149,200
Population structure (%)   17 | 56.1 | 26.3 (17.6 | 56.1 | 26.3)
Distribution built area (%)   B 96 | AP 2 2

TERRITORY

 CYN
Dumfries & Galloway

Area (km²)   6,443
Density (per km²)   23
Population   148,871
Natura2000 (km²)   M 1,543 | T 525

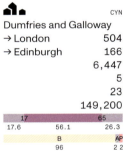

188   Port City Atlas   Atlantic

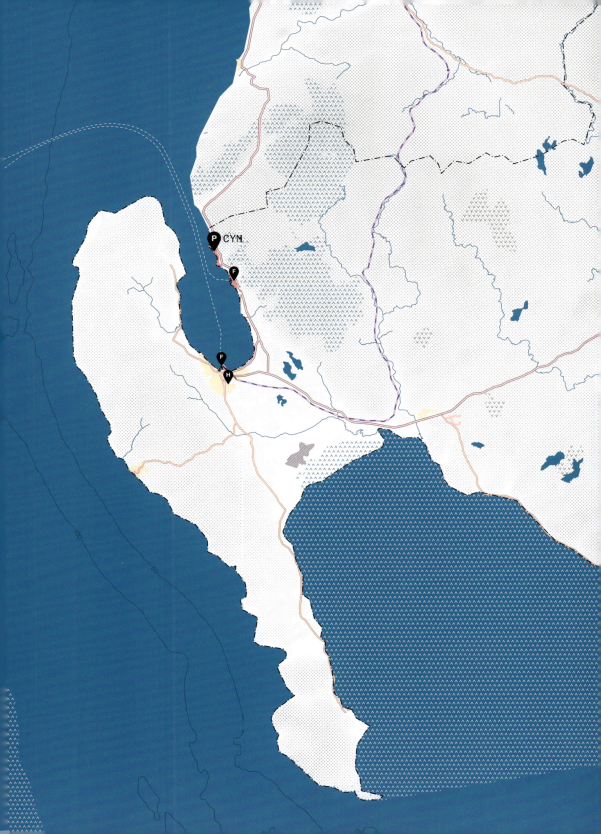

BEL
LAR

Belfast, UK
Larne, UK

Lagan River
Irish Sea

PORT

BEL / LAR (%)   59.0 33.9   2.1 36.8   29.3   38.9

	BEL	LAR			BEL	LAR
Liquid	326	54		Liquid bulk	2,182	5
Dry bulk	140			Dry bulk	6,677	
Container	275			Containers	1,756	
Specialized				RoRo	7,569	2,704
General	4,567	2,272		Other	331	38
Cruise ship	144					
Passenger				Cargo (t)	18,515	2,767
Other	37	3				
Vessels	5,453	2,329		Passengers	1,626	467

CITY

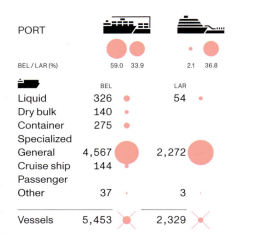
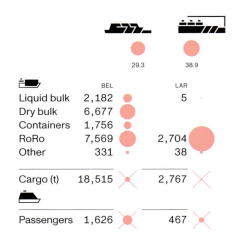

	Belfast / BEL	Mid and East Antrim / LAR
→ Capital national (km) → London	520	532
→ Capital regional (km) → Glasgow	177	147
Area (km²)	138	1,049
Built-up area (km²)	90	50
Density (per km²)	2,477	132
Population	341,049	138,152
Population structure (%)	18.8 66.6 14.7	21.2 60.8 18.0
Distribution built area (%)	B 84 A I P 2 8 6	B 90 I P 7 3

TERRITORY

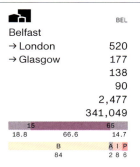
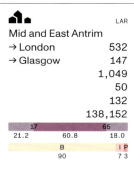

	Belfast / BEL	Mid and East Antrim / LAR
Area (km²)	138	1,049
Density (per km²)	2,482	129
Population	341,506	135,338
Natura2000 (km²)	M 384	M 1,361 T 272

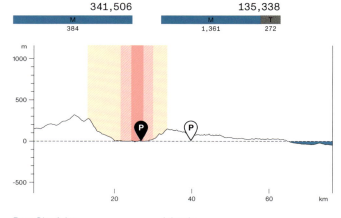

190   Port City Atlas   Atlantic

DUB | # Dublin, IE | Irish Sea

PORT

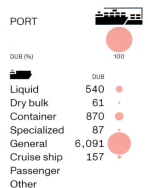

DUB (%)

	DUB
Liquid	540
Dry bulk	61
Container	870
Specialized	87
General	6,091
Cruise ship	157
Passenger	
Other	
Vessels	7,806

	DUB
Liquid bulk	4,652
Dry bulk	1,821
Containers	5,802
RoRo	14,040
Other	17
Cargo (t)	26,332
Passengers	1,991

CITY

Dublin | DUB

	DUB
→ Capital national (km)	
→ Capital regional (km)	
→ Dublin	0
Area (km²)	118
Built-up area (km²)	183
Density (per km²)	11,266
Population	1,325,700
Population structure (%)	15 / 65
	19.3 / 69.7 / 11.0
Distribution built area (%)	B 89 / I 9 / P 2

TERRITORY

Dublin | DUB

	DUB
Area (km²)	925
Density (per km²)	1,500
Population	1,387,606
Natura2000 (km²)	M 478 / T 632

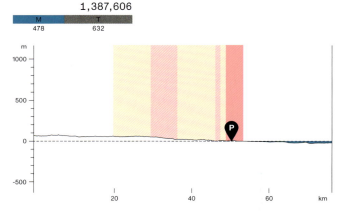

192 | Port City Atlas | Atlantic

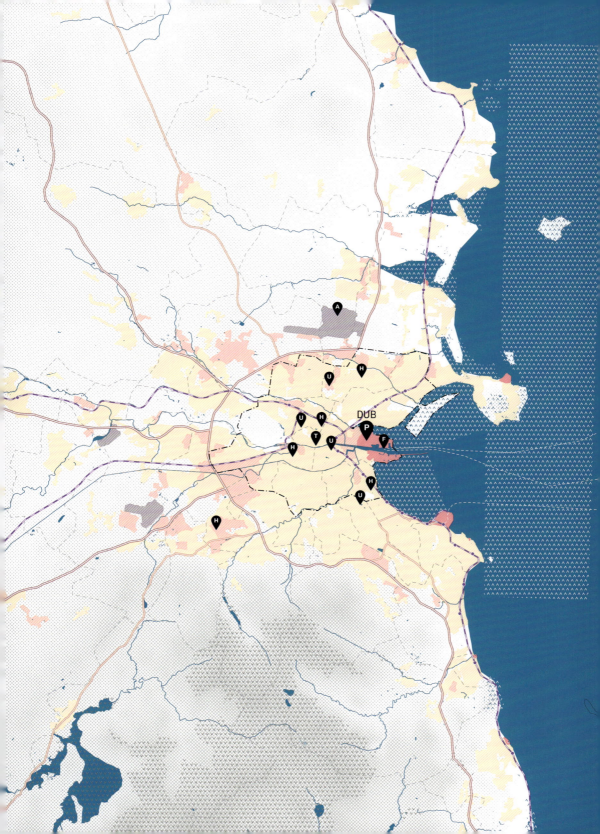

LMK # Limerick, IE  Shannon River

PORT

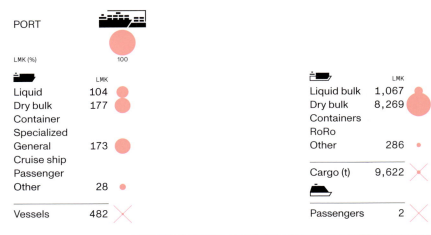

LMK (%) 100

	LMK			LMK
Liquid	104		Liquid bulk	1,067
Dry bulk	177		Dry bulk	8,269
Container			Containers	
Specialized			RoRo	
General	173		Other	286
Cruise ship				
Passenger			Cargo (t)	9,622
Other	28			
			Passengers	2
Vessels	482			

CITY

Limerick LMK

→ Capital national (km)
→ Capital regional (km) → Dublin 176
Area (km²) 19
Built-up area (km²) 27
Density (per km²) 2,168
Population 61,570
Population structure (%) 15 | 65
17.9 | 69.0 | 13.1

Distribution built area (%) B | I P
89 | 10 1

TERRITORY

Mid-West LMK

Area (km²) 10,236
Density (per km²) 47
Population 484,164
Natura2000 (km²) M | T
3,367 | 1,561

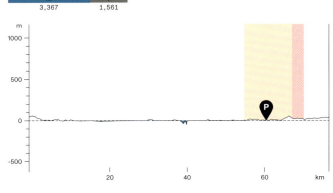

194 Port City Atlas Atlantic

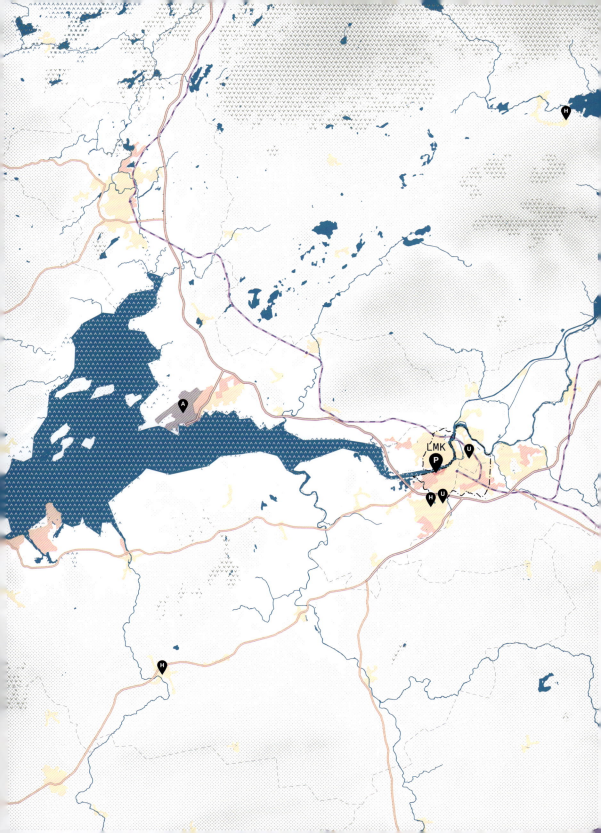

ORK
Cork, IE
Lough Mahon

PORT

ORK (%)   100

	ORK	
Liquid	362	
Dry bulk	135	
Container	398	
Specialized	52	
General	658	
Cruise ship	93	
Passenger	33	
Other		
Vessels	1,581	✕

	ORK	
Liquid bulk	4,884	
Dry bulk	1,526	
Containers	1,890	
RoRo	135	
Other	271	
Cargo (t)	8,706	✕
Passengers	114	✕

CITY

	Cork	ORK
→ Capital national (km)	→ Dublin	218
→ Capital regional (km)		
Area (km²)		40
Built-up area (km²)		40
Density (per km²)		3,285
Population		130,119
Population structure (%)	14.6 / 70.5 / 15.0	15 / 65
Distribution built area (%)	B 85 / I 12 / P 3	

TERRITORY

	South-West	ORK
Area (km²)		12,251
Density (per km²)		58
Population		705,950
Natura2000 (km²)	M 4,047 / T 777	

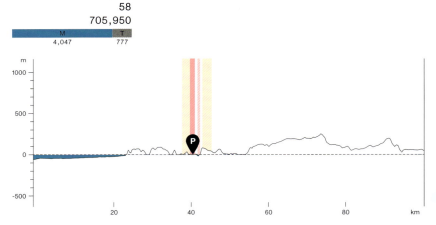

196   Port City Atlas   Atlantic

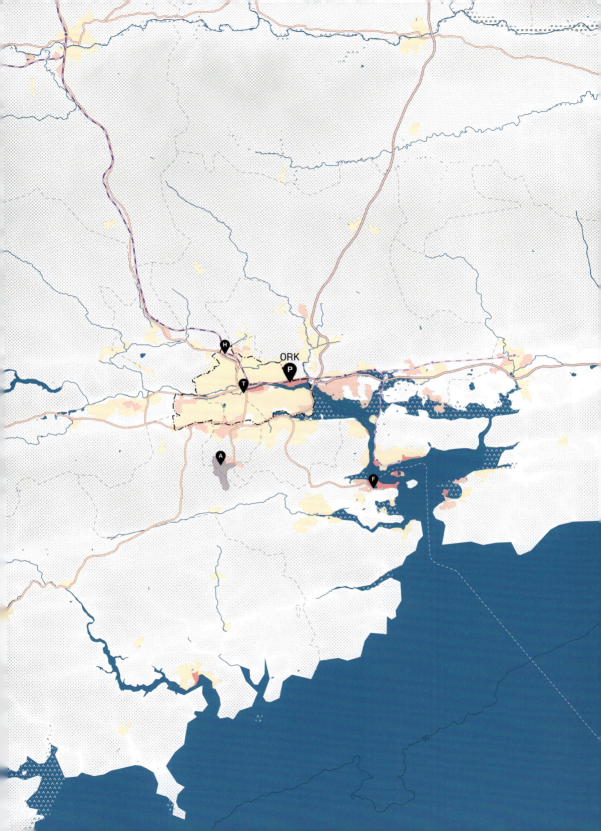

HYM # Heysham, UK  Morecambe Bay

PORT

HYM (%) 100

	HYM			HYM
Liquid			Liquid bulk	
Dry bulk			Dry bulk	
Container			Containers	
Specialized			RoRo	4,538
General	2,040		Other	
Cruise ship			Cargo (t)	4,538 ✕
Passenger				
Other				
Vessels	2,040 ✕		Passengers	284 ✕

CITY

Lancaster — HYM

→ Capital national (km)
→ Capital regional (km) → London 339
Area (km²) → Manchester 75
Built-up area (km²) 578
Density (per km²) 34
Population 247
Population structure (%) 142,487

17 | 65
23.1 | 56.7 | 20.3

Distribution built area (%)
B | I P
80 | 18 2

TERRITORY

Lancaster and Wyre — HYM

Area (km²) 860
Density (per km²) 296
Population 254,791
Natura2000 (km²)

M | T
3,292 | 162

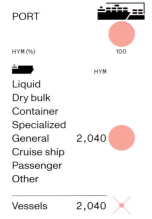
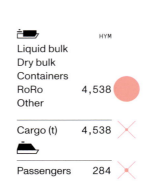

198 Port City Atlas Atlantic

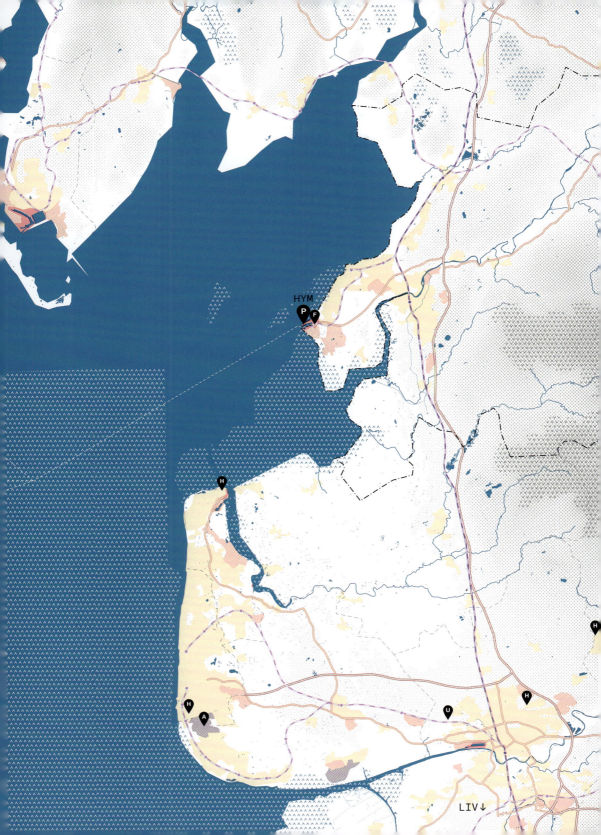

LIV # Liverpool, UK   🚢 ≡ Mersey River

PORT

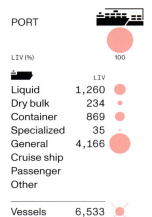

LIV (%)   100

🚢		LIV
Liquid	1,260	●
Dry bulk	234	·
Container	869	●
Specialized	35	·
General	4,166	●
Cruise ship		
Passenger		
Other		
Vessels	6,533	✕

🚢		LIV
Liquid bulk	11,925	●
Dry bulk	7,345	●
Containers	6,274	●
RoRo	7,768	●
Other	1,002	·
Cargo (t)	34,314	✕
🚢		
Passengers	694	✕

CITY

Liverpool   LIV

→ Capital national (km)	→ London	291
→ Capital regional (km)	→ Manchester	50
Area (km²)		646
Built-up area (km²)		333
Density (per km²)		764
Population		493,182
Population structure (%)	15 / 16.9	65 / 64.3 / 18.9
Distribution built area (%)	B 82	A I P / 1 13 4

TERRITORY

Liverpool   LIV

Area (km²)	112
Density (per km²)	4,455
Population	496,784
Natura2000 (km²)	M 2,301

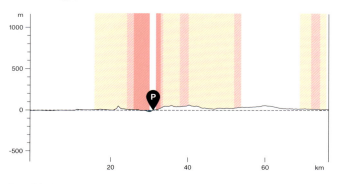

200   Port City Atlas   Atlantic

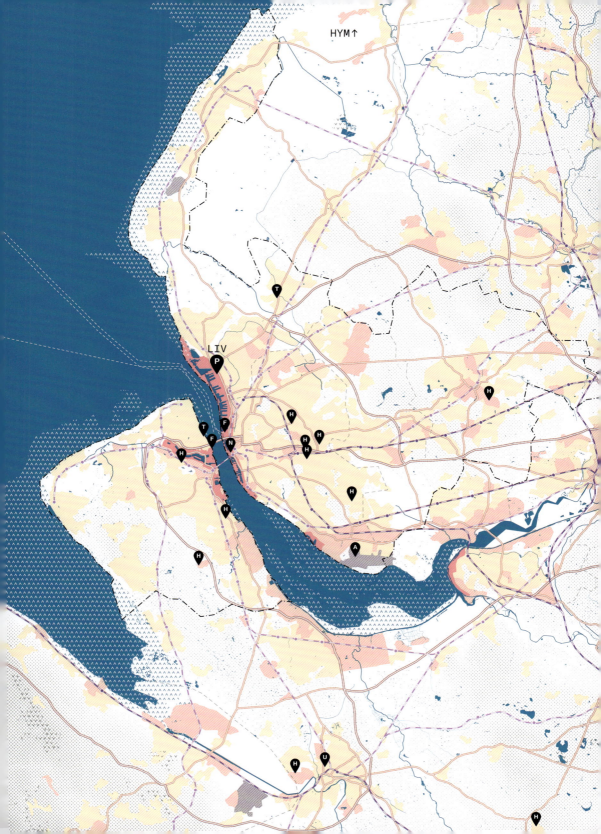

HLY | # Holyhead, UK |  Irish Sea

PORT

HLY (%)   70.4   29.6

	HLY			HLY
Liquid	25		Liquid bulk	
Dry bulk			Dry bulk	
Container			Containers	
Specialized			RoRo	5,323
General	3,083		Other	1
Cruise ship				
Passenger			Cargo (t)	5,324
Other	31			
Vessels	3,139		Passengers	1,886

CITY

Isle of Anglesey   HLY

→ Capital national (km) → London	365
→ Capital regional (km) → Manchester	159
Area (km²)	721
Built-up area (km²)	25
Density (per km²)	97
Population	69,794
Population structure (%)	17 / 65
	23.0 57.8 19.2
Distribution built area (%)	B 72 / A 17 / I 9 / P 2

TERRITORY

Isle of Anglesey   HLY

Area (km²)	721
Density (per km²)	97
Population	70,073
Natura2000 (km²)	M 3,999 / T 5

202   Port City Atlas   Atlantic

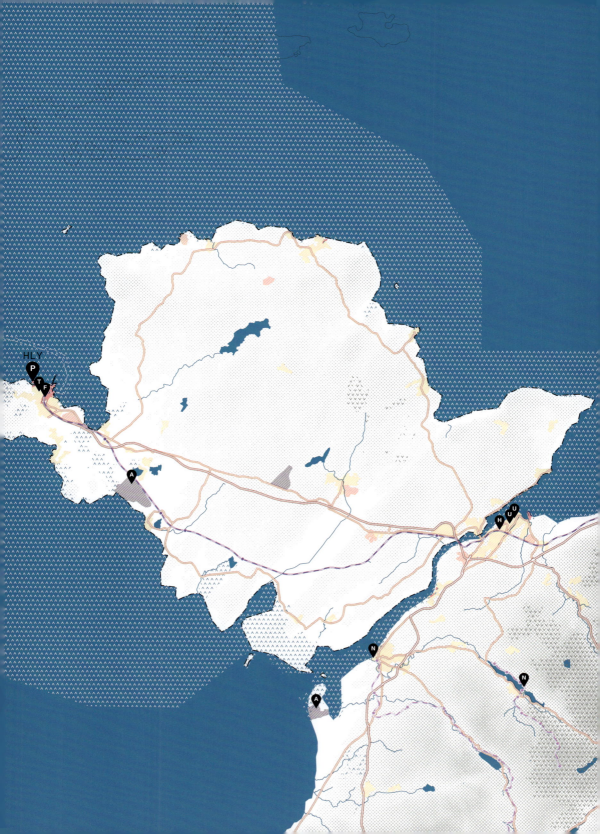

MLF # Milford Haven, UK  River Cleddau

PORT

MLF (%)　　　　　　　　61.6　　　　　　　　　　　　　　34.0　　　　　　　　4.4

	MLF			MLF
Liquid	1,214		Liquid bulk	34,051
Dry bulk			Dry bulk	
Container			Containers	
Specialized			RoRo	853
General	694		Other	
Cruise ship			Cargo (t)	34,952
Passenger				
Other	17		Passengers	327
Vessels	1,925			

CITY

　　　　　　　　　　　　Pembrokeshire　　　　　　MLF
→ Capital national (km)　→ London　　　　　341
→ Capital regional (km)　→ Birmingham　　　230
Area (km²)　　　　　　　　　　　　　　　　1,623
Built-up area (km²)　　　　　　　　　　　　　49
Density (per km²)　　　　　　　　　　　　　　77
Population　　　　　　　　　　　　　　124,711
Population structure (%)　　17　　　65
　　　　　　　　　　　21.5　　56.4　　22.1
Distribution built area (%)　　B　　　A　I　P
　　　　　　　　　　　　　　70　　　8　10　12

TERRITORY

　　　　　　　　　　　　South West Wales　　　　MLF
Area (km²)　　　　　　　　　　　　　　　5,788
Density (per km²)　　　　　　　　　　　　　67
Population　　　　　　　　　　　　　386,480
Natura2000 (km²)　　　　M　　　　　T
　　　　　　　　　　　11,121　　　　487

204　　　　　　　Port City Atlas　　　Atlantic

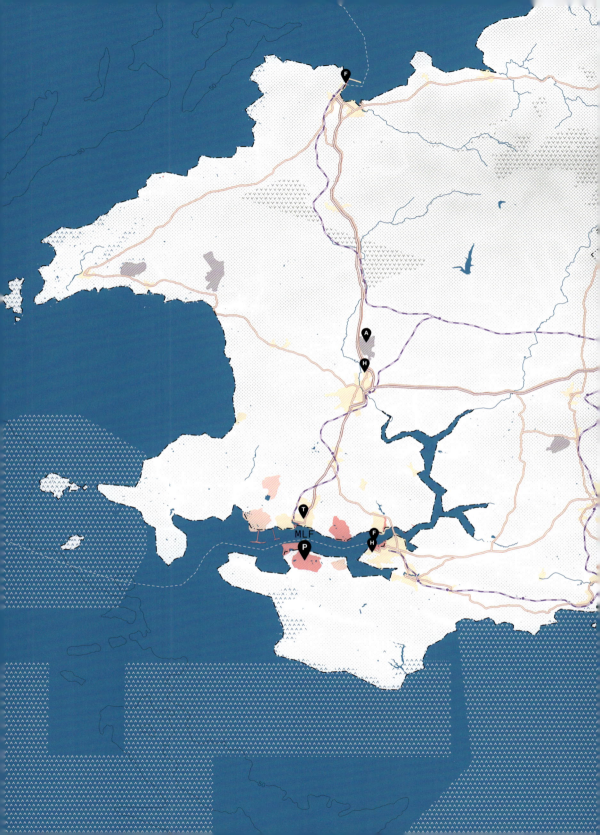

BRS | # Bristol, UK | River Severn

PORT

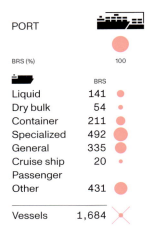

BRS (%)   100

	BRS	
Liquid	141	
Dry bulk	54	
Container	211	
Specialized	492	
General	335	
Cruise ship	20	
Passenger		
Other	431	
Vessels	1,684	

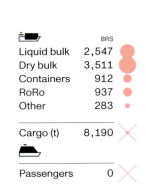

	BRS	
Liquid bulk	2,547	
Dry bulk	3,511	
Containers	912	
RoRo	937	
Other	283	
Cargo (t)	8,190	
Passengers	0	

CITY

Bristol, City of   BRS

→ Capital national (km)	→ London	177
→ Capital regional (km)	→ Birmingham	125
Area (km²)		111
Built-up area (km²)		141
Density (per km²)		4,166
Population		461,329
Population structure (%)	17.7 / 69.4 / 13.0	15 / 65
Distribution built area (%)	B 87	/ P 11 2

TERRITORY

Bristol, City of   BRS

Area (km²)	111
Density (per km²)	4,224
Population	467,099
Natura2000 (km²)	M 1,006 / T 2

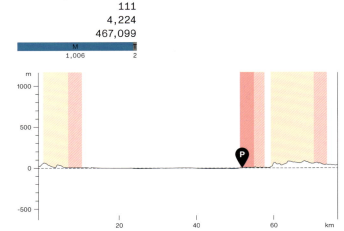

206   Port City Atlas   Atlantic

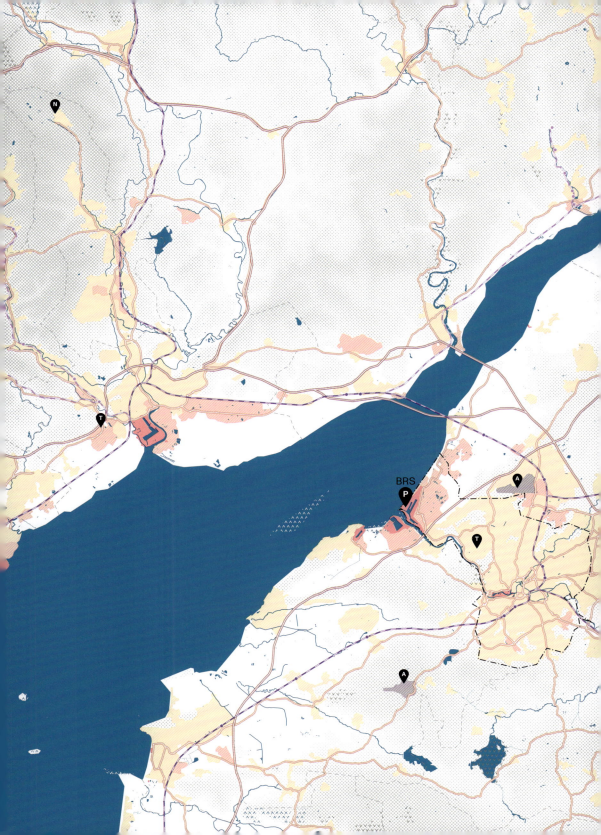

SOU
PME

Southampton, UK
Portsmouth, UK

River Itchen
The Solent

PORT

SOU/PME (%)   0.8   32.7   6.2   2.5   46.0   3.6   6.1   56.5   6.5   30.5   8.6

	SOU	PME
Liquid	1,725	299
Dry bulk	28	
Container	854	90
Specialized	1,001	
General	467	3,031
Cruise ship	454	37
Passenger		
Other	407	
Vessels	4,936	3,189

	SOU	PME
Liquid bulk	20,113	
Dry bulk	2,088	404
Containers	9,029	366
RoRo	1,821	2,635
Other	100	215
Cargo (t)	33,151	3,620
Passengers	1,807	1,754

CITY

	Southampton	SOU	Portsmouth	PME
→ Capital national (km)	→ London	115	→ London	107
→ Capital regional (km)				
Area (km²)		130		196
Built-up area (km²)		85		121
Density (per km²)		1,937		2,760
Population		252,578		542,040
Population structure (%)		17.6 67.2 15.3		16.9 63.9 19.0
Distribution built area (%)		B 88 A I P 2 4 6		B 84 A I P 1 12 3

TERRITORY

	Southampton	SOU	Portsmouth	PME
Area (km²)		50		41
Density (per km²)		5,059		5,321
Population		254,361		216,023
Natura2000 (km²)		M 184 T 3		M 436

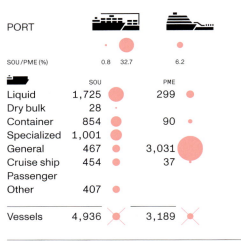
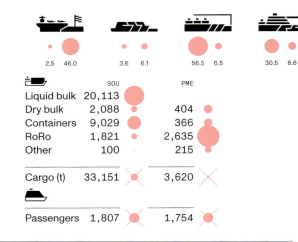
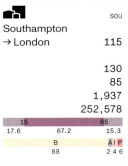
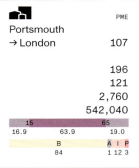
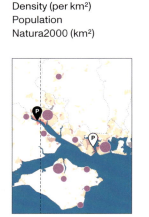
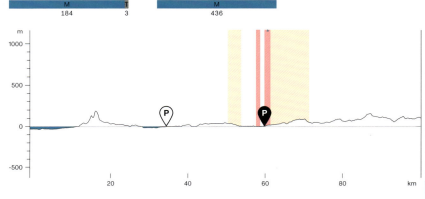

208   Port City Atlas   Atlantic

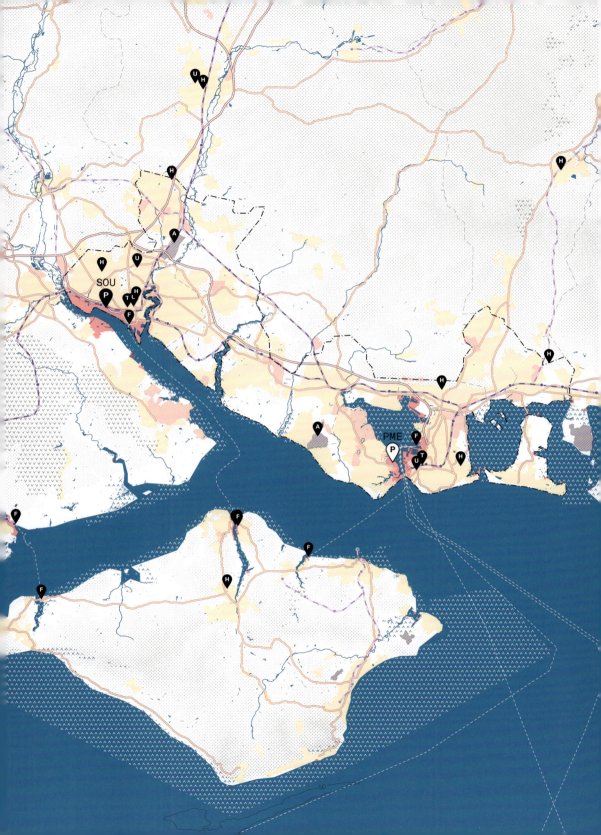

LEH # Le Havre, FR 🚢 📄 Seine River

PORT

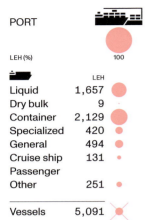

LEH (%) 100

	LEH			LEH
Liquid	1,657		Liquid bulk	36,132
Dry bulk	9		Dry bulk	1,225
Container	2,129		Containers	21,932
Specialized	420		RoRo	844
General	494		Other	40
Cruise ship	131		Cargo (t)	60,173
Passenger				
Other	251		Passengers	172
Vessels	5,091			

CITY

City of Le Havre — LEH
→ Paris 178

→ Capital national (km)
→ Capital regional (km)
Area (km²) 86
Built-up area (km²) 65
Density (per km²) 2,262
Population 195,042
Population structure (%) 18.7 / 62.0 / 19.3 (15 / 65)
Distribution built area (%) B 45 | A 1 | I 34 | P 20

TERRITORY

Seine-Maritime — LEH

Area (km²) 6,301
Density (per km²) 199
Population 1,254,436
Natura2000 (km²) M 2,672 | T 205

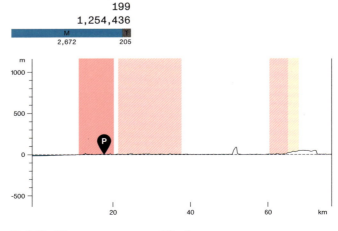

210   Port City Atlas   Atlantic

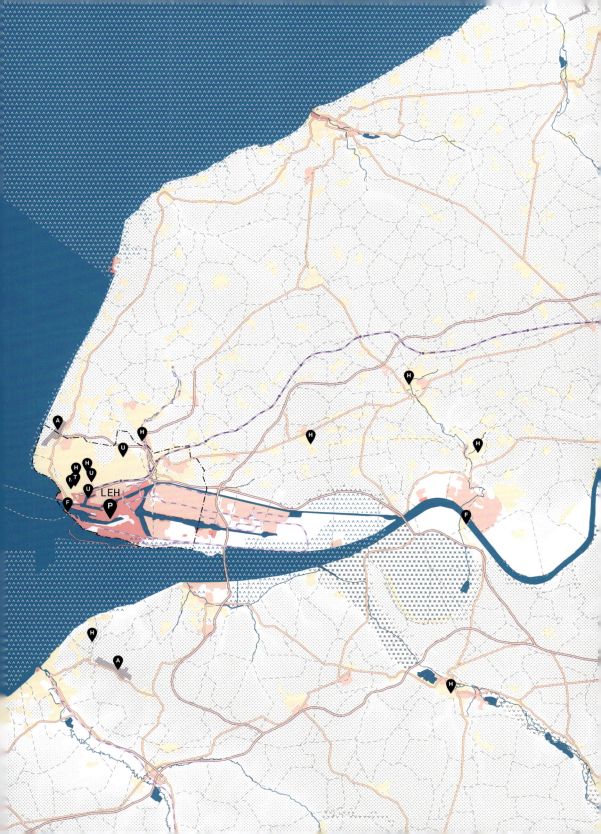

NTE

Nantes Saint-Nazaire, FR

 Loire River

PORT

NTE (%) — 100

	NTE	
Liquid	865	
Dry bulk	679	
Container	250	
Specialized	208	
General	165	
Cruise ship	10	
Passenger		
Other	414	
Vessels	2,591	✕

	NTE	
Liquid bulk	22,633	
Dry bulk	5,339	
Containers	1,404	
RoRo	465	
Other	314	
Cargo (t)	30,155	✕
Passengers	0	✕

CITY

		NTE
	City of Saint-Nazaire	
→ Capital national (km)	→ Paris	382
→ Capital regional (km)		
Area (km²)		48
Built-up area (km²)		31
Density (per km²)		1,461
Population		69,993
Population structure (%)	15 / 65	
	16.9 60.7 22.4	
Distribution built area (%)	B 70 I 25 P 5	

TERRITORY

		NTE
	Loire-Atlantique	
Area (km²)		6,876
Density (per km²)		208
Population		1,427,913
Natura2000 (km²)	M 4,394 T 625	

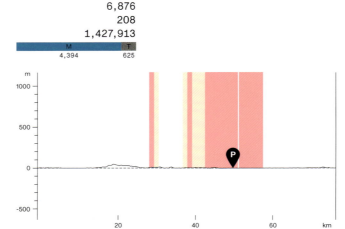

212 — Port City Atlas — Atlantic

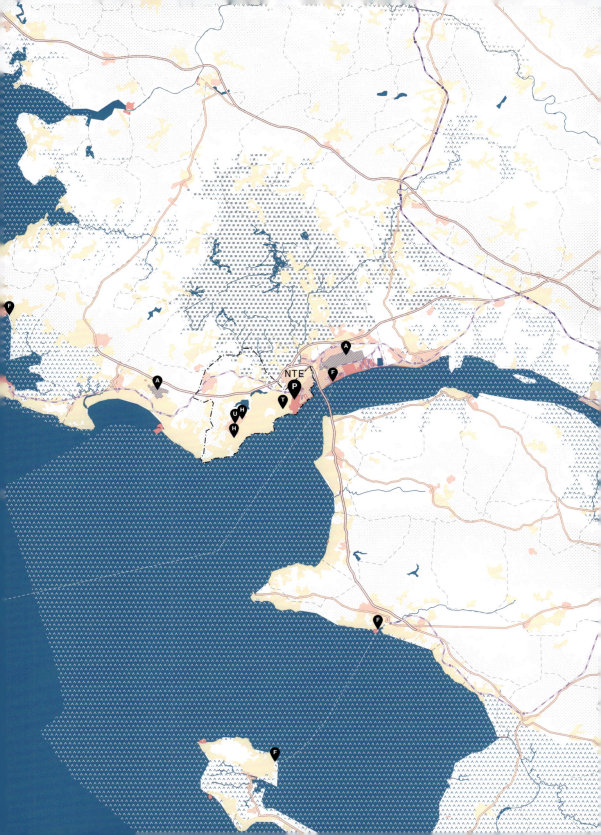

LRH # La Rochelle, FR

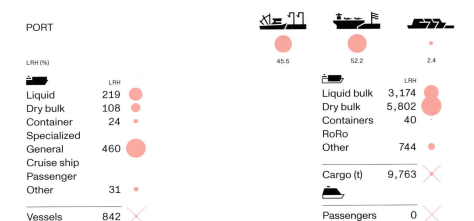

PORT

		45.5	52.2	2.4	

LRH (%)

	LRH			LRH
Liquid	219		Liquid bulk	3,174
Dry bulk	108		Dry bulk	5,802
Container	24		Containers	40
Specialized			RoRo	
General	460		Other	744
Cruise ship				
Passenger			Cargo (t)	9,763
Other	31			
Vessels	842		Passengers	0

CITY

City of La Rochelle — LRH

→ Capital national (km)
→ Paris 400
→ Capital regional (km)
Area (km²) 38
Built-up area (km²) 38
Density (per km²) 2,198
Population 82,783
Population structure (%) 13.1 / 62.6 / 24.3 (15 / 65)
Distribution built area (%) B 59 / A 4 / I 25 / P 12

TERRITORY

Charente-Maritime — LRH

Area (km²) 6,877
Density (per km²) 94
Population 648,837
Natura2000 (km²) M 9,994 / T 647

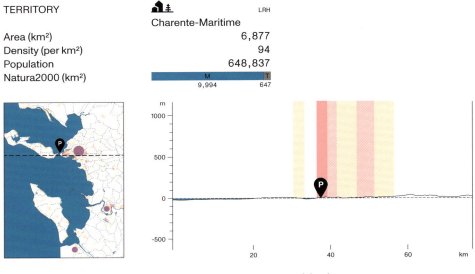

214 — Port City Atlas — Atlantic

BOD
Bordeaux, FR
 Garonne River

PORT

BOD (%) 100

	BOD			BOD	
Liquid	320		Liquid bulk	4,727	
Dry bulk	139		Dry bulk	1,444	
Container	49		Containers	248	
Specialized			RoRo		
General	205		Other	80	
Cruise ship	50				
Passenger			Cargo (t)	6,499	✕
Other	9				
Vessels	767	✕	Passengers	1	✕

CITY

City of Bordeaux   BOD

→ Capital national (km) → Paris	499
→ Capital regional (km)	
Area (km²)	246
Built-up area (km²)	133
Density (per km²)	2,642
Population	650,138
Population structure (%)	15.5 / 68.5 / 16.0
Distribution built area (%)	B 87 / A 7 / I 6

TERRITORY

Gironde   BOD

Area (km²)	10,084
Density (per km²)	161
Population	1,619,190
Natura2000 (km²)	M 9,111 / T 778

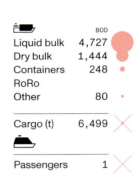

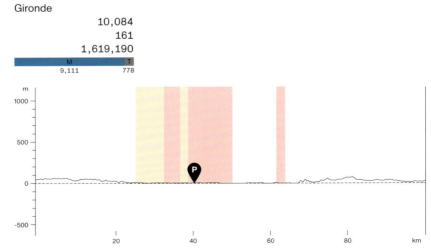

216   Port City Atlas   Atlantic

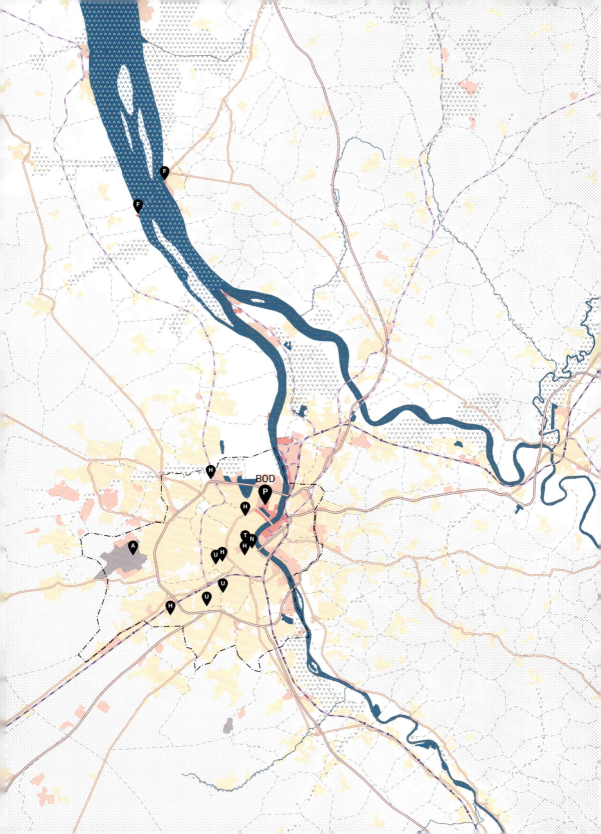

BIO **Bilbao, ES** 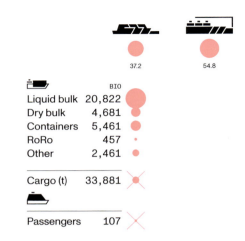 Estuary of Bilbao

PORT

BIO (%)		7.9
	BIO	
Liquid	778	
Dry bulk	500	
Container	614	
Specialized		
General	876	
Cruise ship	59	
Passenger		
Other		
Vessels	2,818	

		37.2	54.8
	BIO		
Liquid bulk	20,822		
Dry bulk	4,681		
Containers	5,461		
RoRo	457		
Other	2,461		
Cargo (t)	33,881		
Passengers	107		

CITY

Bilbao   BIO

→ Capital national (km)		
→ Capital regional (km)		
→ Madrid	332	
Area (km²)	175	
Built-up area (km²)	76	
Density (per km²)	4,532	
Population	792,617	
Population structure (%)	12.0 / 64.0 / 23.9 (15 / 65)
Distribution built area (%)	B 48 / A 5 / I 42 / P 5

TERRITORY

Bizkaia   BIO

Area (km²)	2,213
Density (per km²)	514
Population	1,137,191
Natura2000 (km²)	M 361 / T 213

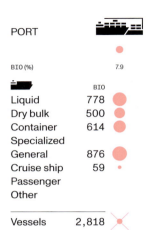

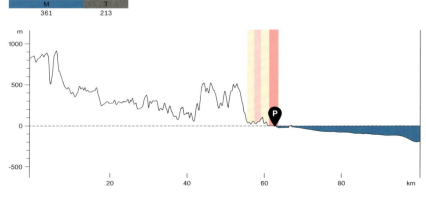

218 Port City Atlas Atlantic

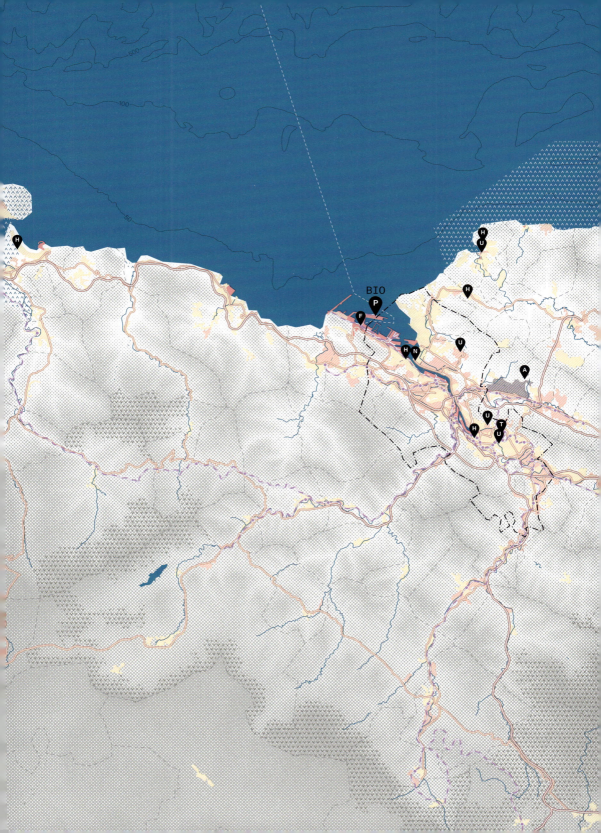

GIJ

Gijón, ES

🚢 🚢 Atlantic

PORT

GIJ (%)		6.5			11.5	82.0
	GIJ				GIJ	
Liquid	93			Liquid bulk	900	
Dry bulk	289			Dry bulk	14,501	
Container	196			Containers	851	
Specialized				RoRo		
General	588			Other	968	
Cruise ship	17					
Passenger				Cargo (t)	17,220	
Other	4					
Vessels	1,187			Passengers	0	

CITY

		GIJ
	Gijón	
→ Capital national (km)	→ Madrid	387
→ Capital regional (km)		
Area (km²)		182
Built-up area (km²)		35
Density (per km²)		1,496
Population		271,780
Population structure (%)	15	65
	11.3 63.1	25.5
Distribution built area (%)	B I P	
	50 44 6	

TERRITORY

		GIJ
	Asturias	
Area (km²)		10,602
Density (per km²)		96
Population		1,022,205
Natura2000 (km²)	M T	
	1,492 5,640	

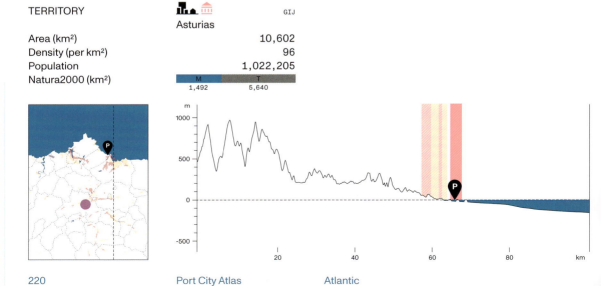

220   Port City Atlas   Atlantic

LCG
FRO

La Coruña, ES
Ferrol, ES

 Ría da Coruña

 Ría de Ferrol

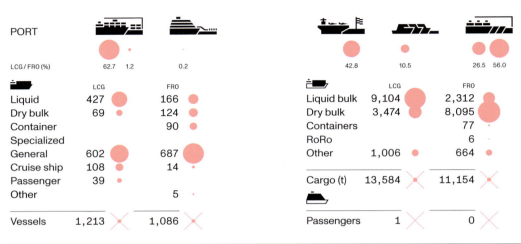

PORT		LCG	FRO			LCG	FRO
LCG / FRO (%)		62.7 1.2	0.2			42.8 10.5	26.5 56.0
Liquid		427	166	Liquid bulk		9,104	2,312
Dry bulk		69	124	Dry bulk		3,474	8,095
Container			90	Containers			77
Specialized				RoRo			6
General		602	687	Other		1,006	664
Cruise ship		108	14	Cargo (t)		13,584	11,154
Passenger		39					
Other			5				
Vessels		1,213	1,086	Passengers		1	0

CITY	LCG	FRO
	Coruña, A	Ferrol
→ Capital national (km)	→ Madrid 507	→ Madrid 507
→ Capital regional (km)		→ A Coruna 21
Area (km²)	38	83
Built-up area (km²)	34	19
Density (per km²)	6,512	800
Population	245,711	66,065
Population structure (%)	12.3 63.4 24.4	10.7 61.5 27.7
Distribution built area (%)	B 75 I 21 P 4	B 68 I 21 P 11

TERRITORY	LCG	FRO
	A Coruña	A Coruña
Area (km²)	7,949	7,949
Density (per km²)	141	141
Population	1,122,006	1,122,006
Natura2000 (km²)	M 4,415 T 400	M 4,415 T 400

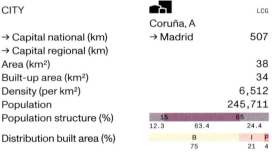
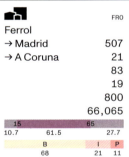
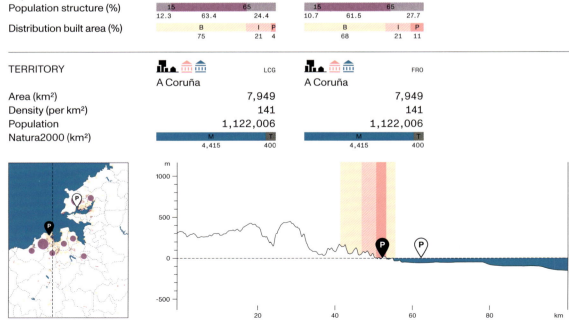

Port City Atlas   Atlantic

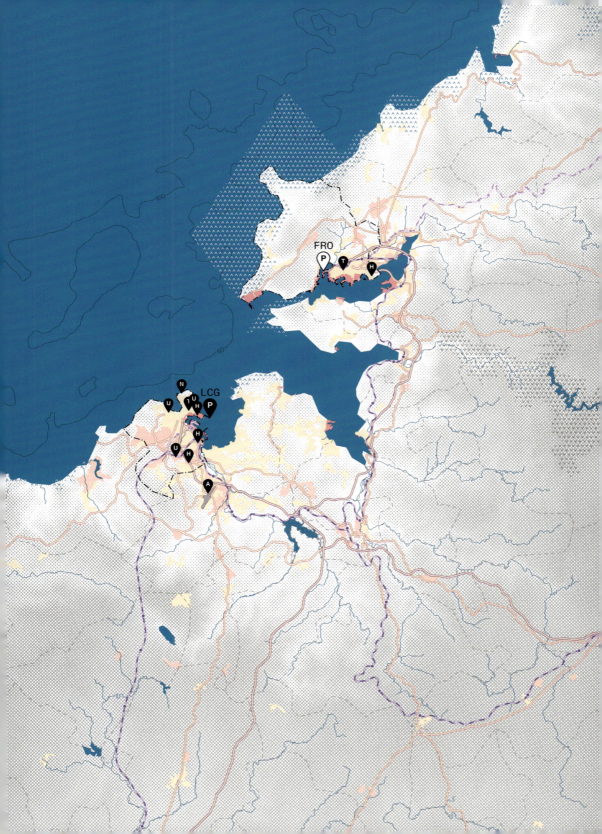

LEI   # Leixões (Porto), PT    Douro River

PORT

LEI (%)   37.4   62.6

	LEI			LEI
Liquid	373		Liquid bulk	7,758
Dry bulk	87		Dry bulk	2,606
Container	1,124		Containers	5,481
Specialized	17		RoRo	1,047
General	853		Other	1,032
Cruise ship	100			
Passenger			Cargo (t)	17,924
Other				
Vessels	2,550		Passengers	1

CITY

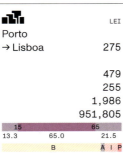

Porto   LEI
→ Capital national (km)   → Lisboa   275
→ Capital regional (km)
Area (km²)   479
Built-up area (km²)   255
Density (per km²)   1,986
Population   951,805
Population structure (%)   13.3 65.0 21.5
Distribution built area (%)   B 86   A I P 1 12 1

TERRITORY

Metropolitana do Porto   LEI
Area (km²)   2,040
Density (per km²)   844
Population   1,722,374
Natura2000 (km²)   M 2,369   T 426

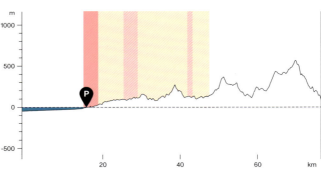

224   Port City Atlas   Atlantic

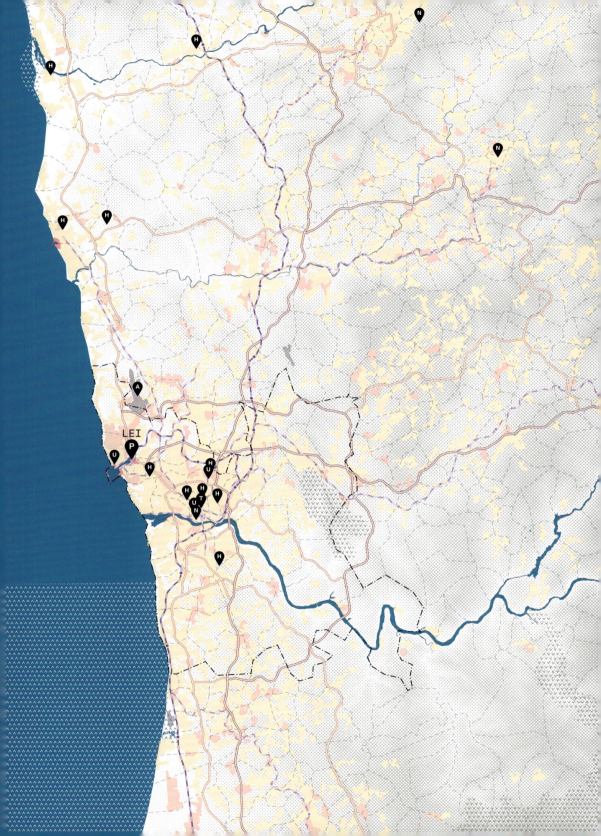

LIS
SET

Lisboa, PT
Setúbal, PT

 Tagus River
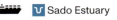 Sado Estuary

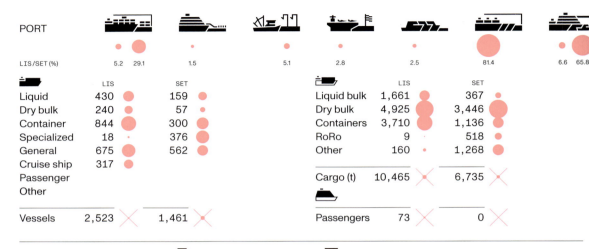

PORT							
LIS/SET (%)	5.2 29.1	1.5	5.1	2.8	2.5	81.4	6.6 65.8

	LIS	SET			LIS	SET
Liquid	430	159		Liquid bulk	1,661	367
Dry bulk	240	57		Dry bulk	4,925	3,446
Container	844	300		Containers	3,710	1,136
Specialized	18	376		RoRo	9	518
General	675	562		Other	160	1,268
Cruise ship	317			Cargo (t)	10,465	6,735
Passenger						
Other				Passengers	73	0
Vessels	2,523	1,461				

CITY	LIS	SET
	Lisboa	Setúbal
→ Capital national (km)	→ Lisboa 0	→ Lisboa 31
→ Capital regional (km)		→ Porto 299
Area (km²)	637	170
Built-up area (km²)	368	49
Density (per km²)	2,921	680
Population	1,859,838	115,758
Population structure (%)	15.8 60.3 23.8	15.5 62.3 22.1
Distribution built area (%)	B 82 A 1 I 16 P 1	B 65 I 33 P 2

TERRITORY	LIS	SET
	Metropolitana de Lisboa	Metropolitana de Lisboa
Area (km²)	2,853	2,853
Density (per km²)	998	998
Population	2,846,332	2,846,332
Natura2000 (km²)	M 3,630	M 3,630

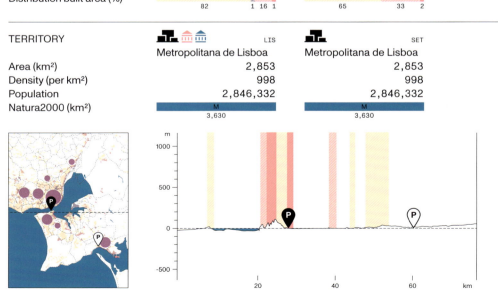

226 · Port City Atlas · Atlantic

HUV # Huelva, ES  Odiel River

PORT

HUV (%)

	HUV	
Liquid	1,557	
Dry bulk	224	
Container	108	
Specialized		
General	593	
Cruise ship	16	
Passenger		
Other		
Vessels	2,491	

	HUV	
Liquid bulk	26,696	
Dry bulk	5,754	
Containers	426	
RoRo	223	
Other	156	
Cargo (t)	33,255	×
Passengers	43	×

100

CITY

Huelva | HUV

		HUV
→ Capital national (km)	→ Madrid	451
→ Capital regional (km)		
Area (km²)		151
Built-up area (km²)		14
Density (per km²)		949
Population		143,663
Population structure (%)	15.6 / 66.4 / 17.9	
Distribution built area (%)	B 50 / I 50	

TERRITORY

Huelva | HUV

	HUV
Area (km²)	10,129
Density (per km²)	52
Population	524,576
Natura2000 (km²)	M 3,045 / T 2,979

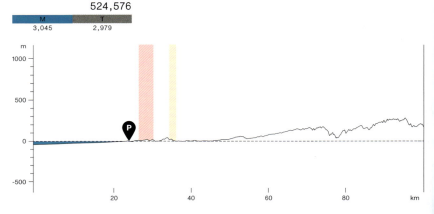

228   Port City Atlas   Atlantic

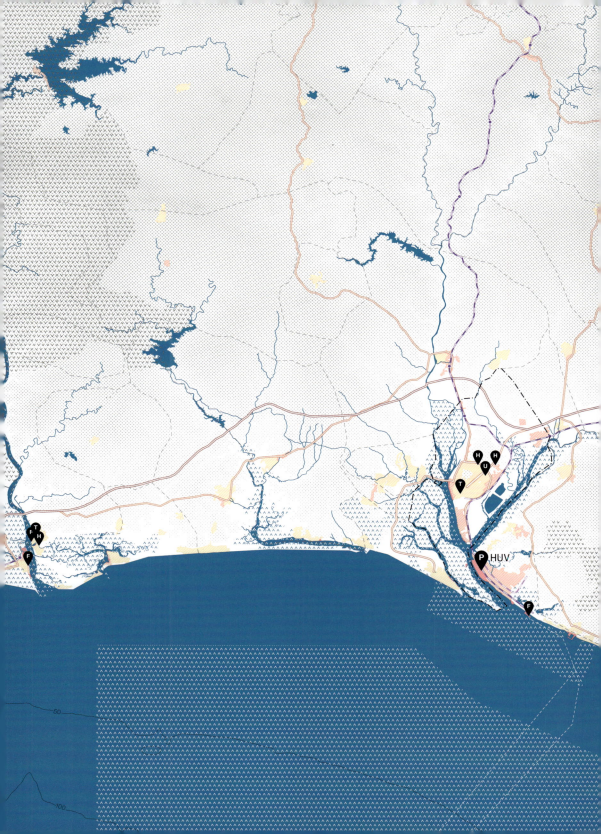

LPA

Las Palmas, ES

 Atlantic

PORT

	LPA
LPA (%)	2.5 / 17.8 / 79.8

	LPA
Liquid	1,432
Dry bulk	1,621
Container	1,915
Specialized	107
General	8,312
Cruise ship	560
Passenger	23
Other	
Vessels	13,959

	LPA
Liquid bulk	8,072
Dry bulk	453
Containers	8,379
RoRo	2,337
Other	609
Cargo (t)	19,850
Passengers	1,994

CITY

Las Palmas

	LPA
→ Capital national (km) → Madrid	2112
→ Capital regional (km) → Santa Cruz	201
Area (km²)	102
Built-up area (km²)	42
Density (per km²)	3,737
Population	379,925
Population structure (%)	12.4 / 69.7 / 17.9
Distribution built area (%)	B 78 / I 14 / P 8

TERRITORY

Gran Canaria

	LPA
Area (km²)	1,560
Density (per km²)	555
Population	865,756
Natura2000 (km²)	M 1,035 / T 508

230 · Port City Atlas · Atlantic

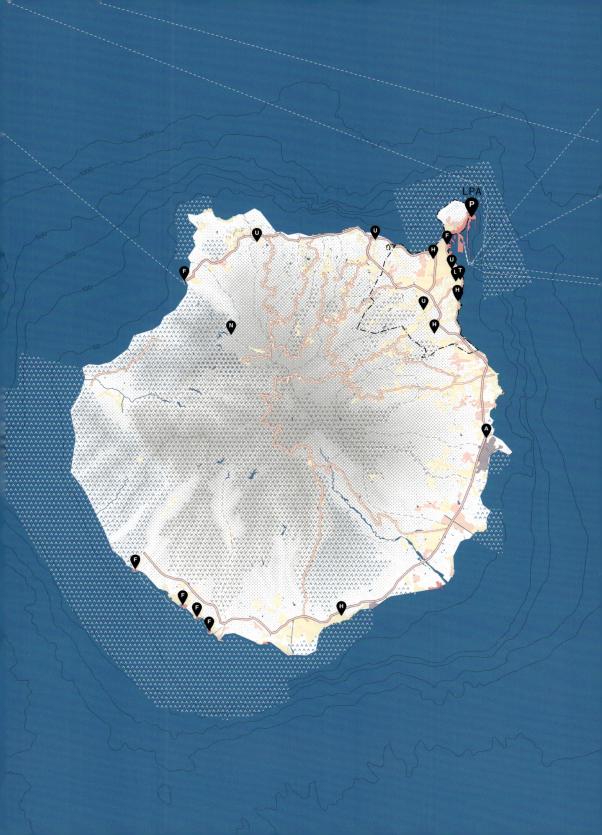

SCT

Santa Cruz de Tenerife, ES

 Atlantic

PORT

SCT (%)   1.8   61.8   36.4

	SCT			SCT
Liquid	814		Liquid bulk	4,812
Dry bulk	149		Dry bulk	422
Container	907		Containers	2,170
Specialized	18		RoRo	2,338
General	6,124		Other	46
Cruise ship	511			
Passenger	7,623		Cargo (t)	9,788
Other				
Vessels	16,132		Passengers	5,615

CITY

	SCT
Santa Cruz de Tenerife	
→ Capital national (km) → Madrid	2136
→ Capital regional (km) → Las Palmas	101
Area (km²)	253
Built-up area (km²)	58
Density (per km²)	1,445
Population	364,815
Population structure (%)	15 / 65
	12.8 69.8 17.4
Distribution built area (%)	B / A / I / P
	77 4 14 5

TERRITORY

	SCT
Tenerife	
Area (km²)	2,035
Density (per km²)	467
Population	949,471
Natura2000 (km²)	M 2,876 / T 675

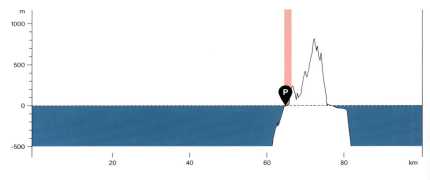

232   Port City Atlas   Atlantic

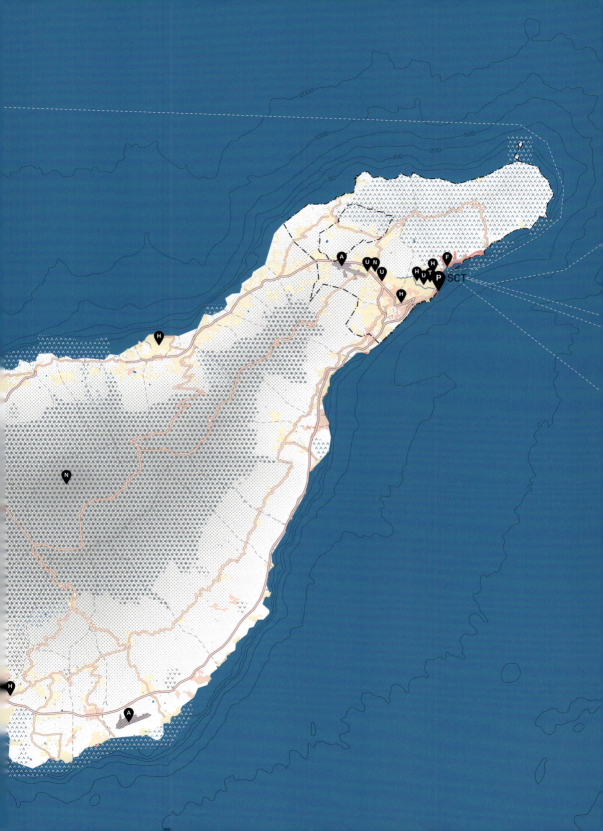

CAD # Cádiz, ES Bay of Cádiz

PORT

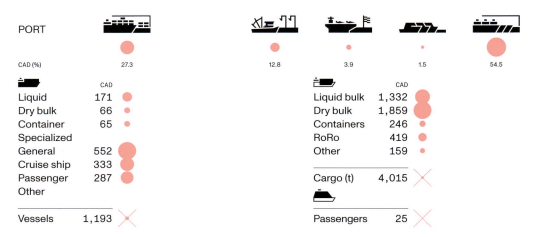

| CAD (%) | 27.3 | 12.8 | 3.9 | 1.5 | 54.5 |

	CAD			CAD
Liquid	171		Liquid bulk	1,332
Dry bulk	66		Dry bulk	1,859
Container	65		Containers	246
Specialized			RoRo	419
General	552		Other	159
Cruise ship	333			
Passenger	287		Cargo (t)	4,015
Other				
Vessels	1,193		Passengers	25

CITY

Cádiz — CAD

→ Capital national (km) → Madrid 486
→ Capital regional (km)
Area (km²) 12
Built-up area (km²) 7
Density (per km²) 9,457
Population 116,027
Population structure (%) 12.3 | 64.7 | 23.1
Distribution built area (%) B 62 | I 18 | P 20

TERRITORY

Cádiz — CAD

Area (km²) 7,438
Density (per km²) 168
Population 1,249,739
Natura2000 (km²) M 4,820 | T 931

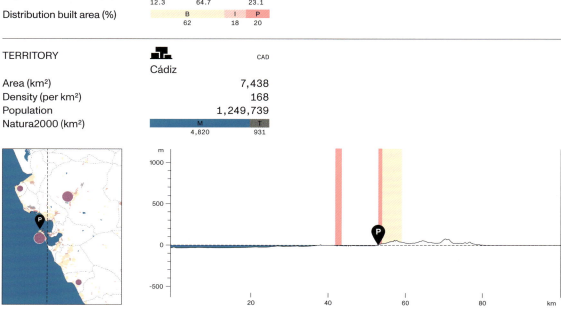

234 — Port City Atlas — Atlantic

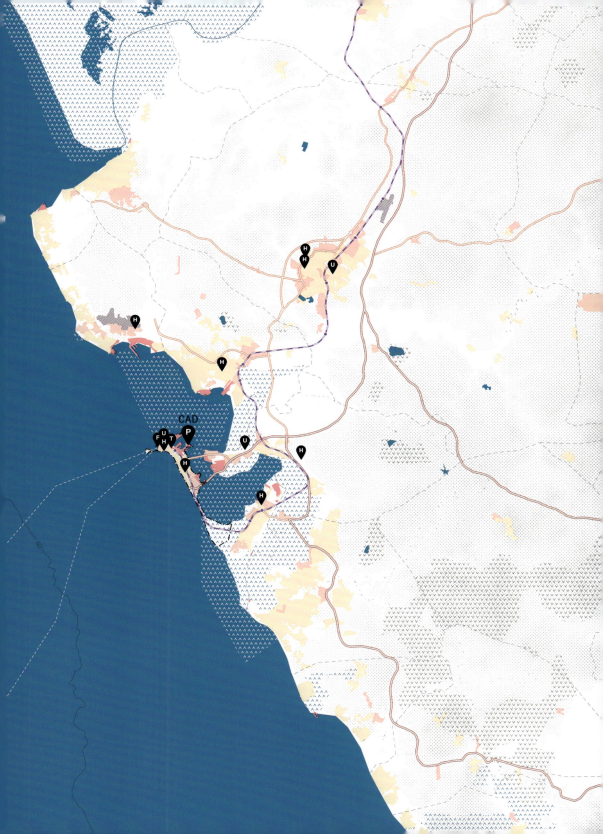

Mediterranean Sea Map and Statistics

ID	Port name	🛢︎[1]		🚢[2]	
ALG	Algeciras, ES	89,908	●	6,148	●
CEU	Ceuta, MA	1,247	·	2,102	●
CAR	Cartagena, ES	33,933	●	1	·
VLC	Valencia, ES	65,308	●	757	●
CAS	Castellón, ES	20,265	●	0	
TAR	Tarragona, ES	32,584	●	31	·
BCN	Barcelona, ES	54,713	●	3,239	●
MRS	Marseille, FR	74,049	●	1,705	●
TLN	Toulon, FR	1,742	·	1,749	●
GOA	Genova, IT	49,698	●	2,881	●
SVN	Savona, IT	13,450	●	806	●
SPE	La Spezia, IT	18,805	●		
LIV	Livorno, IT	36,262	●	2,941	●
CVV	Civitavecchia (Roma), IT	9,527	·	2,886	●
NAP	Napoli, IT	15,431	●	9,257	●
PFX	Porto Foxi, IT	28,818	●		
CAG	Cagliari, IT	12,680	●	389	·
PMO	Palermo, IT	10,047	●	2,017	●
SIR	Siracusa, IT	12,132	●		

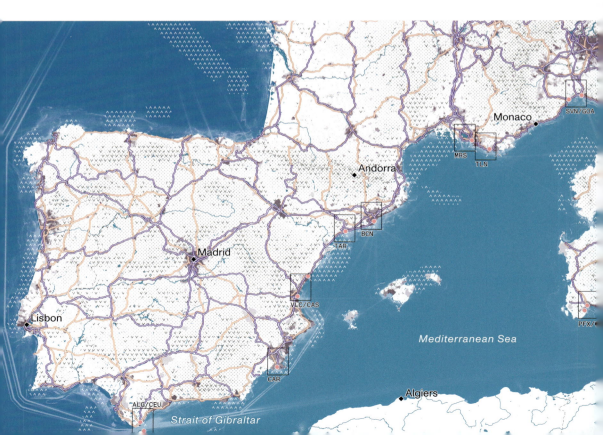

Port name	[1]		[2]	
Messina, IT	7,293	•	11,669	
Milazzo, IT	15,469	•	471	
Gioia Tau, IT	22,694	•		
Reggio di Calabria, IT	4,528	·	10,884	
Taranto, IT	17,608	•		
Ravenna, IT	31,351	•		
Venezia, IT	27,935	•	854	
Trieste, IT	60,332	•		
Koper, SI	22,125	•	0	
Monfalcone, IT	4,485	·		
Rijeka, HR	3,356	·	114	·
Split, HR	1,940	·	4,958	
Peiraias (Athene), GR	56,825	•	9,931	
Perama, GR	3,699	·	6,939	
Elefsina, GR	16,214	•	0	
Thessaloniki, GR	15,172	•	2	

Sea regions[3]
- Atlantic
- Mediterranean Sea

- Altitude in the landscape[4]
- Vessel density, yearly averages of all vessel types[5]
- Natura2000 marine area[6]
- Natura2000 terrestrial area[6]
- Main watercourse[7]
- Main land roads[7]
- Main railroads[7]
- Country border[8]

- Selected port city territory
- Selected port based on tonnage of cargo handled[9]
- Selected port based on number of passengers handled[9]
- Main port outside the EU
- National capital[10]

Population density LAU (in inhabitants per km²)[11]

300   600

0   100 km

[1] tal tonnage of cargo in thousands and in relation to the other selected European ports. Eurostat, 2019.
[2] tal number of passengers in thousands and in relation to the other selected European ports. Eurostat, 2019.
[3] MODnet Human Activities: Regional Advisory Councils, 2014.
[4] A EuroGeographics EuroDEM, 2022.
[5] MODnet Human Activities, Vessel Density Map 2019.
[6] ———, Environment, Natura2000 2015.
[7] ased on Eurogeographics, (2020). EuroGlobalMap. Version 2020 Eurogeographics.
    etrieved from https://eurogeographics.org/maps-for-europe/open-data.
[8] rostat NUTS 1 data.
[9] rostat Maritime transport data, 2019.
[10] atural Earth.
[11] rostat, GISCO LAU, 2019.

ALG **Algeciras, ES**   🚢 ⤴ Strait of Gibraltar
CEU **Ceuta, MA**   🚢 ⤴ Strait of Gibraltar

PORT

ALG / CEU (%) 11.1   73.6   39.5   9.0   6.3   60.5

	ALG	CEU			ALG	CEU
Liquid	2,805	1,017		Liquid bulk	30,703	872
Dry bulk	517	446		Dry bulk	849	24
Container	3,440	62		Containers	53,772	80
Specialized	43			RoRo	1,251	271
General	3,312	9,551		Other	3,333	0
Cruise ship		7				
Passenger	18,840	7187		Cargo (t)	89,908	1,247
Other						
Vessels	28,957	11,084		Passengers	6,148	2,102

CITY

	Algeciras ALG	Ceuta CEU
→ Capital national (km)	→ Madrid 499	→ Rabat 249
→ Capital regional (km)		
Area (km²)	86	20
Built-up area (km²)	19	8
Density (per km²)	1,421	4,287
Population	121,957	84,777
Population structure (%)	17.9 / 66.7 / 15.3	20.9 / 67.7 / 11.5
Distribution built area (%)	B 70 I 13 P 17	B 63 I 28 P 9

TERRITORY

	Cádiz ALG	Ceuta CEU
Area (km²)	7,438	20
Density (per km²)	168	4,241
Population	1,249,739	84,829
Natura2000 (km²)	M 4,820 T 931	M 2,233

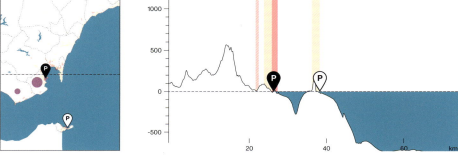

238   Port City Atlas   Mediterranean Sea

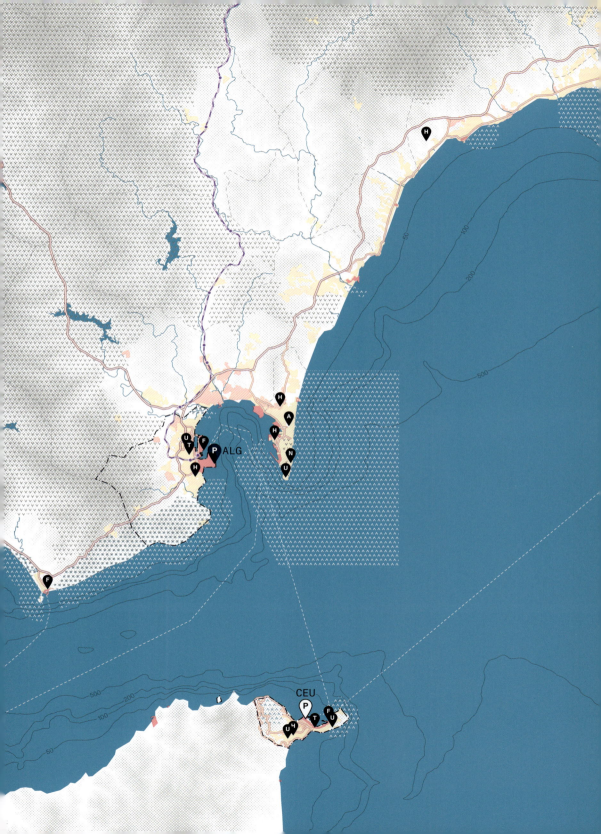

CAR

Cartagena, ES

 Cartagena Bay

PORT

	CAR
CAR (%)	22.8	11.0	14.4	51.7

	CAR			CAR
Liquid	942		Liquid bulk	25,982
Dry bulk	245		Dry bulk	6,837
Container	175		Containers	749
Specialized	19		RoRo	78
General	635		Other	287
Cruise ship	167			
Passenger	126		Cargo (t)	33,933
Other	41			
Vessels	2,169		Passengers	1

CITY

		CAR
	Cartagena	
→ Capital national (km)	→ Madrid	392
→ Capital regional (km)	→ Valencia	215
Area (km²)		558
Built-up area (km²)		58
Density (per km²)		385
Population		214,802
Population structure (%)	17.5 / 66.0 / 16.6	15 / 65
Distribution built area (%)	B 65 / I 31 / P 4	

TERRITORY

		CAR
	Murcia	
Area (km²)		11,315
Density (per km²)		131
Population		1,487,663
Natura2000 (km²)	M 4,136 / T 3,210	

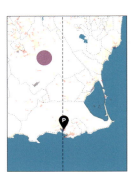

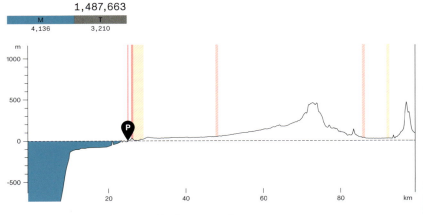

Port City Atlas — Mediterranean Sea

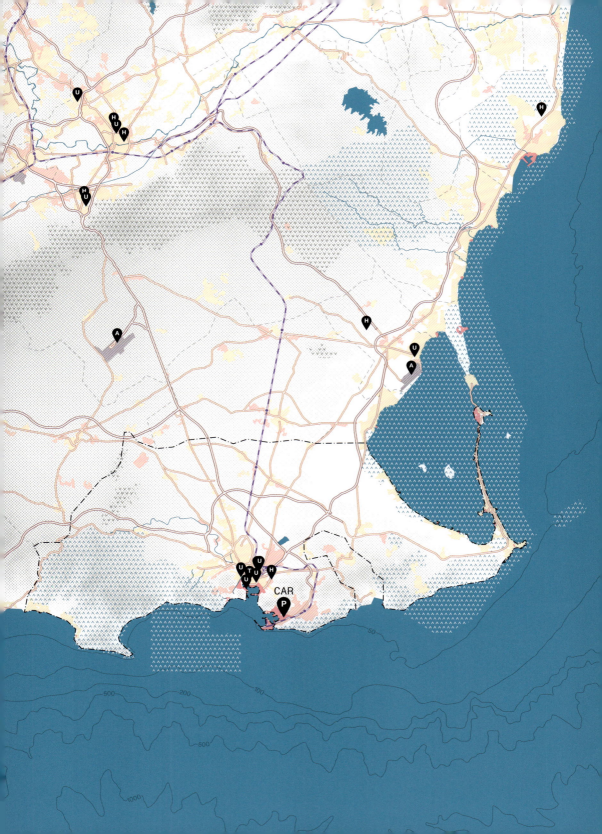

VLC
CAS

Valencia, ES
Castellón, ES

 Balearic Sea
 Balearic Sea

PORT

		VLC		CAS
VLC / CAS (%)		71.4 13.1		1.4

	VLC		CAS	
Liquid	308		531	
Dry bulk	100		313	
Container	3,009		558	
Specialized				
General	4,263		350	
Cruise ship	203			
Passenger	8			
Other			7	
Vessels	7,891		1,759	

| | | 25.1 31.4 | | 2.1 | | 55.5 |

	VLC		CAS	
Liquid bulk	3,120		10,603	
Dry bulk	2,190		7,097	
Containers	49,433		2,330	
RoRo	1,532		4	
Other	9,033		231	
Cargo (t)	65,308		20,265	
Passengers	757		0	

CITY

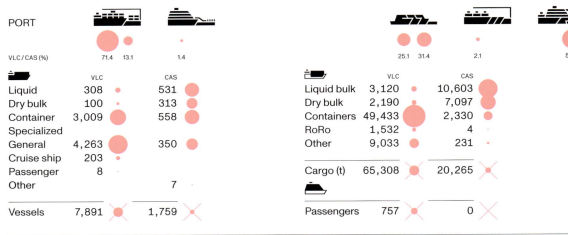

	VLC	CAS
	Valencia	Castellón de la Plana
→ Capital national (km)	→ Madrid 309	→ Madrid 321
→ Capital regional (km)		→ Valencia 65
Area (km²)	401	109
Built-up area (km²)	191	46
Density (per km²)	3,500	1,579
Population	1,403,247	171,728
Population structure (%)	15 65	15 65
	13.7 65.6 20.7	15.3 66.5 18.2
Distribution built area (%)	B A I P	B A I P
	59 3 31 7	65 1 31 3

TERRITORY

	VLC	CAS
	Valencia	Castellón
Area (km²)	10,808	6,634
Density (per km²)	235	86
Population	2,540,588	571,601
Natura2000 (km²)	M T	M T
	1,881 7,282	5,183 5,229

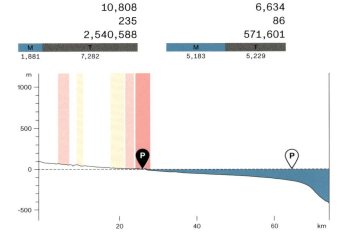

242   Port City Atlas   Mediterranean Sea

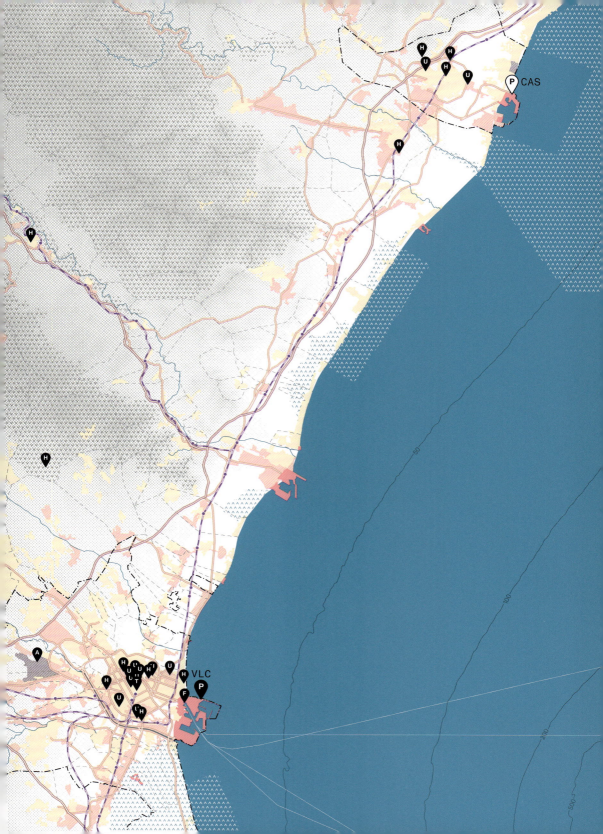

TAR # Tarragona, ES  Balearic Sea

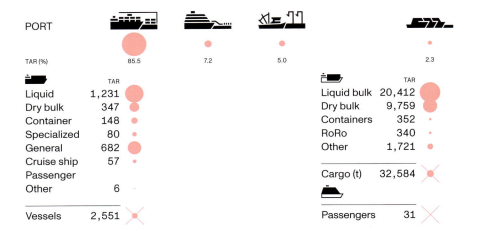

PORT							
TAR (%)		85.5	7.2	5.0			2.3

	TAR				TAR	
Liquid	1,231			Liquid bulk	20,412	
Dry bulk	347			Dry bulk	9,759	
Container	148			Containers	352	
Specialized	80			RoRo	340	
General	682			Other	1,721	
Cruise ship	57					
Passenger				Cargo (t)	32,584	
Other	6					
Vessels	2,551			Passengers	31	

CITY			TAR
→ Capital national (km)	Tarragona		
→ Capital regional (km)	→ Madrid		424
Area (km²)	→ Barcelona		82
Built-up area (km²)			55
Density (per km²)			32
Population			2,444
Population structure (%)			134,515
	15		65
	15.9	65.9	18.1
Distribution built area (%)	B	I	P
	47	34	19

TERRITORY		TAR
	Tarragona	
Area (km²)		6,302
Density (per km²)		127
Population		802,547
Natura2000 (km²)	M	T
	6,146	3,148

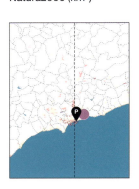

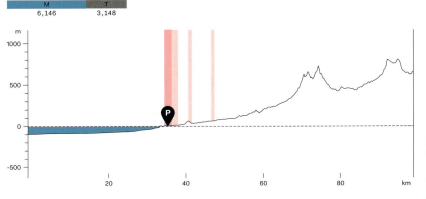

244   Port City Atlas   Mediterranean Sea

BCN # Barcelona, ES

PORT

BCN (%) 13.7 64.1 22.2

	PER			BCN
Liquid	1,042		Liquid bulk	16,134
Dry bulk	98		Dry bulk	4,072
Container	2,313		Containers	27,340
Specialized	435		RoRo	6,340
General	4,213		Other	827
Cruise ship	800			
Passenger			Cargo (t)	54,713
Other				
Vessels	8,901		Passengers	3,239

CITY

		BCN
	Barcelona	
→ Capital national (km)	→ Madrid	507
→ Capital regional (km)		
Area (km²)		599
Built-up area (km²)		307
Density (per km²)		6,182
Population		3,701,270

Population structure (%) 15 65
14.7 65.7 19.5

Distribution built area (%) B 65 A 3 I 30 P 2

TERRITORY

		BCN
	Barcelona	
Area (km²)		7,730
Density (per km²)		721
Population		5,575,204

Natura2000 (km²) M 1,316 T 2,067

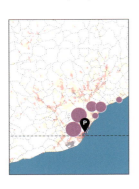

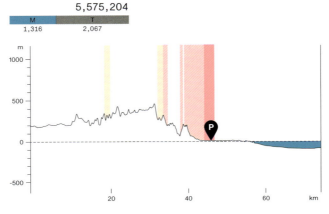

246 Port City Atlas Mediterranean Sea

MRS # Marseille, FR   Gulf of Lion

PORT

MRS (%)   14.9   85.1

	MRS			MRS
Liquid	1,867		Liquid bulk	45,563
Dry bulk	346		Dry bulk	12,595
Container	1,382		Containers	10,861
Specialized	184		RoRo	2,489
General	2,915		Other	2,541
Cruise ship	497			
Passenger			Cargo (t)	74,049
Other	21			
			Passengers	1,705
Vessels	7,212			

CITY

City of Marseille   MRS

→ Capital national (km)   → Paris   661
→ Capital regional (km)
Area (km²)   297
Built-up area (km²)   147
Density (per km²)   3,011
Population   895,431
Population structure (%)   18.3   62.6   19.1   (15 / 65)
Distribution built area (%)   B 88   I 10 P 2

TERRITORY

Bouches-du-Rhône   MRS

Area (km²)   5,248
Density (per km²)   389
Population   2,039,608
Natura2000 (km²)   M 5,377   T 2,517

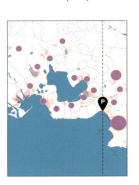
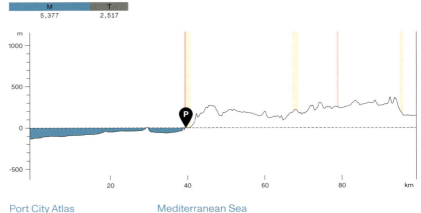

248   Port City Atlas   Mediterranean Sea

TLN   # Toulon, FR    Gulf of Lion

PORT

TLN (%)

	TLN
	70.6
	0.4
	29,0

	TLN			TLN
Liquid			Liquid bulk	112
Dry bulk			Dry bulk	768
Container			Containers	2
Specialized			RoRo	860
General			Other	0
Cruise ship			Cargo (t)	1,742
Passenger				
Other			Passengers	1,749
Vessels	1,675			

CITY

City of Toulon — TLN

	TLN
→ Capital national (km) → Paris	695
→ Capital regional (km) → Marseille	48
Area (km²)	145
Built-up area (km²)	117
Density (per km²)	2,298
Population	334,333

Population structure (%) 15.7 | 59.4 | 24.9
                            15   65

Distribution built area (%) B 79 | I 13 | P 8

TERRITORY

Var — TLN

	TLN
Area (km²)	6,034
Density (per km²)	178
Population	1,076,711

Natura2000 (km²) M 3,052 | T 1,421

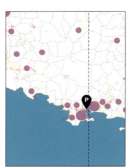

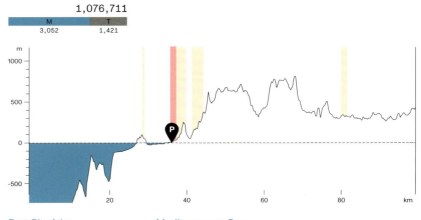

250 — Port City Atlas — Mediterranean Sea

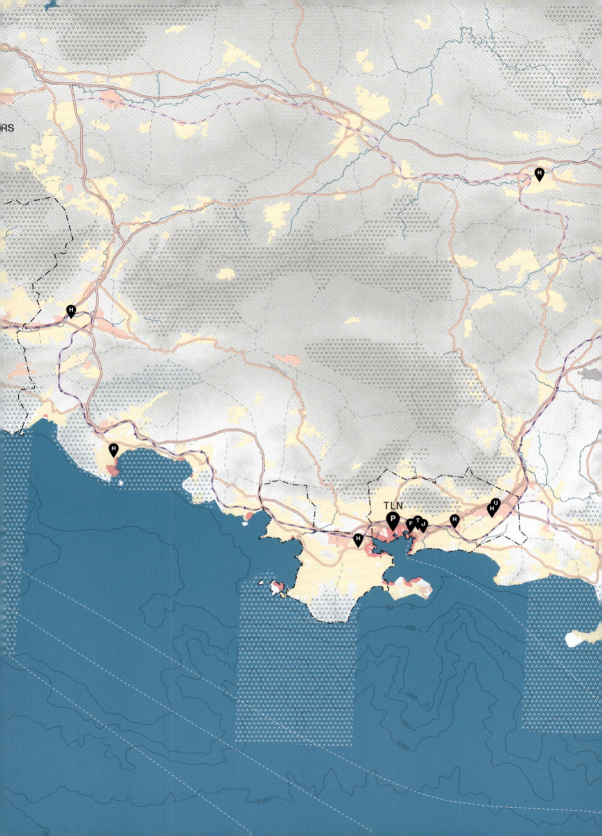

GOA
SVN

Genova, IT
Savona, IT

 Gulf of Genoa
 Gulf of Genoa

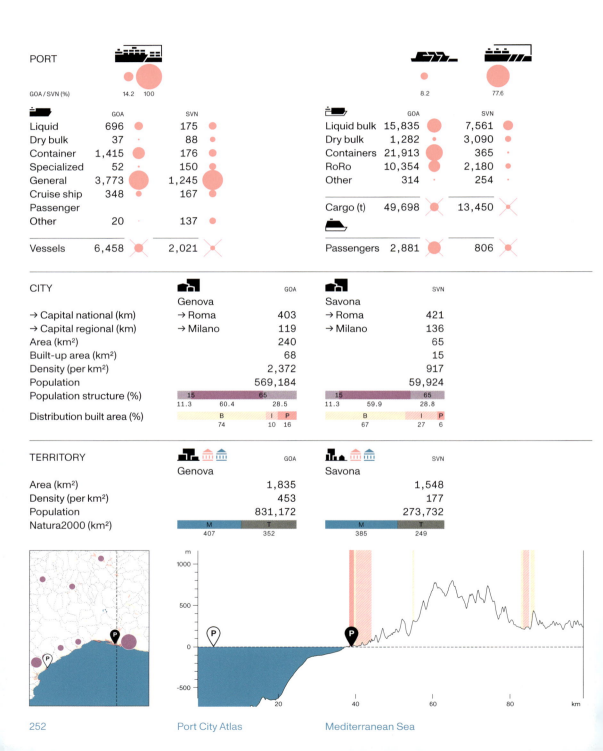

PORT

GOA / SVN (%) 14.2 100   8.2   77.6

	GOA	SVN		GOA	SVN
Liquid	696	175	Liquid bulk	15,835	7,561
Dry bulk	37	88	Dry bulk	1,282	3,090
Container	1,415	176	Containers	21,913	365
Specialized	52	150	RoRo	10,354	2,180
General	3,773	1,245	Other	314	254
Cruise ship	348	167			
Passenger			Cargo (t)	49,698	13,450
Other	20	137			
Vessels	6,458	2,021	Passengers	2,881	806

CITY

	Genova	GOA	Savona	SVN
→ Capital national (km)	→ Roma	403	→ Roma	421
→ Capital regional (km)	→ Milano	119	→ Milano	136
Area (km²)		240		65
Built-up area (km²)		68		15
Density (per km²)		2,372		917
Population		569,184		59,924
Population structure (%)	11.3 60.4 28.5		11.3 59.9 28.8	
Distribution built area (%)	B 74 I 10 P 16		B 67 I 27 P 6	

TERRITORY

	Genova	GOA	Savona	SVN
Area (km²)		1,835		1,548
Density (per km²)		453		177
Population		831,172		273,732
Natura2000 (km²)	M 407 T 352		M 385 T 249	

252   Port City Atlas   Mediterranean Sea

SPE · La Spezia, IT · Ligurian Sea

PORT

SPE (%) 32.6   7.7   41.9   17.8

	SPE			SPE	
Liquid	81		Liquid bulk	2,244	
Dry bulk	12		Dry bulk	421	
Container	941		Containers	16,116	
Specialized			RoRo		
General	78		Other	24	
Cruise ship	210				
Passenger			Cargo (t)	18,805	✕
Other	40				
Vessels	1,362	✕	Passengers		

CITY

La Spezia   SPE

→ Capital national (km)	→ Roma	326
→ Capital regional (km)	→ Milano	159
Area (km²)		51
Built-up area (km²)		17
Density (per km²)		1,803
Population		92,737
Population structure (%)	15 / 65	
	11.7 61.5 26.7	
Distribution built area (%)	B 67 I 11 P 22	

TERRITORY

La Spezia   SPE

Area (km²)	882
Density (per km²)	247
Population	218,094
Natura2000 (km²)	M 143 T 106

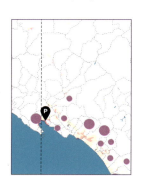

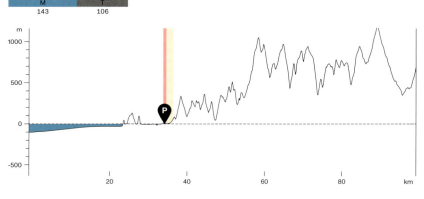

254 · Port City Atlas · Mediterranean Sea

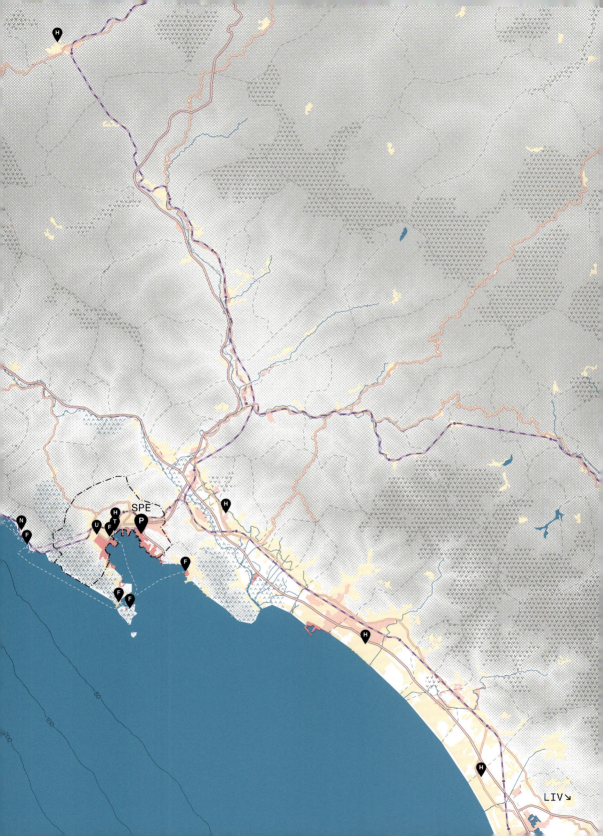

LIV # Livorno, IT Ligurian Sea

PORT

LIV (%) 0.5   3.5   95.9

	LIV			LIV	
Liquid	564		Liquid bulk	5,547	
Dry bulk	31		Dry bulk	722	
Container	622		Containers	16,545	
Specialized	500		RoRo	13,427	
General	6,590		Other	21	
Cruise ship	328				
Passenger			Cargo (t)	36,262	
Other	24				
Vessels	8,659		Passengers	2,941	

CITY

Livorno LIV

→ Capital national (km)
→ Capital regional (km)   → Roma   255
Area (km²)   → Milano 229
Built-up area (km²)   104
Density (per km²)   31
Population   1,514
Population structure (%)   157,457
  15   65
  12.2 61.6   26.1

Distribution built area (%)
  B   I   P
  61   23   16

TERRITORY

Livorno LIV

Area (km²)   1,215
Density (per km²)   274
Population   332,887
Natura2000 (km²)
  M
  1,246   52

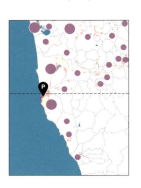
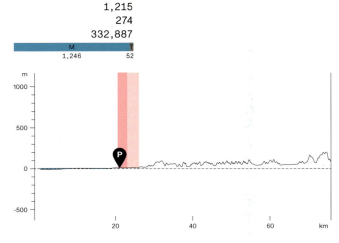

256 Port City Atlas Mediterranean Sea

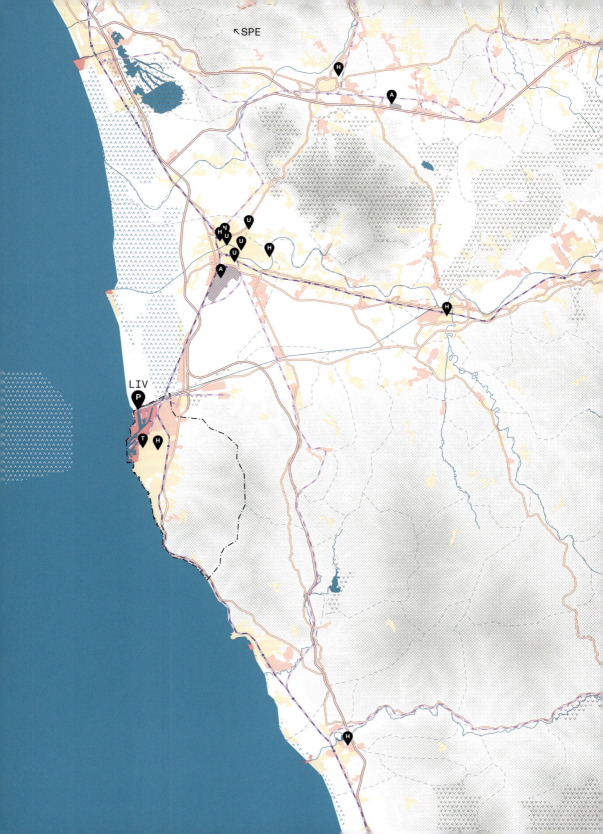

CVV # Civitavecchia (Roma), IT  Tyrrhenian Sea

PORT

CVV (%)   46.9   3.4   4.4   45.3

	CVV			CVV
Liquid	40		Liquid bulk	785
Dry bulk	70		Dry bulk	2,202
Container	227		Containers	1,383
Specialized	178		RoRo	5,152
General	2,984		Other	
Cruise ship	893			
Passenger			Cargo (t)	9,527
Other	4			
Vessels	4,396		Passengers	2,886

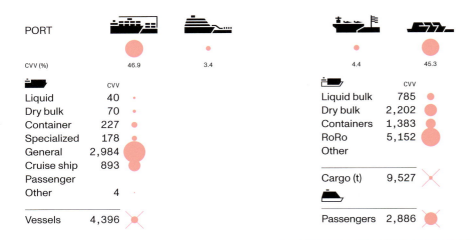

CITY

Civitavecchia   CVV

→ Capital national (km)   → Roma   81
→ Capital regional (km)
Area (km²)   73
Built-up area (km²)   14
Density (per km²)   721
Population   52,716
Population structure (%)   13.8 / 65.2 / 21.0
Distribution built area (%)   B 48 / I 44 / P 8

TERRITORY

Roma   CVV

Area (km²)   5,359
Density (per km²)   796
Population   4,263,542
Natura2000 (km²)   M 1,263 / T 945

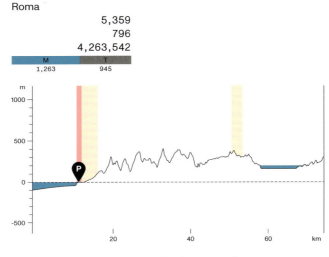

258   Port City Atlas   Mediterranean Sea

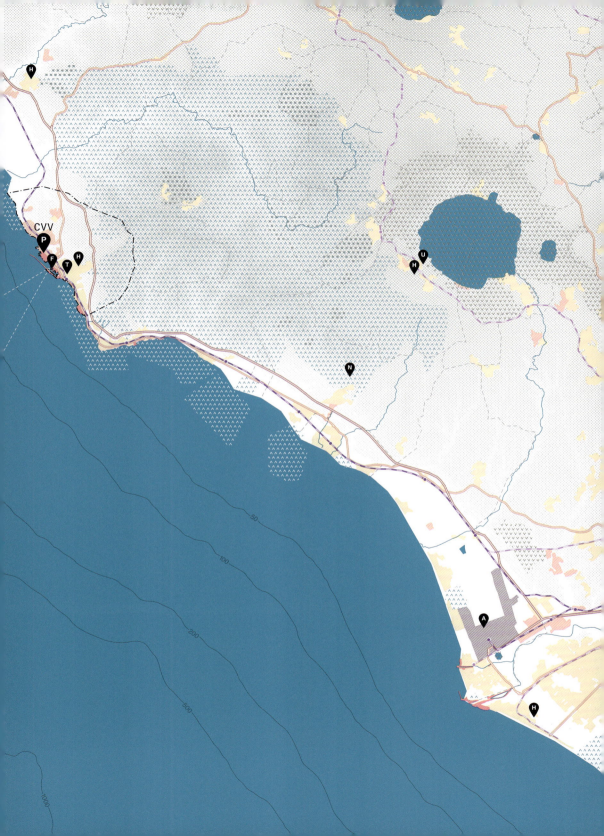

NAP # Napoli, IT Gulf of Naples

PORT

NAP (%)						
	28.6	52.1			8.2	11.1

	NAP			NAP
Liquid	784		Liquid bulk	6,323
Dry bulk	52		Dry bulk	1,246
Container	486		Containers	3,486
Specialized			RoRo	4,161
General	41,536		Other	215
Cruise ship	454			
Passenger	3,133		Cargo (t)	15,431
Other	377			
Vessels	46,822		Passengers	9,257

CITY

		NAP
	Napoli	
→ Capital national (km)	→ Roma	254
→ Capital regional (km)		
Area (km²)		849
Built-up area (km²)		359
Density (per km²)		1,124
Population		954,318
Population structure (%)	15	65
	15.5 67.1	17.4
Distribution built area (%)	B	A I P
	83	1 15 1

TERRITORY

		NAP
	Napoli	
Area (km²)		1,175
Density (per km²)		2,594
Population		3,048,194
Natura2000 (km²)	M	T
	370	400

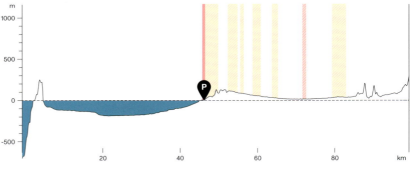

260 Port City Atlas Mediterranean Sea

PFX
CAG

Porto Foxi, IT
Cagliari, IT

 Mediterranean Sea
 Mediterranean Sea

PORT

PFX / CAG (%)   1.9   2.6   21.5   89.6   4.4   78.5   1.5

	PFX	CAG			PFX	CAG
Liquid	1,072	216		Liquid bulk	26,721	1,057
Dry bulk		47		Dry bulk		2,842
Container		114		Containers	57	1,485
Specialized				RoRo		5,129
General		1,793		Other		2,167
Cruise ship		109				
Passenger				Cargo (t)	28,818	12,680
Other	16	22				
Vessels	1,088	2,301		Passengers		389

CITY

	Sarroch	PFX	Cagliari	CAG
→ Capital national (km)	→ Roma	564	→ Roma	544
→ Capital regional (km)	→ Palermo	503	→ Palermo	500
Area (km²)		68		84
Built-up area (km²)		8		44
Density (per km²)		77		1,808
Population		5,266		151,504
Population structure (%)	12.3 61.1 26.5		9.7 63.2 27.0	
Distribution built area (%)	B 45 I 55		B 57 A 1 I 23 P 12	

TERRITORY

	Cagliari	PFX	Cagliari	CAG
Area (km²)		1,249		1,249
Density (per km²)		336		336
Population		419,770		419,770
Natura2000 (km²)	M 378 T 836		M 378 T 836	

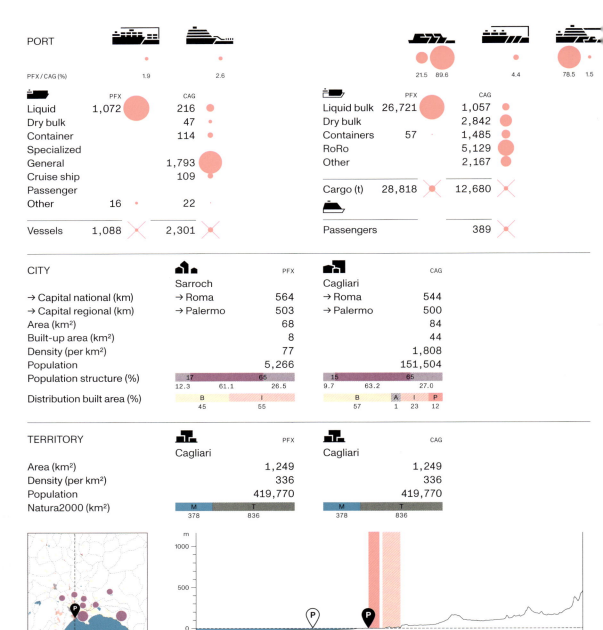

262   Port City Atlas   Mediterranean Sea

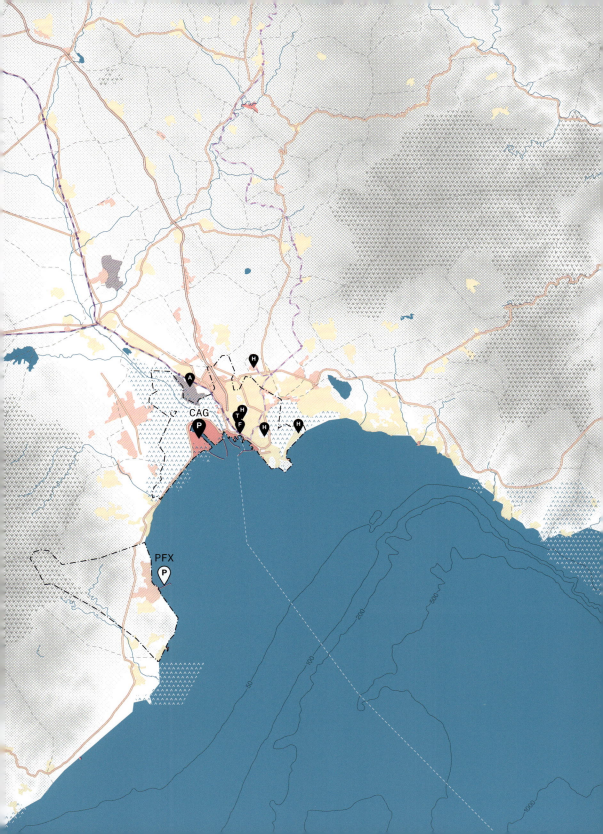

PMO # Palermo, IT

PORT

PMO (%) 29.0 45.9 15.4 9.6

	PMO			PMO	
Liquid	373		Liquid bulk	1,798	
Dry bulk	5		Dry bulk	888	
Container	59		Containers	319	
Specialized			RoRo	6,646	
General	3,289		Other	396	
Cruise ship	230				
Passenger	913		Cargo (t)	10,047	
Other	48				
Vessels	4,917		Passengers	2,017	

CITY

			PMO
	Palermo		
→ Capital national (km)	→ Roma	553	
→ Capital regional (km)	→ Napoli	400	
Area (km²)		160	
Built-up area (km²)		122	
Density (per km²)		4,077	
Population		652,720	
Population structure (%)	14.2	65.4	20.3
Distribution built area (%)	B 96	A I P 1 2 1	

TERRITORY

	Palermo	PMO
Area (km²)		4,996
Density (per km²)		247
Population		1,231,602
Natura2000 (km²)	M 2,243	T 1,588

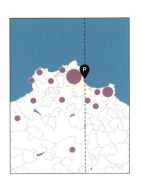
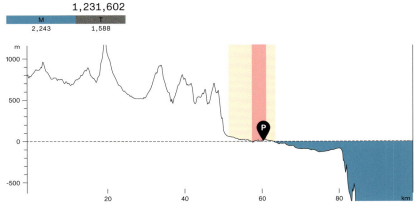

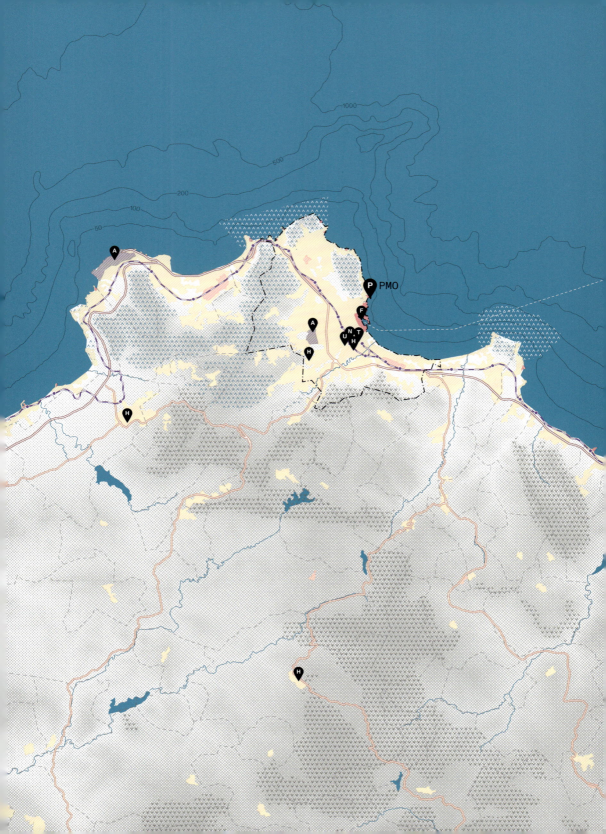

SIR # Siracusa, IT Ionian Sea

PORT

SIR (%)
100

	SIR			SIR
Liquid	336		Liquid bulk	12,132
Dry bulk			Dry bulk	
Container			Containers	
Specialized			RoRo	
General			Other	
Cruise ship			Cargo (t)	12,132
Passenger				
Other	112		Passengers	
Vessels	448			

CITY

		SIR
	Siracusa	
→ Capital national (km)	→ Roma	764
→ Capital regional (km)	→ Palermo	262
Area (km²)		206
Built-up area (km²)		35
Density (per km²)		580
Population		119,710
Population structure (%)	15 / 65
	13.6 64.6 21.7
Distribution built area (%)	B I P
	69 29 2

TERRITORY

	SIR
	Siracusa
Area (km²)	2,110
Density (per km²)	185
Population	391,400
Natura2000 (km²)	M T
	1,092 225

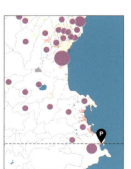
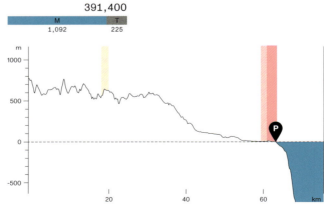

266 Port City Atlas Mediterranean Sea

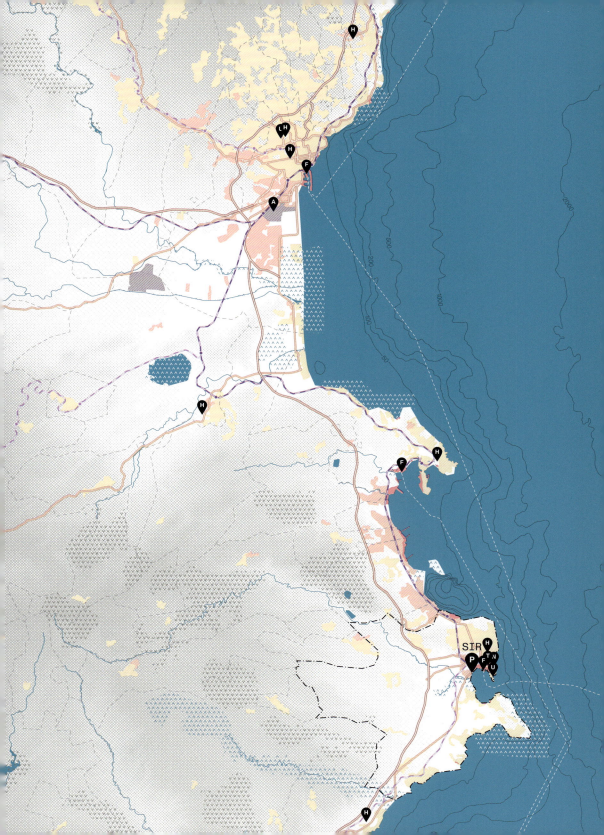

MSN
MLZ

Messina, IT
Milazzo, IT

 Tyrrhenian Sea
 Tyrrhenian Sea

PORT

MSN / MLZ (%) 98.9   100   1.1

	MSN	MLZ			MSN	MLZ
Liquid	9	673	Liquid bulk			15,452
Dry bulk		7	Dry bulk			17
Container			Containers			
Specialized			RoRo		7,293	
General	53,379	2,661	Other			
Cruise ship	140					
Passenger	448	3,223	Cargo (t)		7,293	15,469
Other		4				
Vessels	53,561	6,568	Passengers		11,669	471

CITY

	Messina	MSN	Milazzo	MLZ
→ Capital national (km)	→ Roma	641	→ Roma	617
→ Capital regional (km)	→ Palermo	244	→ Palermo	209
Area (km²)		211		25
Built-up area (km²)		42		13
Density (per km²)		1,084		1,259
Population		229,280		31,028
Population structure (%)	15	65	17	65
	12.8 64.7 22.5		12.8 66.5 20.7	
Distribution built area (%)	B	I P	B	I P
	94 3 3		66 33 1	

TERRITORY

	Messina	MSN	Messina	MLZ
Area (km²)		3,247		3,247
Density (per km²)		191		191
Population		618,713		618,713
Natura2000 (km²)	M	T	M	T
	2,473	874	2,473	874

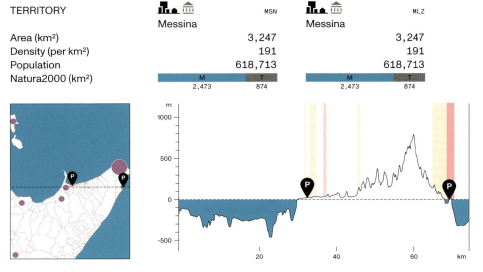

268 Port City Atlas Mediterranean Sea

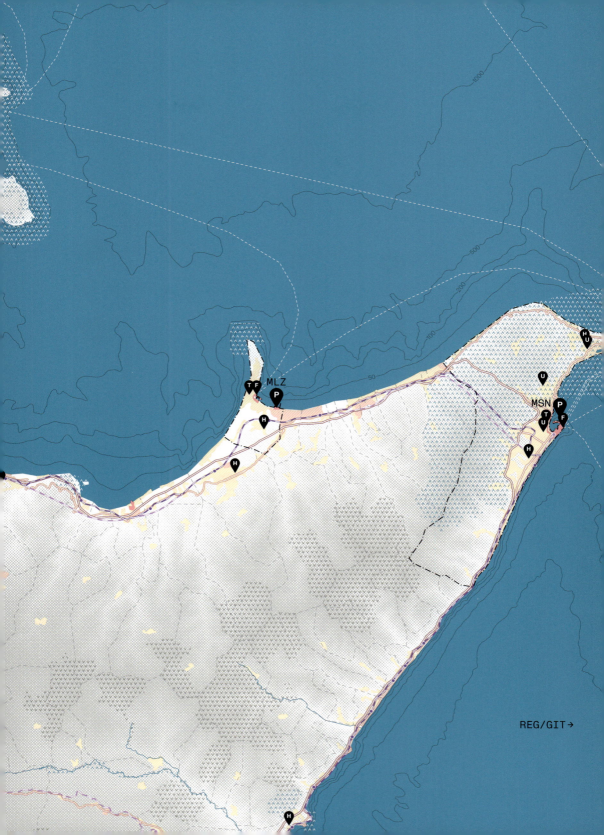

GIT **Gioia Tauro, IT**
REG **Reggio di Calabria, IT**

 Tyrrhenian Sea
 Strait of Messina

PORT

GIT/REG (%) 97.7   2.3   100

	GIT	REG
Liquid	655	
Dry bulk	11	7
Container	1,363	
Specialized	97	
General	144	56,923
Cruise ship		11
Passenger		512
Other	8	
Vessels	2,278	56,934

	GIT	REG
Liquid bulk	1,884	
Dry bulk	2,603	35
Containers	17,677	
RoRo	46	4,483
Other	484	
Cargo (t)	22,694	4,528
Passengers		10,884

CITY

	Gioia Tauro — GIT	Reggio di Calabria — REG
→ Capital national (km)	→ Roma 630	→ Roma 651
→ Capital regional (km)	→ Palermo 286	→ Palermo 254
Area (km²)	38	237
Built-up area (km²)	16	40
Density (per km²)	531	744
Population	20,078	176,299
Population structure (%)	19.7 / 62.3 / 18.0	13.5 / 65.0 / 21.5
Distribution built area (%)	B 33 / I 42 / P 25	B 85 / A 5 / I 8 / P 2

TERRITORY

	Reggio di Calabria — GIT	Reggio di Calabria — REG
Area (km²)	3,180	3,180
Density (per km²)	169	169
Population	536,487	536,487
Natura2000 (km²)	M 847 / T 181	M 847 / T 181

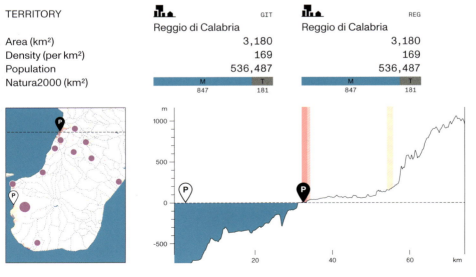

270   Port City Atlas   Mediterranean Sea

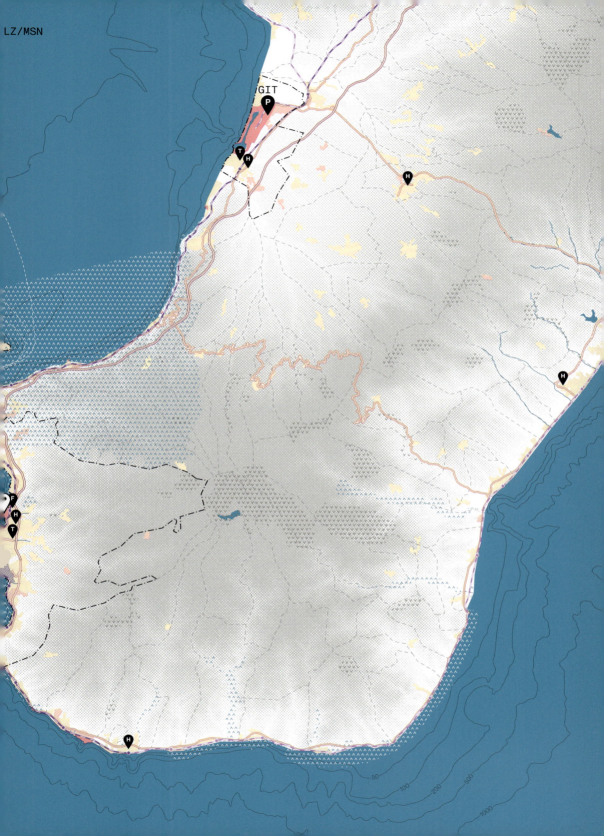

TAR

Taranto, IT

Gulf of Taranto

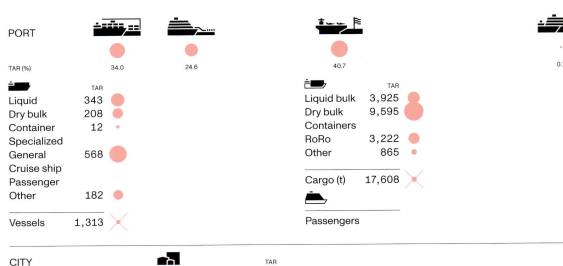

PORT						
TAR (%)	34.0	24.6		40.7		0.7

	TAR			TAR
Liquid	343		Liquid bulk	3,925
Dry bulk	208		Dry bulk	9,595
Container	12		Containers	
Specialized			RoRo	3,222
General	568		Other	865
Cruise ship				
Passenger			Cargo (t)	17,608
Other	182			
Vessels	1,313		Passengers	

CITY		TAR
	Taranto	
→ Capital national (km)	→ Roma	564
→ Capital regional (km)	→ Napoli	327
Area (km²)		247
Built-up area (km²)		83
Density (per km²)		781
Population		192,775
Population structure (%)	15 / 65	
	13.0 63.4 23.5	
Distribution built area (%)	B / I / P	
	36 52 12	

TERRITORY		TAR
	Taranto	
Area (km²)		2,442
Density (per km²)		233
Population		568,258
Natura2000 (km²)	M 804 / T 1,755	

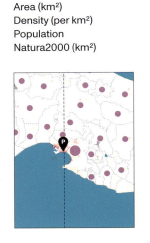

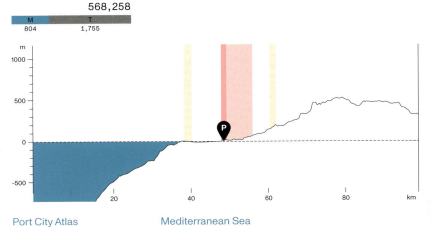

272 Port City Atlas Mediterranean Sea

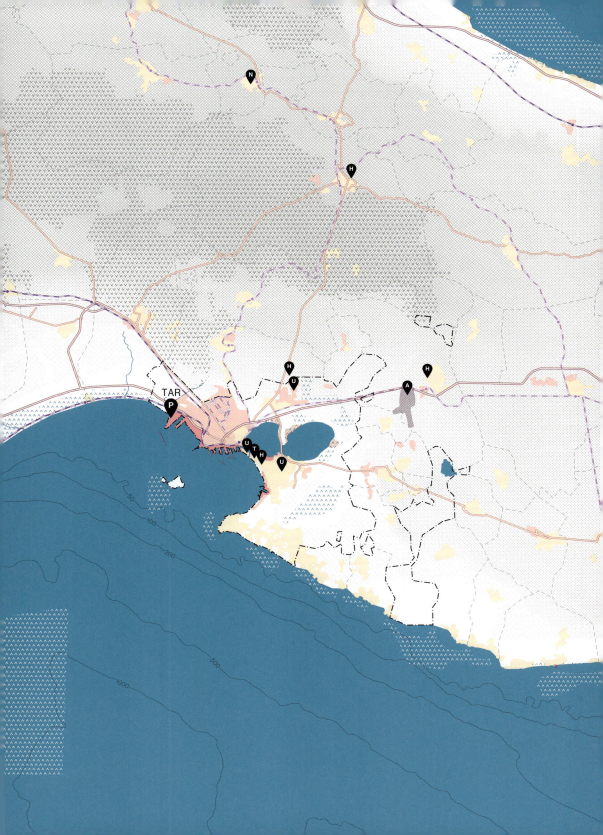

RAN

Ravenna, IT

🚢 Adriatic Sea

PORT

RAN (%)

	RAN	
Liquid	807	
Dry bulk	607	
Container	565	
Specialized	44	
General	1,325	
Cruise ship	15	
Passenger		
Other	719	
Vessels	4,082	

	RAN	
Liquid bulk	7,970	
Dry bulk	15,793	
Containers	2,742	
RoRo	2,740	
Other	2,106	
Cargo (t)	31,351	
Passengers		

100

CITY

	Ravenna	RAN
→ Capital national (km)	→ Roma	594
→ Capital regional (km)	→ Milano	376
Area (km²)		653
Built-up area (km²)		58
Density (per km²)		243
Population		158,923
Population structure (%)	15 / 65 — 12.5 / 63.0 / 24.6	
Distribution built area (%)	B 66 / I 31 / P 3	

TERRITORY

	Ravenna	RAN
Area (km²)		1,859
Density (per km²)		209
Population		388,913
Natura2000 (km²)	M 500 / T 167	

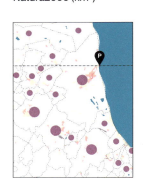

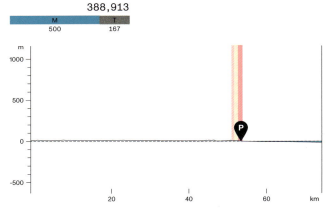

274   Port City Atlas   Mediterranean Sea

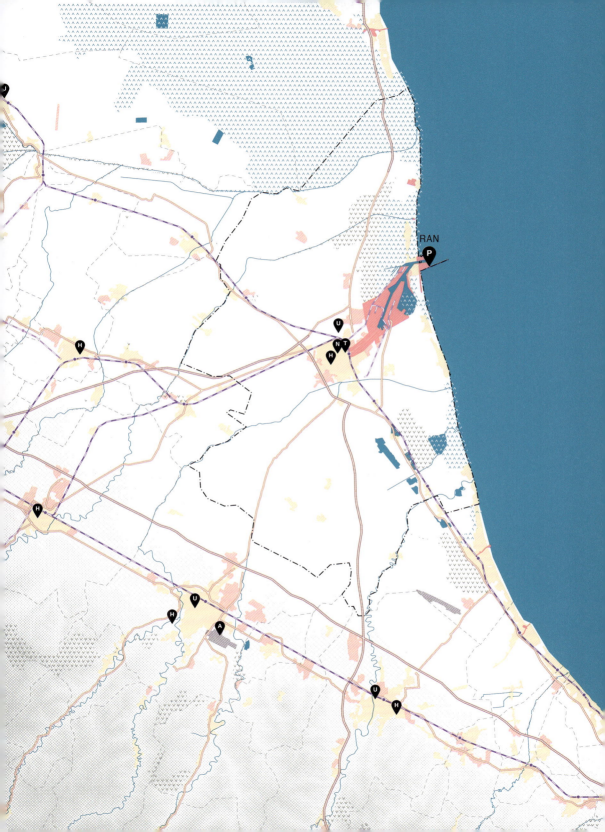

VCE # Venezia, IT Gulf of Venice

PORT

VCE (%) 76.4 1.4 2.3 2.0

	VCE			VCE
Liquid	639		Liquid bulk	8,447
Dry bulk	353		Dry bulk	10,461
Container	945		Containers	5,924
Specialized	30		RoRo	2,186
General	1,322		Other	917
Cruise ship	350			
Passenger			Cargo (t)	27,935
Other	264			
			Passengers	854
Vessels	3,903			

CITY

Venezia VCE

→ Capital national (km) → Roma 546
→ Capital regional (km) → Milano 347
Area (km²) 159
Built-up area (km²) 90
Density (per km²) 1,634
Population 259,961
Population structure (%) 15 / 65
 11.5 60.8 27.7
Distribution built area (%) B A I P
 65 2 18 15

TERRITORY

Venezia VCE

Area (km²) 2,003
Density (per km²) 425
Population 851,057
Natura2000 (km²) M
 1,908 49

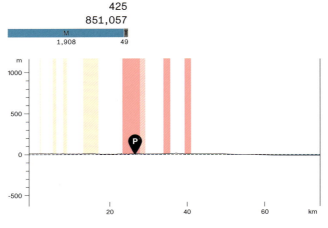

276   Port City Atlas   Mediterranean Sea

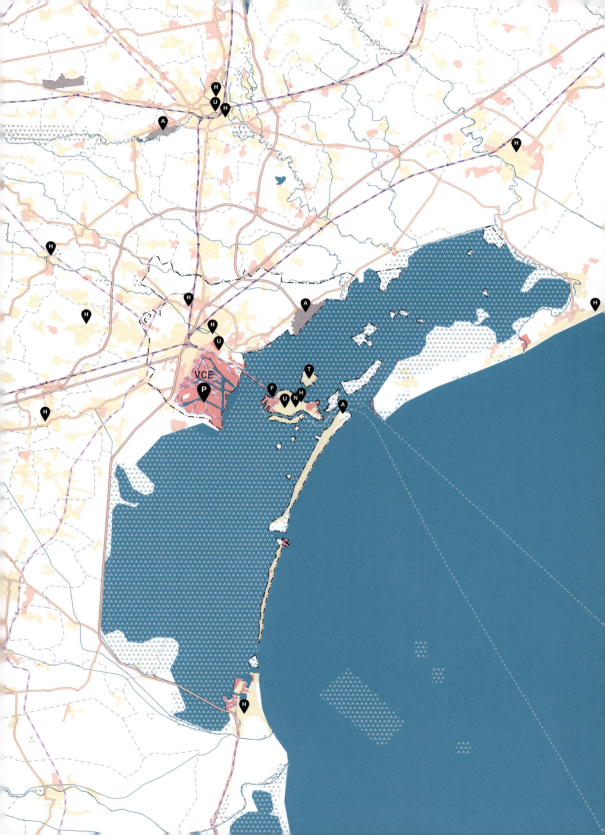

TRS
KOP
MNF

Trieste, IT
Koper, SI
Monfalcone, IT

Gulf of Trieste
Koper Bay
Gulf of Trieste

PORT

TRS / KOP / MNF (%)   83.7   92.7   0.5   14.7   7.3   5.0   1.2   95.0

	TRS	KOP	MNF		TRS	KOP	MNF
Liquid	480	170		Liquid bulk	39,883	4,288	
Dry bulk	54	125	108	Dry bulk	4,300	6,368	3,725
Container	654	621	10	Containers	7,886	8,970	1
Specialized		36	70	RoRo	3,109	1,130	589
General	1,119	554	362	Other	5,154	1,359	170
Cruise ship	55	72					
Passenger				Cargo (t)	60,332	22,125	4,485
Other	168	71	152				
Vessels	2,530	1,649	702	Passengers		0	

CITY

	TRS	KOP	MNF
	Trieste	Koper/Capodistria	Monfalcone
→ Capital national (km)	→ Roma 596	→ Ljubljana 117	→ Roma 612
→ Capital regional (km)	→ Venezia 165		→ Venezia 148
Area (km²)	85	303	20
Built-up area (km²)	37	12	19
Density (per km²)	2,386	172	1,389
Population	202,351	52,234	28,453
Population structure (%)	11.2 60.7 28.3 (15/65)	13.4 63.6 22.9 (17/65)	16.3 60.5 23.1 (17/65)
Distribution built area (%)	B 75 I 2 P 23	B 46 I 40 P 14	B 48 I 20 P 32

TERRITORY

	TRS	KOP	MNF
	Trieste	Obalno-kraška	Gorizia
Area (km²)	5,248	212	1,043
Density (per km²)	389	1,096	110
Population	2,039,608	232,405	115,016
Natura2000 (km²)	M 439 T 1,068	M 4,698 T 1,600	M 513 T 1,208

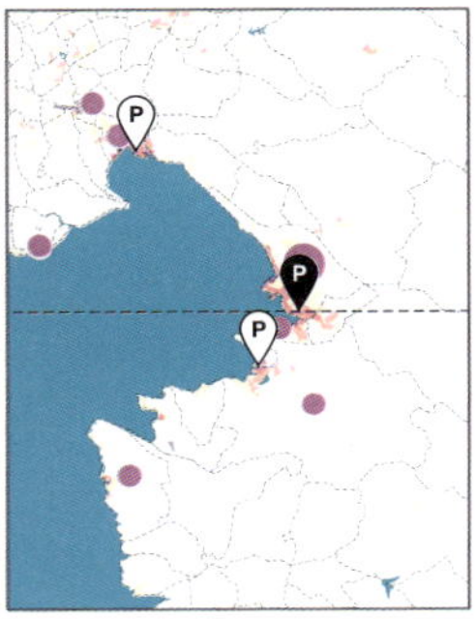

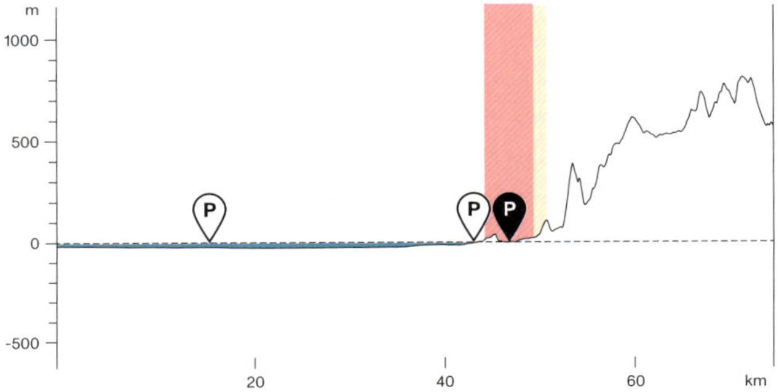

278   Port City Atlas   Mediterranean Sea

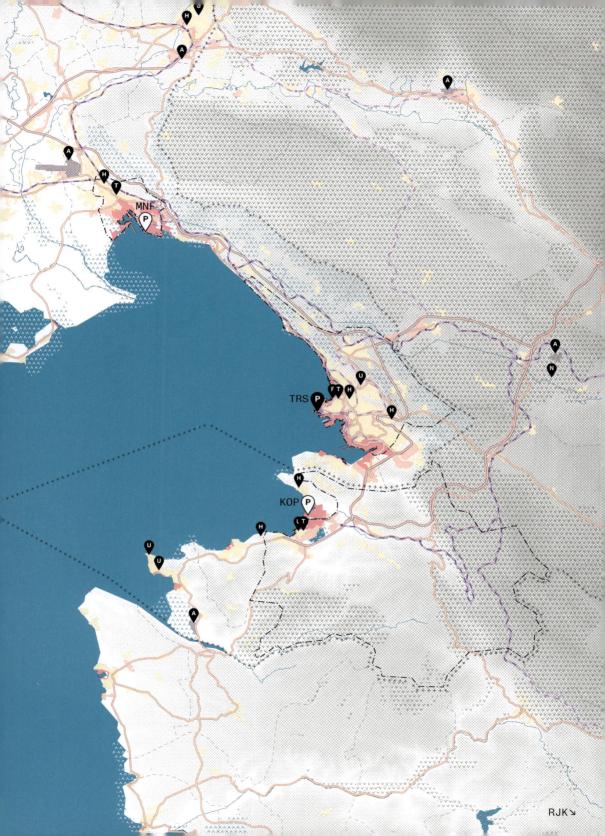

RJK # Rijeka, HR  Rijeka Bay

PORT

RJK (%)   15.4   5.0   79.6

	RJK			RJK
Liquid	26		Liquid bulk	
Dry bulk	23		Dry bulk	198
Container	311		Containers	2,741
Specialized			RoRo	4
General	138		Other	413
Cruise ship	11			
Passenger	1,144		Cargo (t)	3,356
Other	19			
Vessels	1,672		Passengers	114

CITY

Rijeka RJK
→ Capital national (km)
→ Capital regional (km)   → Zagreb   187
Area (km²)   43
Built-up area (km²)   11
Density (per km²)   2,697
Population   116,872
Population structure (%)   15 65
                          11.6 68.6 19.7
Distribution built area (%)   B   I   P
                              74 8 18

TERRITORY

Primorsko-goranska županija   RJK
Area (km²)   3,581
Density (per km²)   79
Population   283,405
Natura2000 (km²)   M   T
                          9,499 1,842

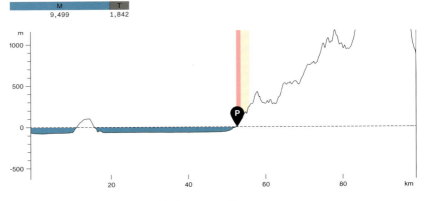

280 Port City Atlas Mediterranean Sea

SPU | # Split, HR |

PORT

SPU (%)

                     SPU
Liquid   139
Dry bulk   222
Container   48
Specialized
General   7,692
Cruise ship   274
Passenger   14,727
Other   43

Vessels   23,145

18.6

	SPU
Liquid bulk	546
Dry bulk	1,122
Containers	93
RoRo	111
Other	68
Cargo (t)	1,940
Passengers	4,958

17.8

63.6

CITY

→ Capital national (km)
→ Capital regional (km)
Area (km²)
Built-up area (km²)
Density (per km²)
Population
Population structure (%)

Distribution built area (%)

Split   SPU
→ Zagreb   364
                     79
                     41
                  2,141
                169,489
        15   65
     14.9 68.2 17.0

        B   I P
        90   7 3

TERRITORY

Area (km²)
Density (per km²)
Population
Natura2000 (km²)

Splitsko-dalmatinska
županija   SPU
                   4,531
                      99
                 447,723
        M   T
      5,230   1,365

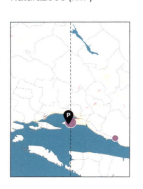

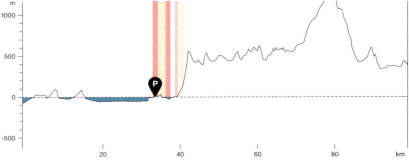

282 | Port City Atlas | Mediterranean Sea

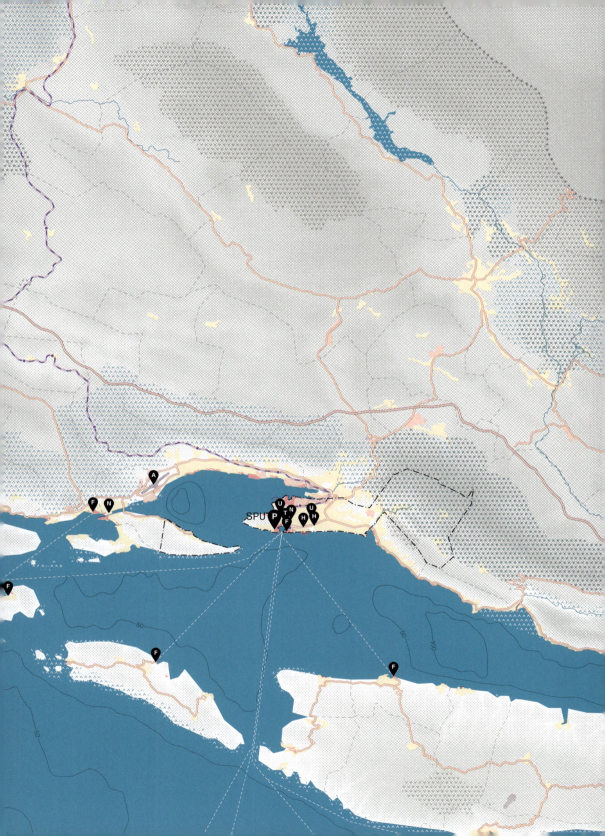

PIR	**Peiraias (Athens), GR**	Aegean Sea
PER	**Perama, GR**	Aegean Sea
EEU	**Elefsina, GR**	Aegean Sea

PORT

PIR / PER / EEU (%) 10.2 98.2 88.6   15.6   15.8 7.9   53.3   5.0 3.4   1.8

	PIR	PER	EEU			PIR	PER	EEU
Liquid	615	1,083	1,437		Liquid bulk	1,314	2,386	12,852
Dry bulk	117		123		Dry bulk	353		2,733
Container	3,481				Containers	49,866		
Specialized	966		194		RoRo	5,276	1,313	46
General	11,460	33,129	559		Other	16		583
Cruise ship	625							
Passenger	9,737				Cargo (t)	56,825	3,699	16,214
Other								
Vessels	27,001	34,214	2,317		Passengers	9,931	6,939	0

CITY

	Athens	PIR	Perama	PER	Elefsina	EEU
→ Capital national (km)	→ Athens	0	→ Athens	9	→ Athens	18
→ Capital regional (km)	→ Thessaloniki	392				
Area (km²)		613		16		20
Built-up area (km²)		402		8		15
Density (per km²)		4,280		1,594		1,253
Population		2,622,404		25,389		24,910
Population structure (%)		13.1 69.0 17.9 (15 / 65)				
Distribution built area (%)		B 81 / A 1 / I 13 / P 5		B 40 / I 5 / P 55		B 27 / A 33 / I 40

TERRITORY

	Peiraias, Niso	PIR	Peiraias, Niso	PER	Dytiki Attiki	EEU
Area (km²)		933.65		933.65		1,005.38
Density (per km²)		530		530		180
Population		494,908		494,908		180,485
Natura2000 (km²)		0		0		M 2,189 / T 219

284 Port City Atlas Mediterranean Sea

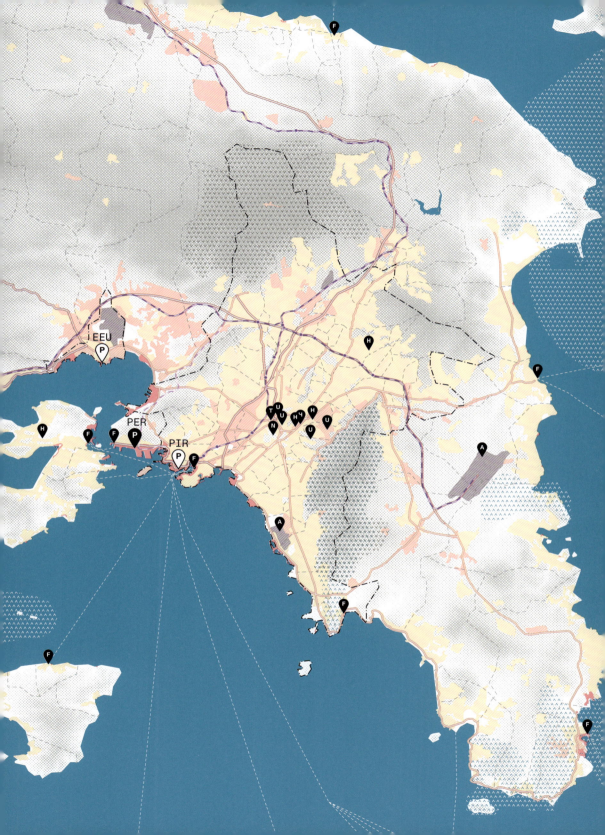

SKG   # Thessaloniki, GR    Thermaic Gulf

PORT

SKG (%) 100

	SKG
Liquid	405
Dry bulk	298
Container	337
Specialized	
General	534
Cruise ship	35
Passenger	
Other	

Vessels 1,585

	SKG
Liquid bulk	6,618
Dry bulk	3,913
Containers	3,876
RoRo	
Other	737

Cargo (t) 15,172

Passengers 2

CITY

Thessaloniki SKG

→ Capital national (km) → Athene	392
→ Capital regional (km)	
Area (km²)	113
Built-up area (km²)	97
Density (per km²)	6,697
Population	754,566
Population structure (%)	10.4 / 68.4 / 21.3 (15 / 65)
Distribution built area (%)	B 60 / I 39 / P 1

TERRITORY

Thessaloniki SKG

Area (km²)	3,685
Density (per km²)	300
Population	1,104,690
Natura2000 (km²)	M 2,496 / T 353

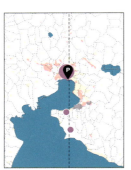

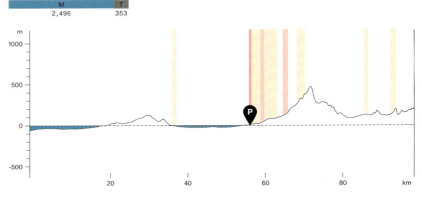

286   Port City Atlas   Mediterranean Sea

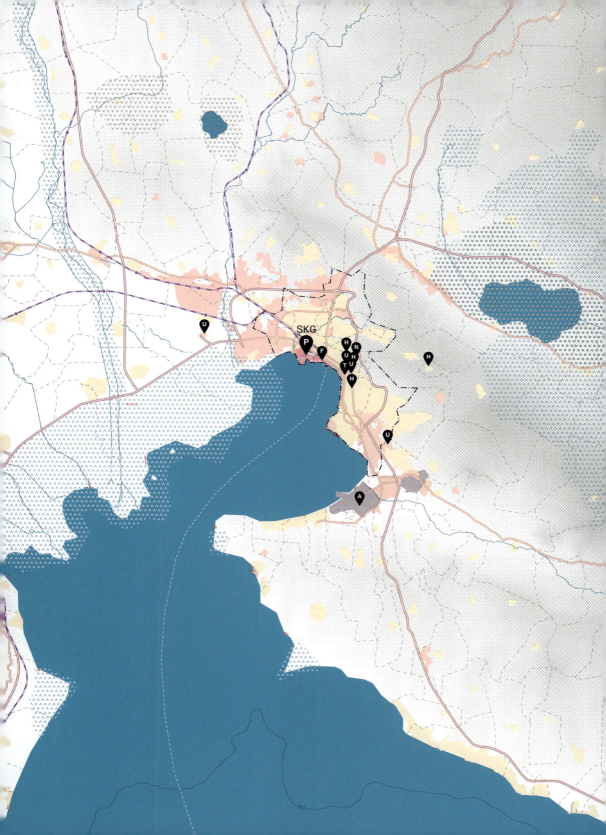

I Interpreting

Planning Challenges and Opportunities in Port City Territories: an Analysis through Infographics and Maps

Abstract

Analysing 100 port city territories through maps and infographics, we can see both planning challenges and planning opportunities. Port authorities are continuously adapting the capacity of their ports to manoeuvre ever larger ships, handle more cargo and improve their operations. As a result, they are constantly seeking to move into adjacent empty land and taking over areas of unused land and water in the port city and port city territory, while moving out of other areas and sometimes giving land back to cities. The maps and infographics provide a basis for the interpretation of future spatial development, illustrating the relationship between the different parts of the port city territory, different relationships between port functions and their impact on the port city territory. Our maps mark the outlines between parts of the territory to help planners and authorities plan connections between ports and the European transport network of motorways and railways. Finally, citizens and planners alike can draw on these maps for co-design, negotiation or citizen science regarding the planning of the port, port city and port territory.

Introduction

Planning has long helped ports adapt to multiple changes, regardless of who or what the drivers of these changes were, whether technological, geostrategic or environmental changes in the Port-CityScape or the changing role of governance and port authorities. On the sea, port authorities have added wharfs to accommodate more ships and moved to deeper waters to accommodate bigger ships; they have expanded their operational coastlines by constructing new structures, such as piers with higher platforms needed because of rising water levels caused by climate change. On land, port authorities have expanded into new territory: adding more rail lines for more and better access to the hinterland, and adding roads within the port territory to connect to national and international road networks.

The following sections explore current and upcoming transitions in port city territories that planners at all levels are facing. Where possible, these transitions are exemplified through our maps and infographics as shown on page 298. The maps can help identify past conditions, some future challenges, and opportunities for developments and strategic decisions. With cartographic features illustrating a territory's built-up area, the area occupied by the port and distribution of industry across the territory, the maps can help port city territory actors site new port areas without encroaching on protected areas or complicating the connection of ports to road and rail networks. Infographics and the data they contain offer an immediate territorial assessment tool planners can use to create scenarios for spatial variations in port city territories, and decision-makers (port authorities, states, city councils, citizens) can co-create new visions for port city territory change and support transformative port planning.

Maps and Infographics for Port Planning and Port City Territory Planning

The maps of the 100 leading port city territories provide information that planners can use at both the cartographic level and the analytical level. They show the relationship today between each port, port city and the rest of their port city territory (including areas on the coast) as a result of the history of port planning, urban planning and spatial planning over time. Though the spatial relations between the different parts of the port city territory vary widely among the 100 ports, we can discern some planning patterns in the maps. In some cases, the city is far from the sea and has no direct access to it at all (e.g., Ravenna, Valencia, Zeebrugge, Riga, Lübeck); usually such a city is connected to the sea by a river or marshes, so port infrastructure was planned and built inland rather than on the coast. Sometimes port development almost completely blocks access from the city to the water (e.g., Trieste, Rijeka, Esbjerg, Helsingborg, Klaipeda, Le Havre), while in other cases the contact between the urban area and the water is extended, and the city and the port share the land-water contact zone (e.g., Livorno). Planners in similar spatial predicaments can perhaps learn from each other.

The infographics offer additional information to planners on a port's predominant cargo, from dry bulk to liquid bulk to containers; on the size of a city, its built-up area and port area; as well as on the size of a territory and its degree of urbanization (e.g., according to Eurostat, a NUTS 3 territory can be urban, intermediate or rural). It is therefore possible to interpret the different relationships among port function and their impact on the port city territory, such as the handling of each type of cargo in relation to the size of the total area of the Local Administrative Unit (LAU) and use this information for planning. In Le Havre, for example, liquid bulk throughput as shown by the infographic is 36.132 tons in an area of 86 km²; in Milford Haven throughput is 34.051 tons in a much larger area of 1.623 km². This means that Milford Haven has 20 times less liquid bulk per square kilometre of total Local Administrative Unit area than Le Havre, which indicates that Le Havre is a *pollution-laden* problem location. Knowing these ratios, port and urban planners might limit industrial development in La Havre LAU, while in Milford Haven, LAU concerns about industrial pollution are not paramount and would not restrict expansion.

Planners may want to rely on the combined information from maps and infographics to limit the impact of port specialization and functions on the environment. They need to acknowledge the delineations between ports, city and territory, all of which are relevant to planning. In commercial ports, the boundaries of the port area are more clearly defined than in other kinds of ports, although those boundaries can also be permeable. Passenger ports are integrated into the city and are the domain of not only port planning, but also urban planning, as for example in Koper.[1] Cruise and ferry terminals, in particular, allow easy access to the city or its most interesting parts.

For future planning proposals, planners can look to the maps for the present configuration of port city territories. In Bristol, for example, the port is indistinguishably merged with other industrial areas; in Milford Haven, the port has expanded outside the old town into previously undeveloped land and has plenty of empty space for further expansion; while in Cairnryan, the port is located completely on its own, directly adjacent to protected areas. In Marseille, the port's further development is restricted by protected areas; in Ravenna, the port has encroached on the fabric of the city, ending the historical separation between the two areas. In Dublin, Clydeport, Liverpool, Helsingborg and Trieste, ports are completely enclosed and surrounded by the urban fabric. In each location there are thus different opportunities and challenges for the development of port city territory.

Land, Water and Air Access to the Port

Our maps show road and rail connections by land, access routes by water, and airports and heliports. They show one or more highway routes through each port city territory and one or more land road accesses to the port, such as in Zeebrugge, Hirtshals and Friederikshaven, Rotterdam, Bristol, Barcelona and Marseille; they also show where such accesses are missing, as in Helsinki, Szczecin, Haysham and others. Such information lets port planners strategically define the most favourable land and water entrances to the port, while planning in the larger port city area to enable access to the port.

L. Ažman Momirski, 'ban waterfronts in Koper: a mparison of spatial issues in initial and current plans for per's port', *Annales: anali za ske in mediteranske študije, ries historia et sociologia* '1 (2015), 19–32.

2   European Commission, 'Ports' (2022). Online. Available HTTPS: https://transport.ec.europa.eu/transport-modes/maritime/ports_en.

3   J.-P. Rodrigue, *The Geography of Transport Systems* (New York: Routledge, 2020).

All this is necessary, if not urgent, because traffic through the hinterland and the foreland to ports is increasing. There is little point in planning and making improvements to port facilities if land transport cannot handle the increased cargo flows. In one recent initiative to address the problem, the EU Commission connected selected seaports in the Trans-European Transport Network (TEN-T), a planned network of roads, railways, airports and waterways and also energy networks and telecommunications networks across EU territory. The TEN-T also provides grants to ports, maritime operators and hinterland transport operators to support infrastructure projects, mainly rail and inland waterways connecting ports with their hinterlands and basic port infrastructure.[2] Ports can also ask the EU Commission to update the TEN-T network, for example to extend the Baltic-Adriatic Corridor, which currently stops in Ravenna, to the entire Italian Adriatic-Ionian side of the Adriatic Sea. The maps do not only show the European infrastructural networks, but demonstrate that the main traffic bottlenecks in most ports are increasingly in the hinterland, not the coast. The maps help planners and authorities to suggest where the European transport network should run in the future.

Today, port authorities and state administration intend to integrate port and airport access,[3] which have been planned separately, and to locate airports close to ports in order to make supply chains more efficient and shorten freight transit times. Our maps identify airports near ports in the port city territories: in some cases, the airports are located either inside the port or they sit at its edge, as in Bremen, Belfast, Nantes Saint-Nazaire, Genova, Barcelona; in other cases, they are located close to the port, as we can observe in Bilbao, Le Havre and Cagliari. There are also some exceptions in which the airports are not present on the maps: on the Mediterranean, the airport of Toulon is far enough east of the city to fall outside the map; in La Spezia there is only one helipad near the port, and the nearest airport is in Pisa, which is beyond the map; for Messina and Milazzo the airport is across the channel in Reggio Calabria; and in the Baltic Sea we cannot see airports at all for Sillamäe, Skoldvik, Kalundborg and Fredericia. This means that the infrastructural links of the port city territory effectively extend beyond the map section.

Infrastructural access to the port goes beyond the land side. Planning for water entrances has to take into account sea depths, not only in the approach to the port but in the port itself, where dredging usually removes underwater sediments to accommodate larger vessels. In addition, maritime traffic also shapes port planning for access. The infographics show the total number (in thousands) of vessels and percentage of vessel types calling at each port from Eurostat Maritime transport data in 2019 (vessels in main ports by type and size of vessels). For example, maritime traffic is heaviest in the port of Santa Cruz de Tenerife in Western Waters, in Reggio di Calabria in the Mediterranean Sea, in Rotterdam in the North Sea and in Helsingborg in the Baltic Sea. Such information complements the view of the maps, which indicate the directions from which ships arrive to the port.

Environmental Issues

Both our infographics and our maps highlight environmental challenges; the first identifies the total area of terrestrial and marine Natura2000 sites in figures and the second the presence or absence of protected areas in the port city territory. The Organisation for Economic Co-operation and Development (OECD), which is an international organization working to set evidence-based international standards and find solutions to a range of social, economic and environmental challenges, defines three subcategories of environmental harms associated with ports:[4] those caused by port activities, those caused at sea by ships entering the port, and emissions from intermodal transport networks to the hinterland. Port planners and port authorities pay close attention to these harms, and to the encroachment of ports on protected areas, and accordingly take special measures in planning. As part of preparing a master plan, experts from different disciplines put together a comprehensive environmental impact assessment—aimed at preventing or reducing the harmful effects of planned activities on the environment and their consequences. These findings must be considered in the planning process. We can conclude from the maps, for example, that planners will have to take extra care in the port of Swinoujscie in Baltic Sea, which is in a difficult situation in terms of further spatial growth and planning, because it is surrounded by marine Natura2000. Similarly, most of the area around the port of Antwerp and the port of Bremen in the North Sea is protected by Natura2000 Terrestrial. Such proximity does not necessarily mean that ports cannot expand. The master plan for the port of Koper included restoration of habitats at its north side that would be damaged by port expansion. This was part of the detailed and in-depth evaluation that won the natural heritage and hydrology sectors' approval to build a third container port pier.

In many port city territories, the energy crisis has made energy production a top priority, pushing port authorities to search for alternative energy sources and planners to implement them in new designs. Another response to the crisis is European circular economy policy, which mandates that ports reform their organization of production and consumption to save energy, but the question remains how to implement the measures. One possible solution in the port city territory, with its concentration of different industries, is industrial symbiosis. This is a concept in industrial ecology (IE) that looks at the stages of the production processes

OECD, 'Environmental impacts of ports' (2022). Online. Available HTTPS: https://www.oecd.org/greengrowth/green-transport/environmental-impacts-of-ports.htm.

of goods and services, and attempts to mimic a natural system through the conservation and reuse of resources.[5] IE is based on the concept of the circular economy, in which different entities form networks of actors to share resources such as materials, energy, information, services or technologies. Eco-industrial parks hosting these activities could be built in areas where ports intersect with industrial areas, as is the case in the port of Rotterdam, where the industrial waste heat of the port refinery fuels the Rotterdam city district heating system.

Waste management is one of the most important planning and environmental issues in port city territories, as resource-intensive industries here benefit from the proximity of ship loading and unloading; but this process cannot be read directly from the maps or infographics. Ports are changing their approach towards waste management. Some authors propose master plans for waste management measures and methods in ports, reporting observed pollution and defining a model for handling the waste, as they have in the Croatian ports Rijeka and Split.[6] A team of French researchers have produced an international overview of port industrial ecology initiatives, looking methodologically at case studies, types of port regions (following the typology of Ducruet et al.)[7] and port IE actors, including port authorities, local authorities, national governments, companies, and researchers.[8] The authors found that many ports in Europe are pursuing IE initiatives, including ports in the Netherlands, Belgium, the UK, Spain and France. The research revealed that ports can make an important contribution to the development of IE by including industrial symbiosis in future transitions.

Partnerships in Planning that Facilitate Transitions: Co-design, Negotiation, Citizen Science

To contribute to contemporary transitions, planners at all levels in port city territories can form multilateral partnerships and collaborations with local people and organizations: co-designing with stakeholders to ensure that outcomes meet their needs; negotiating to reach agreements on plans; and in citizen science, collaborating with citizens on scientific research projects to help solve world problems. In all such partnerships, planners should treat community members as equal collaborators in the planning process. For the most part, however, the foundations for such collaborations, relevant institutions and tools still need to be established in many port city territories.

An example of *co-design* can be found in the port of Hamburg: a maritime laboratory called homePORT, in which the port, citizens, other port stakeholders, research institutions and start-ups work together to design changes in the port.[9] Specifically, this campaign asks what will happen to port areas after the end of the container era, identifies alternative scenarios for the use of those areas and

---

5 M.R. Chertow, 'Industrial Ecology in a Developing Context', in: C. Clini, I. Musu, M. Lodovica Gullino (eds), *Sustainable Development and Environmental Management* (Dordrecht: Springer, 2008).

6 P. Badurina, M. Cukrov and Č. Dundović, 'Contribution to the implementation of "Green Port" concept in Croatian seaports', *Scientific Journal of Maritime Research* 31 (2017), 10–17.

7 C. Ducruet, H. Itoh and O. Joly, 'Port-region linkages in a global perspectives', *MoLos Conference 'Modeling Logistics Systems'* (Le Havre, 2012).

8 J. Cerceau, N. Mat, G. Junqua, L. Liming, V. Laforest and C. Gonzalez, 'Implementing industrial ecology in port cities: international overview of case studies and cross-case analysis', *Journal of Cleaner Production* 74 (2014), 1–16.

9 'homePORT'. Online. Available HTTPS: https://www.homeport.hamburg/.

simulates approaches for a circular economy with zero-emissions. *Negotiations* do not take place very often in port city territory planning; the restructuring and redevelopment of a port in Copenhagen is among a handful of examples of its complexity and success. Important components are participants' learning processes, cooperation and continuous adaptation of approaches to achieve better solutions.[10] In *citizen science*, citizens can be involved at any stage of planning, from defining questions, to developing assumptions, to discussing the results and answering new questions.[11] Citizens can then also initiate projects to improve local spaces. There are many opportunities for planners and communities in port city territories to use citizen science and its findings to influence local policymakers to improve public health, quality of life, social cohesion and awareness of local issues and networks.

Conclusions

Our maps and infographics offer all stakeholders the opportunity to examine individual case studies in depth and with regard to the specifics of their own location and situation, as well as to identify general approaches to addressing planning issues. Port planning practice shows that no single authority controls the form of the port city territory, or its components of hinterland, foreland, port city and port. Rather, that form is shaped by a mixture of bureaucracy and market forces.[12]

New partnerships in planning will change and shape port city areas in the future that are not yet visible on the maps. Global climate change, to which by far the largest contributors are fossil fuels—coal, oil and gas—and sea level rise, caused by global warming, are the latest in the series of changes. Other challenges and tensions facing ports and their territories are the sustainability of spatial development in line with the Sustainable Development Goals,[13] such as Goal 9—developing high-quality and reliable infrastructure—or Goal 13—strengthening resilience and adaptive capacity. Security issues caused by fears of piracy, armed robbery incidents and military combat increase the importance of these issues. Accordingly, the resulting changes are more complex than ever and the interests at play among port city territory actors have multiplied and become more diverse. For example, to become sustainable, ports must incorporate renewable energy and green chemistry, reducing or eliminating the use or generation of hazardous substances. These are changes that can only be achieved and implemented through collaborative planning by all stakeholders.

Maps and Infographics for the Planning of Port City Territories

Helsingborg, SE
 Øresund

Santa Cruz de Tenerife, ES
Atlantic

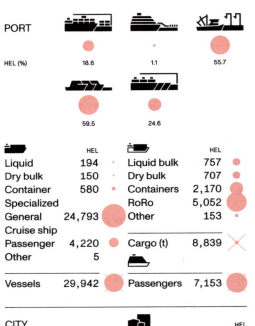

PORT			
HEL (%)	18.6	1.1	55.7
	59.5	24.6	

	HEL		HEL
Liquid	194	Liquid bulk	757
Dry bulk	150	Dry bulk	707
Container	580	Containers	2,170
Specialized		RoRo	5,052
General	24,793	Other	153
Cruise ship			
Passenger	4,220	Cargo (t)	8,839
Other	5		
Vessels	29,942	Passengers	7,153

CITY		HEL
	Helsingborg	
→ Capital national (km)	→ Stockholm	487
→ Capital regional (km)		
Area (km²)		347
Built-up area (km²)		44
Density (per km²)		413
Population		143,304
Population structure (%)	17.8 / 63.4 / 18.7	
Distribution built area (%)	B 72 / I 22 / P 6	

TERRITORY		HEL
	Skåne län	
Area (km²)		11,363
Density (per km²)		120
Population		1,362,164
Natura2000 (km²)	M 2,920 / T 351	

PORT			
SCT (%)	1.8	61.8	36.4

	SCT		SCT
Liquid	814	Liquid bulk	4,812
Dry bulk	149	Dry bulk	422
Container	907	Containers	2,170
Specialized	18	RoRo	2,338
General	6,124	Other	46
Cruise ship	511		
Passenger	7,623	Cargo (t)	9,788
Other			
Vessels	16,132	Passengers	5,615

CITY		SCT
	Santa Cruz de Tenerife	
→ Capital national (km)	→ Madrid	2136
→ Capital regional (km)	→ Las Palmas	101
Area (km²)		253
Built-up area (km²)		58
Density (per km²)		1,445
Population		364,815
Population structure (%)	12.8 / 69.8 / 17.4	
Distribution built area (%)	B 77 / A 4 / I 14 / P 5	

TERRITORY		SCT
	Tenerife	
Area (km²)		2,035
Density (per km²)		467
Population		949,471
Natura2000 (km²)	M 2,876 / T 675	

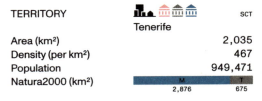

298 Port City Atlas

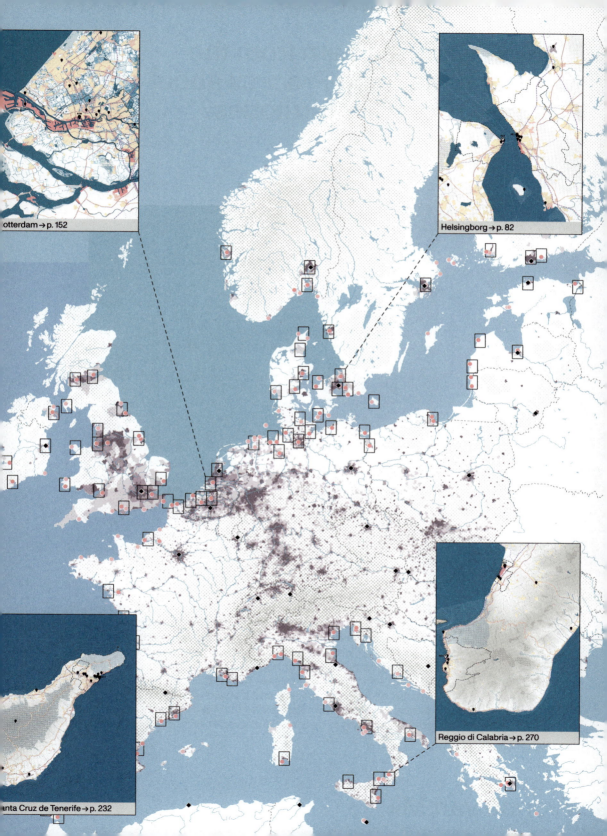

8 What Can We Learn from the Maps and Mapping Process about European Port City Territories?

Abstract

Maps and infographics that translate statistical and spatial data into visual forms offer a wealth of information that requires careful analysis and provides a foundation for research, planning, and sustainable development. This chapter first discusses some initial insights on the benefits of mapping port city territories in terms of the natural geographical conditions on the edge of land and water, and of man-made spatial patterns of port city relations and urban forms. These spatial conditions, clearly identifiable on the maps, give us insight into the spatial and institutional structures that characterize port city territories; thus mapping can help us address future research questions on spatial development strategies or challenges such as energy transition, mass migration and climate change. Based on the observations made during data research, we then discuss insights into data unavailability that have affected the mapping and the mapped results, and address limitations of data and lack of (detailed) data. The chapter concludes that geo-spatial mapping and other visualizations such as infographics can play a key role in the study of port city territories, and in port planning, illuminating complex governance structures and showing the different stakeholders involved in port city territories, and how the natural geographical landscape affects the performance of ports. But we also call for more, and more specific, data.

Introduction

Port city territories all host the same flows of goods and people, yet, as our atlas shows, they are distinctive and complex ecosystems that have evolved over time, connecting natural features of sea and land, urban structures focused on the port and maritime activities, complex governance structures, and actors with different interests and means of power. The uniform mapping of port city territories helps us understand these overlapping patterns, and allows us to describe, define and ultimately classify port city territories according to their spatial characteristics. By looking at (urban)

Yvonne van Mil

morphological patterns, the maps can help us answer questions about port city territories, as these first insights into the spatial and institutional structures of port city territories exemplify.

The chapter starts with the question: looking at the maps, how can we interpret the morphological patterns in the natural topography and geography of port city territories, and in their man-made features such as urban settlements and the port city relation? Second, it addresses what the complexity of data obscures. While working with European datasets, we encountered several challenges. Mapping-based research largely depends on the availability and structure of (existing) datasets and on standardized administrative units. Uniform maps allow for comparison, but also level out individual particularities. We conclude with a call for more available and more detailed data, and a greater awareness of both the possibilities and the limitations of geospatial data.

Deriving Lessons from Complex Spatial Data:
How to Interpret the Morphology of 100 Port City Territories

In reality, port city territories can stretch (far) beyond our 75 by 100-kilometre map-cut-out, but this framing makes it possible to explore complex spatial and institutional relationships, as well as spatial or urban patterns. In the approach chosen for this chapter and applied in the maps on page 308, we highlighted specific map layers to explore select spatial characteristics of port city territories for specific analytical purposes. In this case we chose to focus on the natural geographical conditions on the edge of land and water, and patterns of the man-made relation between port and city, and urban patterns. These morphological patterns allow us to predict some spatial planning challenges; they also illuminate the institutional structures that influence port city territories and point to planning strategies that could improve the performance of the port.

Ports in their Natural Morphology of Land and Water

While we focus on Europe as a whole, our maps also highlight national differences. This becomes particularly clear when examining the length of the coastline in relation to the number of leading ports on our list. Countries with long coastlines have more leading port city territories than those with short coastlines—though the amount of transhipment can be much less. Rotterdam, for example, transits a larger tonnage of cargo per year than all 14 Italian leading port city territories (containing 19 ports) combined. This may be the result of national policies or path dependencies, but we found that natural geographical conditions are also a factor. Increased access to maritime waters, and thus more opportunities for port development, is not a precondition for success. The naturally present limitations and opportunities of such access can also be determinant. By examining the natural morphology of land and water, we observe explainable differences between the four maritime waters: a maritime perspective is more insightful than a national view. France, for example, has eight leading port city territories across three waters. Almost all the ones on the Atlantic coastline (Le Havre, Nantes Saint-Nazaire and Bordeaux but not La Rochelle) are situated in an estuary or on a river, which may be due to the rougher conditions of the Atlantic Ocean. In the Mediterranean Sea, with calmer seas, fewer major rivers and deltas, but more mountains and an irregular coastline, the ports (Marseille and Toulon) are situated in a natural embayment. Dunkirk and Calais are situated on the relatively shallow North Sea where there are multiple deltas and major rivers, but these ports are in a (narrow) strait and have an engineered coastline, as natural protection to safely load and unload ships is lacking. Similar patterns in morphological conditions can also be discovered in other port city territories.

Some patterns are consistent for specific natural morphological conditions. Ports located along a coast (such as Dunkirk or Naples), often block the city's access to the sea. Such a situation can be advantageous for deep-sea ports but can be prone to disasters. Public resistance to further development is also more likely. Ports on rivers and estuaries face different challenges and have different opportunities. They can be developed on both sides of a river and have greater access to nearby territory (such as Antwerp or Hamburg), but face the risk of flooding from the hinterland and from the sea. Similar to ports on a bay (Dublin), the need for continuous dredging causes problems in terms of ecology. Ports on islands (Las Palmas) require good transport connections with the mainland, as a sizeable hinterland is often lacking.

If we read the maps along with port statistics, it becomes clear that the natural geography of port city territories affects port performance as well as the quantity of throughput: of the 15 largest cargo ports in Europe, 11 are located in an estuary or on a river, including the five largest cargo ports in Europe: Rotterdam, Hamburg, Antwerp, Amsterdam and London, all in the North Sea. Here the main river on which they are located serves as a transport connection to the fore- and hinterland, which gives them an advantage over ports that are not located on waterways. The next four largest cargo ports are located in an embayment, including Algeciras and Marseille in the Mediterranean. Most of the largest 15 passenger ports, in contrast, are on a sea strait, an engineered coast or are surrounded by islands. These ports are often closely linked by ferries. So, mapping helps us to better understand the size, function and functioning of specific ports; and that there is no point for some ports to strive to be like Rotterdam, because they are bound by the possibilities and limitations of their location.

Port City Relations in the Territory

Port cities include two key man-made morphological entities—an urban entity and a port entity—plus an institutional entity. Cities developed simultaneously with port terminals, housing and feeding workers, and many terminals were the original reason for a city's existence. Maritime activities have long been a direct driver of urban growth, resulting in a strong, albeit evolving, relationship between the port and the metropolitan area in which they are located. Sometimes the relationship is contentious, as the port continuously encroaches on nearby territories. Nonetheless, the territorial maps show that most ports are still urban, located in and closely linked to the morphology of the city. Indeed, they are connected to a central city with surrounding built-up areas (themselves tied to the city by commuting and other daily interactions),[1] as well as through infrastructure and pollution.

Looking at the scalar relationships between ports, cities and territories, we can observe several morphological patterns on the maps and read them in light of urban histories. The port can be a contiguous morphological zone, expanding (far) beyond the urban morphology of the city, but maintaining the port city relation and remaining within the administrative boundaries of the city, as for instance in Rotterdam and Barcelona. A port city can have moved several (smaller) port function to peripheral locations, some of which no longer have a physical connection with the morphology of the city where they started and are no longer within their administrative boundaries, as in Bordeaux, London and Marseille. Only a few of the 100 leading ports in terms of transhipment have no spatial relationship with an urban centre. These include the transhipment hubs Puttgarden and Sjællands Odde, and the oil port Skoldvik, which were designed and rationally planned in rural locations, away from all the limiting factors of urban areas.[2] Bremerhaven and Zeebrugge can also be included in this category.

Based on the maps, we can argue that a city near a port benefits from having control over port entities and development, for environmental, social and safety reasons. A better understanding of patterns in the scalar development of port city territories from a comparative perspective, as in this atlas, and of the intersection between spatial and social development can inspire better planning in port city territories.[3]

Urban Patterns in the Port City Territory

Ports have a huge impact on the development of a territory, spatially, socially and politically, as well as in terms of air, noise, water or land pollution. Then there is the complexity of shared and conflicting interests of port authorities. The impact of ports on their immediate urban environment calls for far-reaching coordination, even cooperation, between ports and their surrounding municipalities. The infographics show us that more than half of the leading ports are in a predominantly urban territory. About 10 per cent are in predominantly rural territories, often linked to smaller ports that act as transport hubs, or to medium-sized port cities whose community, commercial, recreational, and cultural dynamics make them territorial centres. Moreover, of these 100 leading port city territories, almost 50 per cent consist of more than one port, so that within an area of 75 by 100 kilometres, there are two or more port authorities, all with their own spatial and economic interests. Which calls for inter-port collaboration. In Italy, for example, the government merged several of such smaller port authorities in the Naples area into one larger and stronger port authority. Studying patterns of urban settlements in the territory helps us understand the complexity and difficulties of governance structures, and the distinctive conditions for cooperation between each port, city and territory; it also helps us grasp the degree of urbanization and centralization of the territories.

In the port city territories, we can discern four different morphological urban patterns on the maps: monocentric area with a single port; monocentric area with multiple ports; polycentric area with a single port; and polycentric area with multiple ports.[4] In territories with a *monocentric* urban structure, port cities have a strong centre function, such as in the single port territories Le Havre and Szczecin. Here the urban centre is in the immediate hinterland of the port.[5] Monocentric urban territories with multiple ports are port cities (mostly larger) that have deployed several port sites across or near the metropolitan area, as the result of the changed port city relationship. These include Clydeport, Bordeaux, and Aalborg. In *polycentric* port city territories, several urban cores are located near each other, often in predominantly urban territories. Multiple configurations exist in this category. The most common is a polycentric area with a single port, in which a large non-port city is connected by urban sprawl to a smaller port city, as in Piraeus, 12 kilometres from the centre of Athens, and Leixões, the port of Porto. Administratively, the port is a separate entity, but it is physically and functionally intertwined with the city. Another example of a polycentric port city territory with a single port is two large neighbouring cities of which only one has a port, such as the Liverpool-Manchester agglomeration. Polycentric territories with multiple ports involve at least two port cities in contiguity or proximity, forming a coherent entity in which cities and ports are managed by distinct municipalities and authorities.[6] Examples of this type of coastal agglomerations include Gdynia-Gdańsk, Lisbon-Setubal and Immingham, Hull & Humber. Adjacent port city territories shown in multiple territorial maps can also be considered as one polycentric entity, such as Rotterdam and Amsterdam and Bremen and Hamburg. The four different patterns are characterized

4 O. Merk et al., 'The Competitiveness of Global Port-Cities: the Case of the Seine Axis (Le Havre, Rouen, Paris, Caen)—France', *OECD Regional Development Working Papers* 07 (OECD Publishing, 2011). Online. Available HTTPS: http://dx.doi.org/10.1787/5kg58xppgc0n-en.

5 Merk et al., 'The Competitiveness of Global Port-Cities'.

6 Merk et al., 'The Competitiveness of Global Port-Cities'.

by varying degrees of independence from the surrounding urban centres in the territory, ranging from independent with agglomeration effects stemming from the port city itself to lock-in effects by the nearby metropolis.[7]

Learning from the Mapping Process:
What Does the Complexity of Data Obscure?

Not all spatial conditions that affect or concern port city territories, directly or indirectly, can easily be shown on a map, such as historic events in which a port city territory is locked in development paths, and subsequent path dependency. The lack of specific data can also obscure our ability to interpret the maps. In the mapping of 100 European port city territories, we have learned for example that we need more precise information on land cover, land use and land ownership in ports and more detailed data on the types of transport. We also need more awareness of the limitations of data restricted by administrative borders, and the accuracy of datasets. Most datasets are valuable for a specific purpose, for instance monitoring changes in land cover/land use, but often not suitable for other purposes or for combining and comparing with other data. In addition, datasets and maps are always slightly behind the current situation because it takes time to process data, and institutions revise datasets only every few years. Nonetheless, it is an exciting time in the mapping world, as more and more global and European heterogeneous datasets—such as European Commission data—are becoming openly available, due to new techniques such as satellite imagery, spatial data mining technologies, and ground-based, airborne, and seaborne measurement systems. The European Commission implemented INSPIRE directives in 2007 to establish an infrastructure of spatial data of the European Union; but the Commission has no instruments to oblige member states to provide this data. Our data research shows that many datasets are incomplete as a result, making comparative studies like ours more difficult.

Land Cover

To truly understand the role of ports in their territories, we need comprehensive datasets that identify shipping, industry and logistics-related functions. Ports are identifiable spatial structures; they are often delineated from nearby urban and rural areas by fences or other visible boundaries and have clear functions in the landscape. But this apparent clarity becomes complex when explored through the lens of land cover data.[8] The interpretation of land cover categories differs per dataset (Corine Landcover and Coastal Zone), and land cover categories in general do not match the total footprint or extent of the port. Industries located within the fences or borders of the port, for example, are categorized as industrial or commercial areas, and the port basins (including ships on the water surface) are not indicated as ports, but categorized as water bodies, though they are indeed part of the port. Consequently, the interwovenness of industry and port functions is not clear from the maps and a port—and the size of ships docking—may appear much smaller than it actually is. Also, uniform data showing the total areas controlled by port authorities, including the industries or fallow land et cetera within the port boundaries, is also lacking. Spatial datasets do not include property data or governance structures and maritime statistical data do not include spatial or administrative entities. As a result, the mapping cannot provide insight into the number of stakeholders in the territory or the impact of the port on its surroundings. For the planning of a sustainable future for port city territories, this knowledge is key.

Transport Networks

The online interactive map of European Transport Corridors[9] provides us insight into fore- and hinterland connections. This European Commission network consists of nine corridors, and is a selection of motorways, railways, waterways and short sea shipping routes from the comprehensive TEN-T network that connect all urban hubs in Europe to the main departure and destination points for goods and passengers. The interactive map shows that the ports of Liepaja and Esbjerg, for example, are not connected to these corridors; some ports (including Brünsbuttel) are only connected through water, and others (such as Gijon) only by rail. These kinds of insights can help us to improve the development of future sustainable connections to the fore- and hinterland. This requires that the TEN-T corridor network becomes available as geospatial data (as a download or WMS service) so that it can be integrated into our maps and surveys. In addition, we need more detailed statistical data (meaning information from smaller administrative units) on the transport of goods and people on the various types of infrastructure; this level of detail is now only available for NUTS 1 (country level) at Eurostat. This would make it possible for the impact of transport to and from the port on the territory—inhabitants, Natura2000 areas, et cetera—to be more accurately included in planning and design.

Administrative Borders

To overcome the wide variation in administrative entities in size and population density, we based the classifications of port city territories on Eurostat's Urban Audit categories: Local Administrative Units (LAU), Cities and Greater Cities.[10] Another reason to use the Urban Audit as a basis is that it includes an interpretation of what it describes as the functional area of the city, which is the area we intend to show on the port city territorial maps. According

---

[9] European Commission, 'Mobility and Transport. Interactive Map Viewer' (2018). Online. Available HTTPS: https://ec.europa.eu/transport/infrastructure/tentec/tentec-portal/map/maps.html.

[10] Eurostat, 'Applying the Degree of Urbanisation. A methodological manual to define cities, towns and rural areas for international comparisons' (2021). Online Available PDF: https://ec.europa.eu/eurostat/documents/3859598/12519999/KS-02-20-499-EN-N.pdf/0d412b58-046f-750b-0f48-7134f1a3a4c2?t=1615477801160.

to the Urban Audit, the territory would then be a Functional Urban Zone (FUZ), which is the commuter zone of a City or Greater City. But not all selected port cities meet the indicators for a City or Greater City, meaning that—based on the Urban Audit—there is no statistical data available for either the port cities or their territories. To study the territory, we therefore must rely on the Urban Type of NUTS 3 regions,[11] which often contains a much larger area than the FUZ that extends (far) beyond our map frame, and the size of NUTS regions varies greatly from nation to nation. This standardization keeps us from seeing the dynamics and diversity of port city territories. Ignoring these limitations of data can lead to premature or incorrect interpretation.

Conclusion

Geo-spatial mapping can help stakeholders better understand port city territories and plan their sustainable development, laying the foundation for further research. Many more relevant insights or patterns can be discovered by studying and comparing the maps and infographics in more detail. Consider the overlap of Natura2000 areas with port city territories, for example. Looking at all territorial maps, it is striking that in multiple port city territories conflicts have arisen over whether to preserve valuable maritime landscapes or to further the economic interests of the port, and economic interests often seem to be the winning force. This often means that development at port locations threatens the network of protected areas holding Europe's most valuable and endangered species and habitats.

However, there are still many steps to be taken in order to better understand these kinds of spatial impacts of ports on their surroundings and the complex spatial and institutional structures that underpin them. While our work shows that geo-spatial mapping is an essential tool for the systematic and analytical study of port city territories and a basis for knowledge-based planning and design, it simultaneously provides insight into the limitations and peculiarities of spatial and statistical data.

To better understand the processes that underlie spatial changes, or spatial conflicts and aligned interests in European port city territories, we therefore call for more data: more up-to-date data, including more detailed data on ownership and land use, especially of land controlled by port authorities; and more complete data, that is for all EU nations and seas, and for smaller administrative units.

Eurostat, 'Applying the gree of Urbanisation'.

Interpreting the Morphology of Port City Territories

Ports in their Natural Morphology of Land and Water

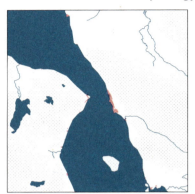

Situated in (narrow) straits
→ Helsingborg and Helsingør, p. 82

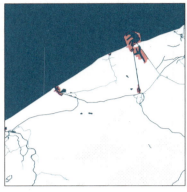

Located along the coast
→ Zeebrugge, p. 158

Located in a estuary or river
→ Riga, p. 104

Port City Relations in the Territory

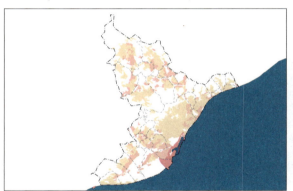

The port as a contiguous morphological zone connected to the city
→ Barcelona, p. 246

Port not interwoven with a city from their foundation
→ Puttgarden and Rødby, p. 120

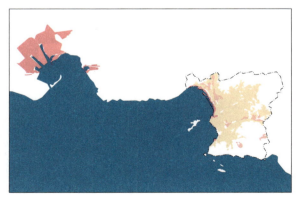

Port area not connected to the city
→ Marseille, p. 248

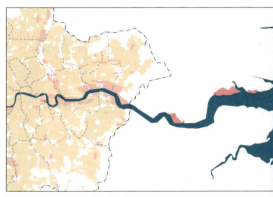

Port area not connected to the city
→ London, p. 166

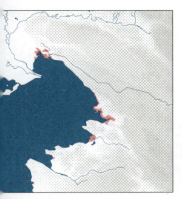
cated in a bay
Trieste, Koper and Monfalcone, p. 278

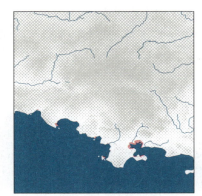
Located on an irregular coastline
→ Toulon, p. 250

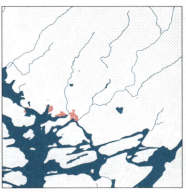
Surrounded by islands
→ Turku and Naatalin, p. 94

Urban Patterns in the Port City Territory

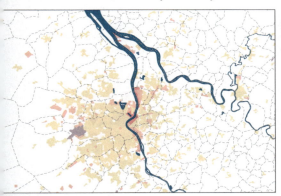
Monocentric urban territory with multiple port sites
Bordeaux, p. 216

Polycentric urban territories with a singel port
→ Leixões (Porto), p. 224

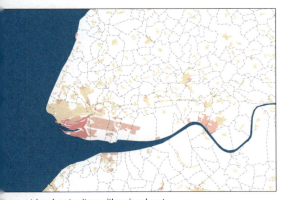
Monocentric urban territory with a singel port
Le Havre, p. 210

Polycentric urban territory with multiple ports
→ Gdynia-Gdańs, p. 112

Interpreting — Interpreting the Morphology of Port City Territories — 309

9 Port City Territories and UNESCO World Heritage Properties: an Opportunity for Implementing the UNESCO Historic Urban Landscape Approach

Abstract
Port city territories across Europe are rich settings for natural and cultural World Heritage properties, many of them related to maritime practices. In protecting and conserving this heritage, and passing it to future generations in line with the World Heritage Convention, territories can face challenges related to water and climate change and to important logistic flows of goods and people between sea and land. On the other hand, they can also have the opportunity to support sustainable development for historic cities and settlements in these areas. To show the intersection of the interests of port city territories and World Heritage sites from a spatial perspective, this chapter focuses on two select areas of the European seas: the first area being a section of the North Sea and the Baltic Sea, the second Italy. We chose these areas for their long coasts, high number of port city territories and long maritime history, as well as their numerous World Heritage properties. In each of these maps, the article explores World Heritage properties where the Outstanding Universal Value (OUV) is specifically related to maritime practices and cultural exchanges. People and institutions protecting World Heritage properties are working to integrate World Heritage properties into their surroundings in line with the World Heritage Convention (Art.5), the UNESCO Historic Urban Landscape (HUL) policy, and the Faro Convention. In port city territories, it is important for these people and institutions to acknowledge the interests of special actors, such as strong port authorities, which can impact policymaking. The chapter invites stakeholders of port city territories to more closely explore the ways in which the protection of World Heritage properties can intersect with the dynamics of port city territories to provide a foundation for discussion.

Introduction
The unique and delicate coastline at the edge of sea and land has attracted people and stimulated urban growth over centuries. Port city territories today are places where different stakeholders and interests intersect and sometimes clash. In particular, maritime

Carola Hein

logistics, industry, urban development, and economic activities can conflict with the historic preservation and local sustainable development of coastal natural and cultural World Heritage properties. This challenge is further exacerbated by the climate crisis and related water changes. The World Heritage Convention of 1972 recognized (p. 1) that "the cultural heritage and the natural heritage are increasingly threatened with destruction not only by the traditional causes of decay, but also by changing social and economic conditions which aggravate the situation with even more formidable phenomena of damage or destruction".[1] The challenges faced by world heritage sites have not decreased over time; on the contrary. Ironically, the maritime practices, flooding, and sea level rise that all threaten the historic city partly result from modern industrial activities in port city territories. By the same token, however, natural and cultural World Heritage properties in port city territories can also be sites for strategic design and planning and for climate action. As the architect Paola Vigano phrased it in an interview: "If we want to save Venice, and I think we should save Venice, we need to save the planet".[2]

The Convention formulated goals to address these challenges and opportunities. One of these goals is "to adopt a general policy which aims to give the cultural and natural heritage a function in the life of the community and to integrate the protection of that heritage into comprehensive planning programmes" (Article 5a). The World Heritage Convention and the UNESCO Historic Urban Landscape (HUL) as well as the Faro Convention also link this heritage protection to sustainable development of local communities. HUL notably aims "at preserving the quality of the human environment, enhancing the productive and sustainable use of urban spaces, while recognizing their dynamic character, and promoting social and functional diversity".[3] These are calls for the diverse stakeholders in port city territories to act together. A port authority, often a large and powerful actor, has the mandate to control and administer the port operation.[4] But the port authority's focus on economic development and throughput has been detrimental to heritage preservation and local sustainable development. Recently, port authorities have started to pay more attention to their neighbouring cities and territories. In light of shared needs for sustainable development, these very different stakeholders can embrace an ecosystem approach to port city territories at the border between sea and land.

To explore the spatial interrelation of port city territories and World Heritage, we opted to make specific map layers that focus on their co-existence. We selected two areas of the European seas (displayed on page 310) that have long coasts, and that are home to both a large number of port city territories and World Heritage properties dating from diverse historic periods. We used two different scales for a closer analysis of the challenges and opportunities relating to World Heritage properties in port city territories. To show the overlap between World Heritage properties and port city territories in different maritime waters, we mapped the two areas respectively at the scales of 1 to 1,350,000 (North Sea and Baltic Sea) and 1 to 10,000,000 (Italy in the Mediterranean Sea). At these scales the maps show us the great number of World Heritage sites located in the port city territories, and raises questions about the historic connections of World Heritage properties around a shared water body. In mapping them, we found that the question of scale remains a challenge. With one exception, each World Heritage property is indicated here as a dot, as the actual extent of each property or its buffer zone would not be visible in a meaningful way at either of our chosen scales. Thus, the scale of the maps invites further, more detailed investigation into the relationship between port city territory and World Heritage property.

The one property that can be made visible at this scale is the Wadden Sea, an area of 1,143,403 hectares along the Dutch, German and Danish coast. UNESCO inscribed the Wadden Sea in 2009 as "the last remaining large-scale, intertidal ecosystem where natural processes continue to function largely undisturbed".[5] It includes Biosphere Reserves and seven so-called Ramsar sites, wetlands designated under the Ramsar Convention. The Wadden Sea is also known also for its Halligen, islands with man-made mounds where people live; the mounds are flooded several times a year, surrounding them with water so that sediment adds to the height of each island. Such practices of living with water require attention and evaluation in a time of climate change and rising sea levels. Moreover, as we can see in the maps, the Sea intersects with or gives shipping water access to several port city territories, defined in the *Port City Atlas* as including the maritime foreland as well as the hinterland. The Wadden Sea is thus part of the port city territories of Esbjerg, Brunsbüttel, Bremerhaven and Wilhelmshaven. Furthermore, it is crossed by the Elbe and Weser Rivers through which ships access the port city territories of Hamburg and Bremen. Ports' dredging and disposal of dredged material in the North Sea; ships' water, air and sound pollution; overfishing; and invasive tourism can all have a direct negative impact on natural sites and their preservation. Organizations like the German NGO Friends of the Earth (Bund für Natur- und Umweltschutz Deutschland, or BUND) regularly decry such activities.[6] Decreasing pollution—for example, through cleaner shipping or smaller ships for fishing or transport—could create healthier futures for local communities.

To be listed on the UNESCO World Heritage list, properties must be of outstanding quality and meet at least one of ten criteria of Outstanding Universal Value (OUV). To better understand how the World Heritage sites in our port city territories are related (or not) to maritime and port city networks, we set out to systematically identify the OUVs for which UNESCO selected them. We manually checked the abstracts of World Heritage properties published on the UNESCO World Heritage Centre website,[7] looking for words

5 UNESCO, Waddensee. Online. Available HTTPS: https://whc.unesco.org/en/list/1314https://whc.unesco.org/en/list/1314

6 Bedrohungen und Belastungen des Lebensraums Wattenmeer. Online. Available HTTPS: https://www.bund-hamburg.de/themen/naturschutz/wattenmeer/bedrohungen-und-belastungen-des-lebensraums-wattenmeer/.

7 UNESCO World Heritage List. Online. Available HTTPS: https://whc.unesco.org/en/list/.

associated with port functions and activities.[8] The OUV of some heritage sites in the Atlas are explicitly connected to maritime infrastructure, including wharfs, cranes and quays, canals, rail and road infrastructure, warehouses, and administrative buildings. Many other World Heritage sites are located in our port city territories but don't have an obvious link to the maritime past. Nonetheless, their preservation may be affected by it, notably in light of climate change.

A First Exploration of the Relation between Port City Territories and Maritime-related World Heritage Properties
We first wanted to explore how widespread the co-existence of port city territories and World Heritage sites actually is. So, we selected an area that includes a part of North Sea and Baltic Seas centred on the Skagerrak strait. These seas surround the peninsula of Jütland and the Danish islands, spanning from the adjacent port city territories of Kent and Calais on the Straight of Dover in the West to the port city territories of Gdansk and Gdynia on the Baltic Sea in the East. This area has long been home to maritime practices and shipping-based exchange, which partly explains its density of port city territories—38 of 50 port city territories mapped in the whole *Port City Atlas*—and of World Heritage properties—23 natural and cultural sites.

Second, we wanted to see whether these World Heritage properties were selected for their maritime connections, and what those histories could tell us about port city territories. Here we can only briefly explore four select World Heritage properties that specifically mention shipping, maritime or port city functions as part of their OUV in the UNESCO World Heritage description. Each site merits further individual analysis to explore both the historic relation to shipping and maritime practices, and the challenges and opportunities of the current relation. These four World Heritage sites are: the historic cities of Lübeck and Brugge, and the cities of Amsterdam and Hamburg, located in Germany, Belgium and the Netherlands. The historic centres of the smaller cities of Lübeck and Brugge have been kept intact as the working port has been moved (in different degrees) to the nearby seaside. The larger cities of Amsterdam and Hamburg have also detached the historic areas from active shipping, with the exception of cruise shipping.

The Hanseatic City of Lübeck was listed by UNESCO as a World Heritage site in 1987 based on criterion iv: an outstanding ensemble. The city's function as a port city has played an important role in the city's historic development as "the former capital and Queen City of the Hanseatic League" that "has remained a centre for maritime commerce to this day, particularly with the Nordic countries."[9] The historic city centre is an 81.1-hectare site with a 693.8 buffer zone that encompasses the Trave and Wakenitz water-ways and the canal surrounding the city; it is detached from Travemünde, a borough of Lübeck at the mouth of the Trave River that has emerged over time as Germany's major ferry port. The further develop-ment of the port along the Trave and in Travemünde continued this separation, which ultimately helps those working to preserve the historic city, as the big ships, major land infrastructure and traffic are located at some distance from it.

The Historic Centre of Brugge was inscribed on the World Heritage list in 2000, for criteria ii, iv, and vi, which emphasize the city's cultural links to other parts of the world, its typology and its artistic achievements. It covers 410 hectares and has a 168-hectare buffer zone.[10] As one of the commercial and cultural capitals of Europe, Brugge developed cultural links, plus land- and sea-based infrastructure networks, with different parts of the world. In the greater Brugge region, the 1907 construction of new port infrastructure called Zeebrugge, or the seaport of Brugge, separated the active port from the historic city. The port is today among Europe's leading ports. Meanwhile, the city government promotes sustainable tourism in the historic city.

UNESCO inscribed the seventeenth-century walled canal ring area of Amsterdam, with 198.2 hectares and a buffer zone of 481.7 hectares, in the World Heritage List in 2010 according to criteria I, ii, and iv, as a human masterpiece, a result of cultural interchange and a unique typology. It described it as a network of canals "with a medieval port that encircled the old town and was accompanied by the repositioning inland of the city's fortified boundaries, the Singelgracht". The city lost direct access to the sea with the closure of the IJ River in 1872, and today IJmuiden acts as the port of Amsterdam, hosting the Tata steel factory and large cruise ships. That site is also the access point for ships to the North Sea Canal with its large locks.[11] Cruise and leisure shipping are a challenge in Amsterdam due to the already high pressure from tourism. However, innovative activities can provide creative solutions. Plastic fishing—cleaning the waste from Amsterdam's canals—is just one approach to relating heritage preservation and maritime awareness.[12]

The Speicherstadt and Kontorhausviertel with Chilehaus in Hamburg were jointly named as a World Heritage site in 2015. It is recognized according to criteria iv as "one of the largest coherent historic ensembles of port warehouses in the world (300,000 m^2)" and is included for the Kontorhaus (office) district "featuring six very large office complexes built from the 1920s to the 1940s to house port-related businesses".[13] With 26.08 hectares and a buffer zone of 56.17 hectares, it is smaller than the other three sites, yet located in a much bigger city and integrated into ongoing maritime and urban activities. Hamburg's World Heritage property has a shorter history than the others. At the turn of the last century, the removal of port functions from the north side of the River Elbe to the south side, with the exception of cruise shipping, set the stage for the creation of a multifunctional district; here, heritage ships create new relationships between the historic city and the water. The nearby HafenCity development invokes this maritime history in names, styles, and architecture, links that are valuable

---

10 UNESCO, Historic Centre of Brugge Online. Available HTTPS: https://whc.unesco.org/en/list/996

11 UNESCO, Seventeenth-Century Canal Ring Area of Amsterdam inside the Singelgracht Online. Available HTTPS: https://whc.unesco.org/en/list/1349/ https://whc.unesco.org/en/list/1349/

12 Plastic Whale "Come Fishing … for Plastics". Online. Available HTTPS: https://plasticwhale.com/plastic-fishing/.

13 UNESCO, Speicherstadt and Kontorhausdistrikt with Chilehaus. Online. Available HTTPS: https://whc.unesco.org/en/list/1467

both to remaining maritime activities, notably cruise ships, and the preservation of World Heritage property.

The four case studies briefly explored here show that even when maritime practices radically change and active ports are moved away from historic settlements, a site's historic relationship to water remains. Water constantly flows and continues to link ports and cities, opening several opportunities for stakeholders to work together: to include water in heritage management plans; to apply the UNESCO Historic Urban Landscape approach to promote inclusive local development of port city territories; and to not only preserve World Heritage properties but activate them to address the climate crisis. Port development and preservation alike require citizen participation, community-based planning, and an approach that includes socio-cultural values.

A National Approach to Port City Territories and World Heritage Properties: the Case of Italy

We then wanted to explore how port city territories and World Heritage sites interrelate in a national setting, such as Italy, where both are particularly abundant. The right site of the map (Map 114) explores port city territories and World Heritage sites in a single country—Italy—focusing on the southern waters surrounding its boot-shaped peninsula with the Tyrrhenian Sea, the Ligurian Sea, Tuscan Archipelago and Ionian Sea in the west and south, and the Adriatic Sea in the east. Italy alone is home to 14 (including the border crossing Trieste/Koper area) of the leading 25 port city territories of the Mediterranean, which may not be a surprise given its long coastlines and central location. Except for Porto Foxi & Cagliari and Gioia Tauro & Reggio di Calabria, each of these port city territories is also home to a cultural World Heritage property, in part because Italy has a long and outstanding history, and it was among the first countries to propose sites to UNESCO for World Heritage status. Three of these heritage sites are closely related to maritime and shipping practices: Venice and its lagoon (1987), Genoa: Le Strade Nuove and the system of the *Palazzi dei Rolli* (2006), and the historic centre of Naples (1995).

The descriptions of these sites on the list of the World Heritage Convention note their historic links to maritime and shipping practices, even if UNESCO did not list them for these links. For example, the description of Venice states: "Founded in the 5th century and spread over 118 small islands, Venice became a major maritime power in the 10th century."[14] The presence of the Port of Marghera in the Venice Lagoon is now highly debated, because it pollutes the water and disrupts the ecosystem of the lagoon. Nonetheless, it is notable that the Port Authority of Venice is involved in the management plan for the World Heritage property. Naples identifies itself as a port city, the "Historic Centre of Naples, one of the foremost Mediterranean port cities."[15] Nowadays, the port and the World Heritage property often come into conflict here, as both

[14] (UNESCO, Venice and Its Lagoon. Online. Available TTPS: https://whc.unesco.org/n/list/394/)

[15] (UNESCO, Historic Centre Naples. Online. Available TTPS: https://whc.unesco.rg/en/list/726/)

strive to claim space along the coast and in the hinterland. The story of the construction of the metro line in the historic city documents the long history of the site, the challenges of preservation and the careful integration of the cruise ship terminal nearby into the historic urban fabric. In Genoa, the World Heritage site is "The Strade Nuove and the system of the Palazzi dei Rolli in Genoa's historic centre date from the late 16th and early 17th centuries"; the abstract links it to the period "when the Republic of Genoa was at the height of its financial and seafaring power."[16] (The World Heritage property abuts a revitalized waterfront and a partly active port with all the challenges of pollution.

Port authorities have the opportunity and the responsibility to work with cities and metropolitan governments as well as territorial authorities to implement the UNESCO Historic Urban Landscape approach to balance development with historic preservation of World Heritage properties. In the case of Italy, multiple ports are managed in port clusters, opening up opportunities for comprehensive approaches to protecting World Heritage. Indeed, as this chapter and these maps demonstrate, heritage sites are more than simply places to be protected from development; they can drive a better kind of development. Port city territories can mobilize their heritage, honour the maritime culture that has allowed them to thrive, and use these historic sites as foundation for sustainable and inclusive development and for climate action. This work of preserving World Heritage, and of attracting and distributing touristic flows, can also catalyse the emergence of port city territorial governance. Re-thinking existing ports and cities in sustainable ways requires investing in new infrastructure, urban developments and buildings; it also requires European-wide planning and policy-making.

Goals

Understanding, recognizing, and preserving these historic maritime connections, planners and politicians can position World Heritage properties for local sustainable development, whether as sites of education on maritime awareness or as creative hubs. Such solutions need to go beyond attracting cruise and leisure ships, which are particularly prominent in the Mediterranean. In fact, cruise and leisure shipping are not sustainable development, as they are major threats to World Heritage properties. Modern ports must also acknowledge and address the impact of their shipping, dredging, and water pollution on nearby natural World Heritage properties. Actors in port city territories need to carefully balance the positive and negative externalities of tourism on World Heritage properties. New, carefully managed forms of ecotourism and slow tourism—including non-polluting boats—could add value to preservation.[17] Stakeholders must tie new activities to their sites' preservation. Today's interventions often focus on festivals, harbour birthdays, and other tourist events that nostalgically celebrate traditional forms of shipping. It may be possible to mobilize these maritime

---

16 UNESCO, Genoa: *Le Strade Nuove* and the system of the *Palazzi dei Rolli*. Online. Available HTTPS: https://whc.unesco.org/en/list/1211

17 *Sustainable Tourism Charter for the Northern Lagoon in Venice.* Online. Available PDF: https://www.veneziaunica.it/sites/default/files/33.pdf

[3] The European Lighthouse project *Bauhaus of the Seas Sails* explores this approach.

activities for broader education on maritime practices, including sustainable food from the sea.[18] More largely, in line with the UNESCO Historic Urban Landscape (HUL) approach, heritage sites can help redefine maritime culture as innovative, and focused on preservation of water-related infrastructure.

We envision a kind of heritage protection and sustainable development that is like the ecosystem approach of our Atlas: networked, multi-scalar, and understanding current conditions both as the outcome of path-dependent past developments and the frame for future transformations. Given the need for collaboration within and among port city territories, and the necessity for sustainable practices across complex territories, the *Port City Atlas* proposes conceptual and methodological innovation to complement and support other tools that are currently being developed. Providing standardized geospatial maps of port city territories as a visual foundation for discussion within their territory and across territories, it will help planners overcome siloed approaches to spatial planning. The *Port City Atlas* helps to envision tourism and creativity, mobility and connectivity on the sea and in the hinterland, a key element for port city territories and at the heart of European Union policy.

We hope that port authorities, and urban and territorial leaders will use this book as a point of discussion for conversations on shared goals. First, we suggest that stakeholders start to think of port city territories as sites where multiple domains come together: past, present and future; heritage preservation and sustainable economic development; ecological riches and climate change. The *Port City Atlas* invites these stakeholders to have conversations, to (re)imagine port, city and territory as a single spatial unit with long histories, diverse heritage and shared values. All this may require some ports (or cities) to adjust their preservation and development plans to adapt to a shared future, and specifically to adopt a maritime perspective.

Second, we hope that different port city territories will explore shared challenges and opportunities together. One positive outcome could be a partnership between communities that have shared maritime connections and World Heritage properties, engaging with historic shipping networks for contemporary (touristic) activities. Finding shared strategies to engage with underwater archaeological sites or Natura2000 sites next to working ports could be another positive outcome. Working groups on the role of shipping channels, or road- or rail infrastructure or warehousing or tourism, as part of an ecosystem approach may be developed based on this atlas. An ecosystem approach is also at the heart of the UN Sustainable Development Goals (SDG), established in 2015 to address global challenges. A better understanding of specific values or identities inherent in port cities can help stakeholders develop shared strategies as an inherent part of balanced and sustainable development in line with SDG 11.7 to protect and safeguard the world's cultural and natural heritage.

European Port City Territories and UNESCO World Heritage Properties

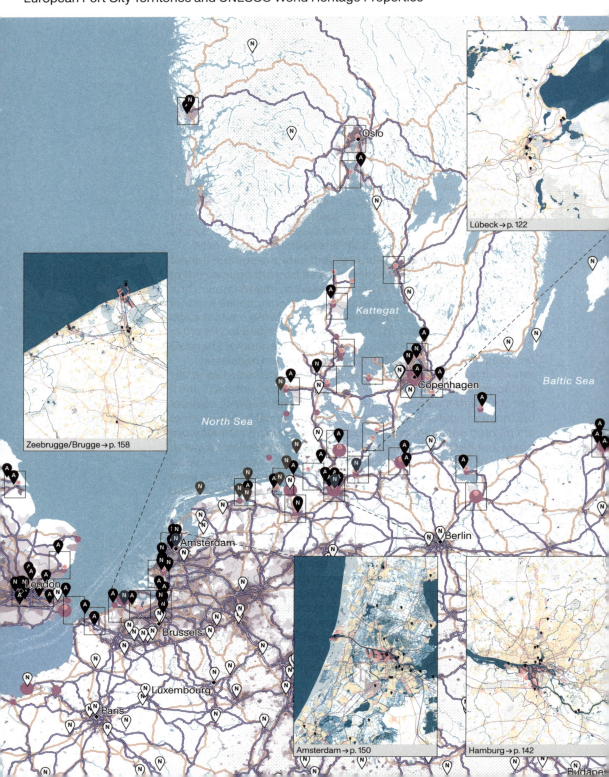

Comparative Analysis of the Port City Territory

Waterside
Port main typology
City typology
Territory typology (NUTS 3)

BALTIC SEA

ID	Port Name	W	P	C	T
HEL	Helsingborg, SE				
HLS	Helsingør, DK				
CPH	Københavns, DK				
TRG	Trelleborg, SE				
MMA	Malmø, SE				
RNN	Rønne, SE				
STO	Stockholm, SE				
LLA	Luleå, SE				
TKU	Turku, FI				
NLI	Naantali, FI				
HEL	Helsinki, FI				
SKV	Sköldvik, FI				
TLL	Tallinn, EE				
RIX	Riga, LV				
VNT	Ventspils, LV				
LPX	Liepaja, LV				
KLJ	Klaipeda, LT				
BOT	Butinge, LT				
GDN	Gdansk, PL				
GDY	Gdynia, PL				
SZZ	Szczecin, PL				
SWI	Swinoujscie, PL				
RSK	Rostock, DE				
ROF	Rødby, DK				
PUT	Puttgarden, DE				
SLM	Sillamäe, EE				
LBC	Lübeck, DE				
KEL	Kiel, DE				
FRC	Fredericia, DK				
AAR	Århus, DK				
SST	Statoil-Havnen, DK				
SJO	Sjaellands Odde, DK				

NORTH SEA

ID	Port Name	W	P	C	T
AAL	Aalborg, DK				
FDH	Frederikshavn, DK				
HIR	Hirtshals, DK				
EJB	Esbjerg, DK				
BRB	Brunsbüttel, DE				
HAM	Hamburg, DE				
BRE	Bremen, DE				
WVN	Wilhelmshaven, DE				
BRV	Bremerhaven, DE				
DZL	Delfzijl, NL				
EME	Emden, DE				
AMS	Amsterdam, NL				
RTM	Rotterdam, NL				
ANR	Antwerp, BE				
GNE	Ghent, BE				
ZEE	Zeebrugge, BE				
DKK	Dunkirk, FR				
DVR	Dover, UK				
CQF	Calais, FR				
MED	Medway, UK				
LON	London, UK				
FXT	Felixstowe, UK				
HRW	Harwich, UK				
IPS	Ipswich, UK				
IMM	Immingham, UK				
HUL	Hull, UK				
MME	Tees & Hartlepool, UK				
TYN	Tyne, UK				
FOR	Forth (Edinburgh), UK				
BGO	Bergen, NO				
TON	Tønsberg, NO				
OSL	Oslo, NO				
GOT	Göteborg, SE				

ATLANTIC

ID	Port Name	W	P	C	T
CYP	Clydeport (Glasgow), UK				
CYN	Cairnryan, UK				
BEL	Belfast, UK				
LAR	Larne, UK				
DUB	Dublin, IE				
LMK	Limerick, IE				
ORK	Cork, IE				
HYM	Heysham, UK				
LIV	Liverpool, UK				
HLY	Holyhead, UK				
MLF	Milford Haven, UK				
BRS	Bristol, UK				
SOU	Southampton, UK				
PME	Portsmouth, UK				
LEH	Le Havre, FR				
NTE	Nantes Saint-Nazaire, FR				
LRH	La Rochelle, FR				
BOD	Bordeaux, FR				
BIO	Bilbao, ES				
GIJ	Gijón, ES				
LCG	La Coruña, ES				
FRO	Ferrol, ES				
LEI	Leixões (Porto), PT				
LIS	Lisboa, PT				
SET	Setúbal, PT				
HUV	Huelva, ES				
LPA	Las Palmas, ES				
SCT	Santa Cruz de Tenerife, ES				
CAD	Cádiz, ES				

MEDITERRANEAN SEA

ID	Port Name	W	P	C	T
ALG	Algeciras, ES				
CEU	Ceuta, MA				
CAR	Cartagena, ES				
VLC	Valencia, ES				
CAS	Castellón, ES				
TAR	Tarragona, ES				
BCN	Barcelona, ES				
MRS	Marseille, FR				
TLN	Toulon, FR				
GOA	Genova, IT				
SVN	Savona, IT				
SPE	La Spezia, IT				
LIV	Livorno, IT				
CVV	Civitavecchia (Roma), IT				
NAP	Napoli, IT				
PFX	Porto Foxi, IT				
CAG	Cagliari, IT				
PMO	Palermo, IT				
SIR	Siracusa, IT				
MSN	Messina, IT				
MLZ	Milazzo, IT				
GIT	Gioia Tauro, IT				
REG	Reggio di Calabria, IT				
TAR	Taranto, IT				
RAN	Ravenna, IT				
VCE	Venezia, IT				
TRS	Trieste, IT				
KOP	Koper, SI				
MNF	Monfalcone, IT				
RJK	Rijeka, HR				
SPU	Split, HR				
PIR	Peiraias (Athene), GR				
PER	Perama, GR				
EEU	Elefsina, GR				
SKG	Thessaloniki, GR				

CAROLA HEIN is Professor and Head of the Chair History of Architecture and Urban Planning at the Delft University of Technology and Professor at Leiden and Erasmus University. She holds the UNESCO Chair of Water, Ports and Historic Cities and leads the LDE PortCityFutures Centre. She has published widely in the field of architectural, urban and planning history, tying historical analysis to contemporary development. Among other major grants, she received a Guggenheim and an Alexander von Humboldt fellowship. The latter resulted in her edited book Port Cities: Dynamic Landscapes and Global Networks (Hein, 2011) where she first proposed the concept of the spatial impact of port related flows on cities and territories, the Port-CityScape. Over the next decade, she continued her work on commodity flows in port cities and territories, focusing on the importance of long-term development and path dependencies. Following her appointment as professor at Delft University of Technology in the Netherlands in 2014, she has combined her interest in port cities with the GIS-based research tradition of the Chair History of Architecture and Urban Planning. Her article 'Oil Spaces: The Global Petroleumscape in the Rotterdam/The Hague Area' (Hein, 2018) describes the close link between water and oil. The co-edited book *Urbanisation of Sea* (Couling, Hein 2020) and the recent books *The Routledge Planning History Handbook* (2018), *Adaptive Strategies for Water Heritage* (2020), and *Oil Spaces: Exploring the Global Petroleumscape* (Hein 2021) analysing the close link between shipping, water, oil and ports set the stage for an atlas exploring and visualizing maritime flows on ports, cities and territories. Her many honours include the Sarton Medal in 2020, awarded to an outstanding scholar in the history of science.

YVONNE VAN MIL is a Researcher and Cartographer at Delft University of Technology at the Chair History of Architecture and Urban Planning, and the Chair Complex Projects. Her research interests lie in spatial history and spatial planning, and specifically in regional development and geospatial mapping. She is co-author of several books, including *Driven by Steel. From Hoogovens to Tata Steel 1918–2018* (2018), *Atlas van het Westland, 10.000 ruimtelijke ontwikkeling* (2016), and contributed chapters to the *Atlas of the Dutch Urban Landscape* (2014) and *Atlas van de Schie. 2500 jaar werken aan land en water* (2016). She has always been fascinated by ports, and joined the discussion on port cities professionally when she started working with Carola Hein in 2019. Her passion for maps and mapping as a means of studying and communicating spatial processes and expertise in systematic, spatial analyses led to shared publications on mapping and port city territories, and has paved the way for the *Port City Atlas*. Her co-authored articles include 'Towards a Comparative Spatial Analysis for Port City Regions Based on Historical Geo-spatial Mapping' (2019) (with Hein) and 'Straddling the Fence: Land Use Patterns in and around Ports as Hidden Designers' (2021) (with Hein and Ažman-Momirski).

LUCIJA AŽMAN-MOMIRSKI is Associate Professor of Urban Design at the University of Ljubljana. Her research interest is the spatial development of port city territories. She has explored port expansion in studies of the Port of Koper and the city of Koper. Lucija Ažman-Momirski won the design competition for that port's new master plan in 2007. She was the project leader for drafting professional guidelines in the spatial reorganisation of the Port of Koper, Slovenia, from 2007 to 2011; this work also won the International Maks Fabiani Award in 2015 and International Urban Planners Exhibition Award in 2015. She has expanded her work on port cities to education and research, publishing 'The Resilience of the Port Cities of Trieste, Rijeka, and Koper' in a special issue of *The Journal of Urban History* on port cities and resilience. Her (co-)authored published research papers include 'Shifts in Governance: Who Governs and What is Governed in the Port of Koper' (2020) 'Straddling the Fence: Land Use Patterns in and around Ports as Hidden Designers' (2021) (with Van Mil and Hein) and 'Port City Resilience: Piloting a socio-spatial method for understanding comparing and representing linked maritime heritage' (2022) (with Hein and Van Mil).

STEPHAN HAUSER is a postdoctoral researcher in the fields of urban planning and sustainability science at Helsinki Institute of Sustainability Science, University of Helsinki; he previously worked as a lecturer and researcher at the Chair of History of Architecture and Urban Planning at the Delft University of Technology on the influence of the industrial sector on the development and application of laws in Europe.

LUKAS HÖLLER is a doctoral student at Delft University of Technology, conducting research on second-tier port cities as gateways to healthy territories, as part of the LDE PortCityFutures Centre. He holds a B.Eng. in Landscape Architecture from Weihenstephan-Triesdorf University and an MSc in Urbanism from Delft University of Technology.

DOUWE DE JAGER is a student-assistant at the Chair of History of Architecture and Urbanism, contributing to research projects through geospatial data visualization. He is pursuing an MA in Architecture.

HÜLYA LASCH is a research associate at the Chair of Urban Development and Quantitative Methods and at the Chair of Digital City Science at HafenCity University Hamburg where she studies geospatial data visualization, digital planning tools, urban health and socio-spatial inequalities. She holds an MA in urban planning from Hafencity University.

CENK BATUHAN ÖZALTUN has been active for three years as a student-assistant at the Chair of History of Architecture and Urban Planning. After his Master's in Management in the Built Environment at Delft University of Technology, he started as a trainee at a real estate consultant in Amsterdam.

MYRTHE PEET is a Master's student in Building Technology at Delft University of Technology; as a student-assistant at the Chair of History of Architecture and Urbanism, she has contributed spatial analysis to research on maps.

MEES VAN RHIJN is a Bachelor student at the Faculty of Architecture in Delft and works as a student-assistant at the Chair of History of Architecture and Urban Planning. In 2022 he studied at the İTÜ in Istanbul, where history, culture, diversity and disorder ceaselessly amaze and continually give new insights.